"I JUST HAPPENED TO BE THERE..."

"I JUST HAPPENED TO BE THERE..."

Making Music With the Stars

Dear Dolores,

Hope you enjoy my stories. Keep singing and bringing joy to all.

All the best

Nick Perito

Nick Perito

To order additional copies of this book, contact:
Xlibris Corporation
1-888-795-4274
www.Xlibris.com
Orders@Xlibris.com
23341

CONTENTS

NYC Blackout
Judy Garland (Vegas—"Thunderbird")
San Carlos, California
Hollywood, Florida
Judy and Perry (NYC)

Como's First Summer Tour
Bea Arthur
Early Grammy Shows
Gilbert Becaud
Harry Warren (1967)
Jane Jarvis and Muzak (1969-70)
The Hollywood Palace
"White Christmas"
The Accordion

Como in Vegas
Don Knotts TV Show—Como in London—
The "Big 3" Christmas TV Specials
Louis Jourdan (1972)
Shirley Bassey (1973)
Anthony Newley (1975)
Como Concerts in England
Festival Hall
Moscow, Russia
Como in Mexico

Don Ho (Hawaii)
Como in Australia
Vienna and Salzburg
Evel Knievel TV Special (1977)
Bing Crosby 50th Showbiz Anniversary

ACKNOWLEDGEMENTS

Thank you Giovanna Bonaventure, Lee Hale, Terry Woodson, Linda Hope, Ward Grant, Stephen Pouliot, my three children and my cousins, John and Robert Perito, for your suggestions and editorial help.

Thank you Scott Citron of Scott Citron Design for the cover design of this book.

Thanks to Bill DiCicco and Paul Surratt of Research Video for their show business archival knowledge, cooperation and assistance over the years.

Thanks to the very cooperative and talented staff at Xlibris Corporation—namely, Melissa DiLeonardo, Tracy Festinger, Jen Harmon and John MacDonald. Also of invaluable help was Robert Ceballos of Kinko's in Calabasas, Calif.

A very special thank you to my daughter, Jennifer. Without her dedication and creative guidance, this book would never have become a published reality.

Thanks to Scott Record for taking me along as his pianist on a Caribbean cruise in January of 2002. That was when I first put pencil to paper and actually began writing this book. If you like what I have written, I'll take a bow. If you don't, then blame it all on Scott.

PREFACE

In my wildest dreams I never thought that I could, or would ever be able to write a book. The power of "the word" has always intrigued me. My father could tell a story and give people so much pleasure just by what he said and how he said it. Hopefully, I have inherited some of his talent for story telling

Several years ago, I was having dinner in Washington, D.C. with my cousin, Paul Perito, and a couple of his friends. After hearing me tell some humorous stories about growing up in an Italian family, they all agreed that I should write a book. A friend of one of Paul's clients named Lisa Grunow, turned out to be a real "nudge." I am forever grateful for her constant support and encouragement. She insisted that I tell about my childhood growing up in an Italian-American family and also, the wonderful experiences I have had throughout my years in the music business.

Shortly after I started writing, anxiety set in because I couldn't think of a good title for this book. While explaining my frustration to a successful writer friend of mine named Stephen Pouliot, I mentioned that I didn't want my stories to come off sounding like "Hey, look at me—how wonderful I am! The fact is, I just happened to be there and I want to write about it." After a short pause, his face lit up and he said, "There's your title—*I just happened to be there.*"

At first, I was concerned that maybe those words sounded too much like false modesty. But that is hardly the case. I have been fortunate to work with many talented and high profile artists but that is a direct result of the personal drive and commitment instilled in me by my parents. After years of practicing and hard work, I was able to produce when opportunity presented itself.

This book consists of two major parts. The first deals with my growing up in a strict Italian family. All of the old customs and beliefs from Potenza, Italy were strictly adhered to, even though we lived in Denver, Colorado.

The second part tells (in chronological order) about my leaving home—serving in the army for three years, then on to the Juilliard School of Music and many of my personal and professional experiences that have taken me all over the world.

If the show business portion is what you are curious about, then start with the Juilliard chapter. However, I humbly recommend that you take it from the top and, hopefully, you will find it worth your while.

Many fabulous teachers have shown me the way and I thank them all from the bottom of my heart. I am also grateful for the love and encouragement that I've received from my family and close friends.

I dedicate this book to my dear sister, Marian—my brother, Mike—and my loving parents, Jennie and Rocco

CHAPTER 1

HELLO WORLD

Someone was holding me in their arms . . . I was looking up at a beautiful blue ceiling . . . drops of cold water were falling on my face—I heard soft voices—more cold water . . . I was crying!

I was two weeks old at the time and I was being baptized at Mt. Carmel Church in Denver, Colorado . . . many long years ago.

OK—OK, I'm not crazy—please don't close the book. Give me a chance and continue on for a while because I have many stories to tell that I hope you will find interesting and amusing. They might even help to bring back some fond, personal memories for you.

Aside from the discomfort I experienced at my baptism, I knew I was surrounded by love right from the moment I drew my first breath.

The first big thrill I had occurred at the age of four when I heard my father's friend play what I later learned was an accordion. He held this "magic box" on his lap, and by squeezing it in and out and pressing some buttons on both sides of the instrument, beautiful music filled the room. It always seemed to make people happy. My parents, both music lovers, were delighted to see my reaction, and at the age of five, I was given a small twelve-bass accordion.

Ernest Bonvicini, the son of my father's friend, became my first teacher and he believed in the old school of teaching music. I was not allowed to actually play the instrument until after he taught me *solfeggio*—which meant that I first had to learn the basics of music like reading notes and understanding their rhythmic values. My father took a dim view of this approach, because he was paying fifty cents for each of my weekly lessons and he was anxious to hear me play some of his favorite old Italian melodies. After three months or so of *solfeggio*, I was finally allowed to play the instrument. Later on, we got into the study of harmony, intonation, and melodic development.

At first I found it very difficult to coordinate my left hand, which was pushing down little buttons that I couldn't even see, while my right hand was pressing down keys resembling a piano keyboard. At the same time, I had to push and pull the bellows in and out in order to create a sound. After a lot of tears and frustration, the love and encouragement I received from my parents helped me through the entire ordeal. Much of it was like learning to ride a bicycle—one day, I got the idea—and then life was worth living again.

I was determined to make my family proud of me so I practiced a lot. It was gratifying to know that I could entertain people and make them happy by simply playing songs on this instrument. Like every child, I was always told to be quiet and not make any noise. But now, with this new instrument, I could make a lot of noise and get away with it. I loved the idea! More about that later, but first, let me tell you about my parents and our family tree.

ROCCO and JENNIE

Sometime around the year 1845, a baby was abandoned on the steps of a Catholic church in Potenza, a little town in south central Italy. That baby was my grandfather, my father's father. A poor family named Perito, adopted him when he was only one week old. Not much else was known about him except that he grew up to marry a young lady named Marianna Cardillo, a true "fireball of energy." They lived a life of poverty, and like so many other Catholic families of that region, they immediately started to raise a family—a large one that they could not provide for.

As a result, my father, Rocco, the youngest of their eight children, was rented out to a local sheepherder. He was seven years old and his job was to tend a herd of sheep and goats grazing on the nearby hills. His only possessions were the clothes he wore.

Once a week, someone brought him a loaf or two of bread and maybe some leftover food scraps from the landowner's table. Other than that, he had to sustain himself with fruits and vegetables that he stole from neighboring orchards anf farms. Water was available at a local stream. Since he only had one year of proper schooling, he learned to live by his wits. Whatever money he earned was paid directly to his mother, who was also employed as a servant. He was allowed to see her for a few hours once every two or three weeks. It's difficult to imagine a child of that age forced to be *out on his own*.

Many of his young friends had to do the same for other landowners. Survival was their number one priority. In order to stay warm on cold nights, they snuggled with the animals they tended. Life was incredibly grim and lonely for all of them.

After several years, he managed to find other menial jobs that allowed him to stay down in the village with his mother. One day he and his friends were thrilled to hear a marching band at a local Catholic feast celebration. They could not afford to buy any instruments, so my father taught them all to imitate musical sounds by using their lips and voices. Soon they were able to march down the street imitating, visually and audibly, the actual instruments of the band.

His love of music immediately became an escape for him. Along with that came a natural talent to tell stories and make jokes about whatever was pertinent at the time. The joy and laughter he was able to bring to his friends gave him a lot of personal pleasure.

At that time, life in Potenza was rough for all the poor peasants. Over a period of several years, five of his older brothers and sisters individually managed to accumulate enough money to "escape" to the wonderful new country across the sea—America! Four of them migrated to Denver, Colorado, and one older brother, Paul, ended up in Boston, Massachusetts. The Great European Migration was in full bloom at that time and in the year 1898, Rocco, at the age of fifteen, was also on his way to a magical place called "Denver, Colorado." He spent twenty-nine agonizing days in steerage on a ship from Naples, Italy, to New York City. Coming through Ellis Island and the train trip to Denver took another three weeks.

Like so many of his family and friends, he was amazed when he finally arrived in Denver to see how similar the nearby mountains were to those of Potenza. He soon found a job for one dollar a day as a scab laborer, helping to build a railroad over the Rocky Mountains. Again, he was forced to survive under extremely harsh conditions. Up in the high country, there was very little food or shelter provided for the workers. Whether you lived or died depended on whatever your own ingenuity and energy could provide. He, along with thousands of other poor immigrants from all over Europe and Asia, are the true heroes who built the railroad over the Rocky Mountains through Colorado to California.

Rocco gradually worked his way back to Denver and found a job cleaning out railroad cars. All this time, he was obsessed with learning his new language.

One day he met an attractive young lady named Gerada Comnillo, and he was immediately taken by her beauty and charm. Her mother and father also came from Potenza, Italy. She was born in Denver, the next to oldest of eighteen—that's right, eighteen children! Her father was a drunkard and was not able to earn much money. As a result, the family lived in poverty—like many other Italian immigrants in the area. After only two or three years of elementary school education, Jennie, which became her American name, was forced to quit school and stay home to help her mother raise their extra-large family. Her childhood was filled with a great deal of pain, sorrow, and anguish, and she grew up learning how to cope with the harsh realities of everyday life. Only thirteen of her siblings survived to adulthood.

Jennie spoke English and also Italian (with a perfect Potenza accent). I was told that she fell in love with Rocco at their first meeting. He offered her an escape from the drudgery of her daily family life. They were married while both were still in their teens, and like so many of their peers, they immediately started to raise a family in a house just a couple of blocks away from where Jennie grew up.

Wedding photo of my parents Rocco and Jennie 1903

MY SIBLINGS

Their first child, John died two weeks after birth. Shortly thereafter, a son, Mike was born and was followed two years later by another son, Nick (not me—I'll explain later). After five or six years, they were blessed with twin girls. But again tragedy struck. One twin died at birth, which left only "Marianna" (namesake of Rocco's mama). Marian became her American name.

Rocco found a new job selling fruits and vegetables at a store on Broadway, way over on the American side of town. Business was good, and Rocco was soon renamed "Perry" by all of his new customers. On weekends, the family helped out by working at the store. Brother Mike, in his early teens, was not much help because (according to Mama) he was too busy chasing pretty girls. He also loved music and was quite precocious—like father, like son. Nick, on the other hand, was the perfect son. Intelligent, loving, and dedicated—all that my parents ever wanted in a child. He enjoyed selling popcorn from a small streetcar-looking wagon in front of the store. Marian was very young at the time and was tied to Mama's apron strings.

All seemed to be going well until Nick became ill with pneumonia. His condition worsened day by day until he tragically passed away at the age of thirteen. My entire family was devastated by his death. The world of medical science that we all know now was in its embryonic stage at that time, and those kinds of tragedies occurred frequently in many indigent families.

At that point, I felt that fate stepped in—and guess what? I was born two years later in our house at 3321 Osage Street.

As was the custom in many old Italian families, I was given the same name as my deceased brother. I can gratefully say that never, during my entire life, has anyone in my family ever made any comparisons between me and the other Nick. They loved him dearly for what he was and they let me grow up just being me.

CHAPTER 2

GROWING UP IN TWO

DIFFERENT CULTURES

Italian was the main language spoken in our home. My sister and I soon became bilingual, because we were comfortable with whatever tongue our parents chose to speak.

Many of the older Italians who migrated to Denver brought with them nicknames that they had acquired while growing up in Italy. Many of the sobriquets were very funny, and for some unknown reason, I never bothered (in my mind) to translate them into English. One day my mother and I were walking past a neighbor's house. She, a very fat lady, was sitting out in her front porch. Thinking I would make my mother proud of my good manners, I shouted up to the lady, "Good morning, *coola grosso!*" I had heard all of her friends call her that, not realizing that it was always done behind her back. Well, my mother was terribly embarrassed by my greeting and she gave me a slap that I would never forget. To make matters worse, I yelled back at Mama, "Why are you mad at me? That's what everybody calls her?" BAM! I got another slap and she carted me away. It was *then* that I made the translation in my mind. I had said to the lady, "Good morning, big ass!"

My father sold his interest in the fruit store and started selling his produce door to door via horse and wagon. He became quite successful with his new American customers, and soon he was able to trade in the horse and wagon for a small Model T Ford truck.

He also moved our family to a new house on the upper north side of town.

When I started at Columbian Elementary School, at the age of six, I began to realize that I was part of a distinctly different culture. From 8:30 AM to 3:15 PM, Monday through Friday, I was an American. Otherwise, our family could have been living in Potenza, Italy.

Being of Italian heritage and growing up in American neighborhoods was sometimes difficult, emotionally, for many of us kids coming from foreign families. We were surrounded in school by American culture and values, which was as it should have been. But sometimes we were made to feel that we weren't as good as the other kids. Hollywood movies and radio dramas often depicted Italians as gangsters and urban tough guys who weren't respectable people. Therefore, we clung to our European heritage. Our lifestyles, customs, and culture (religious and familial), the food we ate, the music we heard, our special Catholic outdoor feast days—all of these only strengthened the fact that we were different, *and* we were poor. Our older male family members and friends were farmers, craftsmen, or just plain laborers. None were lawyers, doctors, or accountants. The women stayed home, took care of the kids and all of the household problems.

I remember coming home from school one afternoon, after having had a fight with one of my classmates. My nose was bleeding slightly and I suffered some scratches on my arms. When my father first saw me, I expected a comforting hug, but instead, he gave me a little slap across the face. When he noticed the tears in my eyes, he pointed his finger at me and said something like this (half in Italian and half in English), "When are you going to start using your brain? Violence solves nothing! Stop and think first! Try to make people understand that any problem can be settled much better by intelligent reasoning and discussion." My tears stopped, and when I stood up and started to walk away, he gave me a gentle Italian *shkaf* (love tap) on the back of my head. It didn't hurt and I could see a smile on his face. He had made his point.

OUR NEW HOUSE

Our new house had two levels. The upper floor, had a kitchen (it was used only to make coffee in the morning), dining room, front room, three bedrooms, and a bathroom. The basement had another kitchen, a laundry room, a furnace room, and an unheated room where all our food was stored. That's also where we kept the icebox. There was no electrical home refrigeration in those days. Upstairs was only for sleeping and using the bathroom. The front room was off-limits, except for my daily accordion and piano practicing and, on the rare occasions, when American or nonfamily guests paid us a visit.

Otherwise, we lived in the basement and the kitchen was the main room in the house, as it was in all Italian families.

Every fall Papa made homemade wine and it was fun helping him stomp on the grapes in a big vat in our fruit room. We always wore rubber boots, because he didn't think that using our bare feet was the sanitary thing to do. After the initial pressing was over, he saved the residue from the grapes and stems, added more water, let it all steep for a couple of days, and then we stomped all over again. He called the wine that came from our second stomping *sotto apera*. It was naturally not as good as the first pressing and he carefully labeled the different bottles. I soon discovered who his best friends were by what specific bottles of wine he asked me to get when they came over to visit.

Although we had a washing machine, our clothes still had to be hung outside to dry on the clothes lines. In the freezing cold of Colorado winters, it was funny to see Papa's long white underwear hanging down from the line—frozen solid—greatly resembling a large slab of salted dry codfish *(bacala)*.

We had two empty lots next to our house where we grew all kinds of fruits and vegetables. It also had a small animal pen that housed our goat, Stella. Mama saved the water in which she boiled the pasta, because she used it to mix in with the food scraps that she had for our goat's daily meals. Stella, in turn, rewarded us with milk that allowed Mama to make delicious ricotta cheese.

BOZO

When I was about seven years old, we had a small white spitz dog named Bozo. After several months, he became my best pal. One day Papa took me and Bozo in the car and I thought we were going for a drive out to the countryside. I had no idea what was about to happen.

When we got to what seemed like the middle of nowhere, Papa suddenly stopped the car and without a word of explanation, he opened his car door, took Bozo out of the backseat and set him gently out on the ground. He quickly got back into the car, slammed his door shut and we sped away. I cried bitterly as I stared out of the back window at my little dog who was futilely chasing our car. I vaguely remembered Papa trying to explain his reason for abandoning Bozo, but I was too heartbroken to listen to him.

Years later, I learned that he was told by some of his old cronies that Bozo, being a spitz dog, might have some kind of disease that could be very harmful to all of us. Apparently Papa panicked, and since he felt he couldn't afford to take the dog to a veterinarian, that was his way of solving the problem. I honestly felt that deep down inside, he was as sad about the entire incident as I was.

FOOD

We rarely went to a grocery store except to buy eggs or a bottle of milk. All other staples were purchased in bulk at special wholesale places. A few times a year, my father brought home a couple of large wooden boxes of spaghetti. Mama made all the other pasta by hand. There was always a large sack of flour kept in our basement storeroom along with all of the canned goods. Mama and Marian canned thirty or forty bushels of tomatoes every fall so that we would have enough sauce for whatever meals they chose to cook the remainder of the year. Also, any "day-old" fruit that was not sold on Papa's truck was canned and stored away for the cold winter months.

The older Italian women made bloomers (underwear) out of the leftover cloth from flour sacks. All of us kids liked to tease them about that, because one windy day, they were bent over working in a large vegetable farm and a strong gust of wind blew their dresses up over their heads. There, clearly printed on their bloomers, we all saw the slogan of the flour company across their buns—and it said "Pride of the Rockies."

Mama always had lots of delicious homemade Italian cookies in the house, just in case somebody came over to visit. Her assistant in all this cooking wizardry was my sister Marian, who years later was regarded by all of her friends and members of our family as the No. 1 *chef di Potenza*. We ate all kinds of fruits and vegetables, many of which we grew in our gardens. Long, thin sweet peppers were, and still are, my favorite summertime treat. (Fry them in a large pan until they are practically burned, then gently place them on paper towels to remove any excess oil. Then add salt to taste. Try it sometime—you'll love it.) Mama used cheap cuts of meat like pork neck bones or homemade sausage to spice up the *minastra*—the Italian word for any coarse green leafy vegetable like kale, chicory, cabbage, or endive. Garlic, of course, was a dietary staple. The growing, preparing, and general discussion of food was one of the most important parts of any Italian family get-together.

Sunday was the most special day of the week. I remember waking up smelling the garlic and onions frying and then hearing the hissing sound when Mama added the tomatoes to the sauce. Later in the day, after coming home from church, I would eat the pasta. It seems I accidentally dropped some of the sauce on every white shirt I ever owned. This happened in spite of the fact that Mama always tied a large *mahpeen* (napkin) around my neck.

As a surprise, sometimes Papa stopped by the Happy Home Bakery and purchased (at a cheaper price, of course) a day-old coffee ring sprinkled with raisins, pecans, and white icing. That was regarded as our American *treat*.

But the ultimate dessert for all of us kids was ice cream. It was an absolute luxury because we didn't know how to make it ourselves at home. One had to go to the store and buy it, and that seemed to happen only on birthdays. Mama and Marian shared my love for this heavenly delight.

The Meadow Gold Creamery was a small store near our house that made and sold ice cream. My favorite was the combination of vanilla, strawberry, and chocolate (Neapolitan). Many nights, when we were returning home from visiting family friends or some function where I had played the accordion, I would start to plead with my father to please stop and buy us a pint of ice cream. My pleading would begin when we were about a mile away from the creamery. From the backseat of the car I would start by softly asking, "Paaa . . . ?" He always knew, by the tone of my voice, what I was hopefully suggesting. As we got closer to the creamery my pleas of "Paaa . . . ? Paaa . . . ?" occurred more frequently and with more urgency. But on most nights, knowing we couldn't afford it, he pretended not to hear me and we'd go straight home. Those were some of the saddest moments of my childhood.

But there were nights when my pleas *were* honored. As soon as Marian and I felt the car slowing down, a block or so before we reached the creamery, we'd start to giggle, laugh, and cheer. Papa would pull over to the curb and give me the necessary fifteen or twenty cents. Marian then walked me across the street (like a good sister), and we'd buy a pint of *frozen delight!*

When we got home we divided the pint three ways—Mama, Marian, and me (Papa always gave us his share)—and the taste was something I couldn't begin to describe. The sheer ecstasy of it all! At that time, my biggest ambition in life was to one day be able to make enough money to buy all the ice cream I could eat.

THE PIG

The fall of the year was the time that all Italian families harvested and canned fruits and vegetables for the cold winter months ahead. Many of the farmers who lived outside of the city limits also raised pigs. Once a year, generally around October or November, they slaughtered one of their animals. It was a big event with many friends and family members present to help with the many chores that had to be done.

The actual slaughter of the pig was a terrifying experience to witness, but somehow, at the age of seven or eight, I was both frightened and intrigued by it all. Those who were invited assembled early on a Saturday or Sunday morning, in this case at the Satriano farm in Welby, a farm community outside of Denver. Several of the younger able-bodied men had the difficult task of isolating the fattest pig and tying its front and hind feet together with baling wire. Also clamping and wiring its mouth shut. A pig can be a terribly dangerous animal when provoked, and these were frightening moments for both man and beast. When the pig was finally subdued, it was placed on a large wooden plank and horse drawn up to the barn next to the main house, squealing hysterically all the way!

All the women were advised to stay in the house. Everyone was told, "Please do not say '*poor pig*' because that will cause him to die more slowly." It was an old Italian belief.

Because of his years of experience, the patriarch of the family, nicknamed "Padre Shid," was the one who knew where to plunge the knife into the pig's throat so that it would die quickly with minimum suffering. I managed to sneak up near the old man to get a close up look at exactly what was about to happen. I will spare you the gory details of the actual slaughter. But please understand that to all concerned, this entire event was not for any macho or hunter-like gratification. The sole purpose was to provide the family with food for the following winter and spring months. Now, I shudder when I think of the horror of the actual killing.

My father kept a low profile at times like this because, deep down in his heart, he had a love for animals. It stemmed from his early days as a child when he tended the goats and sheep in Italy. He always referred to an animal as a *povera creatura* (poor creature).

Meanwhile, everyone was kept busy for the rest of the day preparing for dinner. Then cutting up the meat and frying the fatty sections to make lard. Every part of the pig was either salted, cured, or preserved in one way or another—nothing was wasted, even the skin, feet, ears, tail, and the blood that was used to make *sanguinacia* (blood sausage).

A farmer's life was, indeed, a rough one. I remember several times when in the middle of summer, and without warning, a devastating hailstorm would wipe out their entire vegetable crop— many times, on the day before the harvest. All their hard work for the year went for naught, and their income was next to zero.

I soon understood why my parents constantly encouraged me to practice, study, and learn a craft so that my destiny would not be determined by the fickle finger of Mother Nature.

My new accordion—I was 8 or 9 years old

ACCORDION

Ernest Bonvicini, my accordion teacher, and his dad loved to take me on trips up into the mountainous coal mining regions of

Colorado where they were able to sell accordions to many lonely miners who loved hearing any kind of live music. Even though I was considered small for my age, Earnest would literally tie the accordion to my body and then, very carefully, lift me up by my ankles so that while I was hanging upside down in midair, I was able to play a song or two that they all knew.

We were a big smash, and as a result, the Bonvicinis sold a lot of accordions. They always gave me a couple of dollars as payment for my performances, and that made Mama, my banker, very happy. On our return trips to Denver, we often stopped at some old mountain café with a sign out front that simply read "eats." The chili and small saltine crackers were to die for! That was considered to be American food (which we rarely had at home). I also loved peanut butter and jelly on white American bread simply because it was different.

Earnest went to Italy several times with his father to buy more accordions and while he was away, I studied with a man named Joe Grande. His home was in Globeville, a section of Denver where many Polish families lived. He was a dear man and he taught me a lot about the instrument.

Henry Gentile and Anthony Stone were two of my young friends who also played the accordion. Henry was a couple of years older than me and I was very impressed with his ability on the instrument. We learned to play a couple of duets together and we won an amateur contest at the Rivoli Theatre on Curtis Street. We were thrilled to split the first prize money of five dollars! To this day, Henry plays the accordion in Denver and gives his followers a great deal of musical enjoyment.

Anthony Stone was another duet partner of mine. He also played very well and we performed together at many local functions. As little kids, we both loved to set off firecrackers when our families got together for Fourth of July celebrations. But getting the money to buy the fireworks was always a big problem. One year, my father got me and Anthony a job playing our accordions out on the sidewalk in front of a big firecracker store on Twentieth and Larimer Street. Many customers were attracted to the store by seeing and hearing us play the popular tunes of the day. We didn't earn much money but we did get all the firecrackers we wanted—*for free!* In later years, Anthony became very successful as an academic educator in the Denver public school system.

In addition to playing the accordion, I loved playing baseball, as did my cousins, Joe and Gene Carpinello. In the summer time during our school vacation, we desperately wanted to play on a little league baseball team, but we had to stay home and work in our gardens—or go along on our fathers' trucks and help them sell fruits and vegetables. When we did get some free time, we played "catch" for hours—just throwing the ball back and forth, teaching each other how to catch high flies and field fast grounders. The New York Yankees was our favorite team because it had two famous Italian players, Tony Lazzeri and Frank Crossetti. And later when Joe Di Maggio came on the scene, we were delighted because we now had our own heroes to root for. I knew the batting averages of all the players in the major leagues. My favorite position to play was shortstop. Mama was forever telling me to "drop that damn ball and get in here and practice your accordion!"

Papa enjoyed telling me (in Italian) many old fairy tales that he had heard when he was a little boy back in Italy. All that folklore he remembered was verbally handed down from generation to generation, and he loved playing the role of the *bard*. The stories he told were incredibly exciting, with lots of gory details. I retold them to my classmates at Columbian grade school during a class we had called auditorium. It was for the benefit of kids who were shy and possibly had difficulty in communicating. I'm happy to say that was never one of my problems. Mrs. Casey often let me speak the last five minutes of a class session in order to bring everyone up on the latest episode of *"Rocco's Imagination,"* which was a lot like today's Harry Potter stories.

THE "EVIL EYE"

My uncle Jimmie took me to many different parties for family and friends, and because I could play the popular songs of the day on the accordion, I was the star of the show. But often times, I came home with a bellyache. Firmly believing in lots of old Italian superstitions, Mama was convinced that somebody there had given me *Mal Occhio* (the evil eye), and that's why I was sick. She would insist that I lie down in bed next to her, and while quietly reciting in Italian a lengthy prayer called La Razione, she would wave her hand gently over my face and begin to yawn frequently. It was an involuntary reaction on her part. She had been told that the more yawns she made, the more effective the prayer would be. It was very comforting for me, and I always fell asleep in her arms. The following day, I'd try to tell her that maybe the reason I got sick the night before was because I had eaten lots of dill pickles and American snacks followed by ice cream. She totally dismissed that theory because she was convinced that somebody had "taken my eyes." As I grew older, Mama was still concerned about people giving me the evil eye. Being a very religious person, she gathered up several small pictures of various saints, sewed them into a small cloth packet that she called "La Dabatheena" (American spelling). She insisted that I pin it to the inside of my underwear to keep me *safe* from *harm,* and nobody could see it. I didn't mind wearing it until I went to junior high school, and that was because every day after our gym class, we had to take a shower and I dreaded undressing in front of my school pals, knowing that it would be impossible for me to explain what the heck that thing was pinned to my underwear.

P.S. No, I do not still wear "La Dabatheena." Shortly after entering high school, I abandoned that habit and realized that I was not getting *Mal Occhio* anymore. OK, use your own imagination as to why, in later years, it could be very embarrassing under certain circumstances.

In those early preteen days, my storytelling and accordion playing gave me an opportunity to be the center of attention and that, I must admit, I really enjoyed. But looking back on it all now, there were times when I wonder why somebody didn't just squash me for being so damn precocious.

However on certain occasions, Papa did take me to task. It was generally after we got home from a family get-together. I had either disregarded his eye signs and took too many pieces of candy, or I did something that he knew I had been told not to do. Whenever I heard him address me by using the words, "Eh, *professore*," I knew I was in trouble. What really got my attention was not the little slap I received, but the fact that he wouldn't talk to me sometimes for two whole days afterward. That always made me sad. The word *respect* was very important to him and he made sure that I understood it. If I ever complained about a teacher at school or anyone older than me, he emphasized that *respect* was the first rule in communication. After that, you could get into the actual substance of the problem.

PAPA

He was fascinated by new thoughts and inventions. When I was very small, I remember how excited he was listening to a small crystal radio set that one of his friends had rigged up for him. Radio was in its embryonic stage and he was enthralled by its possibilities for entertainment and education.

Somewhere along the way, he learned to play the harmonica. I think it was given to him by a customer who owed him some money.

Whenever I wasn't around to play the accordion, he entertained his friends by playing a couple of tarantellas on his new toy.

The airplane was also a topic of enthusiastic discussion. We couldn't understand this phenomenal invention that would actually allow people to fly and travel by air. Lowry Field was a small air strip on the outskirts of town and many Sunday afternoons, Mama would pack a lunch and we'd all go out to the airfield and sometimes wait for hours, along with many other Denverites, in order to watch "the plane land." I shared Papa's fascination and enthusiasm about airplanes and air travel, but Mama and Marian were frightened by the whole idea.

The great financial depression of the early thirties took a toll on all of our friends. Being a peddler of fruits and vegetables was not a lucrative job for Papa at that time. Large supermarkets became popular and the competition was intense. Many late afternoons he came home with lots of produce that he wasn't able to sell during the day on his normal route.

I had learned early on that I could take my little red wagon, go knock on the doors of our American neighbors and sell not only things that we had grown in our garden, but also much of Papa's leftover produce. I remember the neighbors saying that I was "so cute," and as a result, they bought things they really didn't need only because they loved to see me smile. Well, I played along with that idea and as a result, I often made more money after school selling fruits and vegetables out of my little red wagon than my father did all day on his truck.

Papa slowly became more and more depressed. For days on end, he stayed home and refused to go out and peddle his produce. We finally realized he was having a nervous breakdown. He was under a great deal of stress because of the economic depression, and many of his childhood memories were coming back to haunt him. As a result, he developed a serious case of hypochondria. I was convinced that he suffered from imaginary diseases that hadn't been discovered yet. Times were tough for all of us and we had to borrow five hundred dollars from a relative in order to pay the rising doctor bills. Eventually, Papa went back to peddling intermittently, but life was still grim because we owed money and it would take us years to pay off our debts.

Many of my close cousins were experiencing similar situations in their families. But we managed to cling together and cheer each other up.

In all those years, it seemed my sister and I never got to eat a whole peach, plum, or apple. We always had to eat those pieces of fruit that had a worm hole or a bad spot cut out of them. Papa kept all the good ones to sell to his customers. My favorite fruit of all was the banana. It seemed bananas were always too expensive, so we never had any, except on holidays. Before dinner, Mama allowed me take one from the fruit bowl and place it beside my plate. I was not allowed to eat it until after I finished all my other food. What a treat that was for me.

THE WATERMELON STORY

Sundays in the summertime were often spent on the farm of our old family friend, "Padre Shid" Satriano (the same man with the pigs). Nobody ever bothered to translate that nickname. It didn't seem important.

Many Italian families would show up. The men just sat around, played cards and drank homemade wine, while the women assembled in the kitchen (naturally), shared family stories and cooked delicious dinners. The young boys always found a ball and went outside to play catch. After dinner, the kids set up in the front room to listen to the radio, while the older folks remained in the kitchen. Papa would then tell funny stories, in Italian of course, many of which were on the naughty side. Opportunities like this always brought Papa out of his funk. The older folks all loved to hear his stories and their roars of laughter often drowned out the radio show the kids were listening to. I would laugh because I understood Papa's stories. When I refused to translate for my young friends, they beat up on me.

On one particular Sunday, I was asked to bring my accordion and play some songs for the older folks. I really wanted to be outside playing baseball with my pals, but one look from my father—he had deadly eyes that could either charm or destroy you—and I knew my fate was sealed. I had to stay inside and play the accordion for the older folks. Mr. Satriano sensed my frustration and he said, in Italian, "Nicolo, for every song you play, I will give you a watermelon." Well, that really got my attention because I realized with all of that produce, along with *my smile* and the little red wagon, I could make a lot of money the next day with our neighbors. I proceeded to play all of the twelve songs I knew, announcing loudly (after each one) exactly how many I had already played. I soon ran out of songs, but since the men were all having a good time with their card games and wine drinking, I decided to repeat all of the tunes I had already played. Nobody knew the difference— except my mother and father. They kept giving me severe looks, which I pretended not to notice. Finally, someone forcibly removed the accordion from my grasp and I bellowed out, "You owe me thirty-five watermelons!"

The old man, Satriano enjoyed the entire caper. When we left to go home, he made sure that thirty-five watermelons were loaded into the backseat of our family car. My sister and I had no place to sit, so we crawled on top of the melons, and all the way home we listened to Mama tell us what a rude little bastard I was. When we finally got home, I was lucky not to get a big *shkaf* from Papa, because I think he was silently proud of me for what I was able to accomplish with my nerve and persistence. This time I got off easy.

PICNICS

Denver is situated at the foot of the Rocky Mountains, and to be able to go up there on a picnic in the summertime was a dream come true for me, my sister, and my cousins from Auntie Ange's and Auntie Rosie's families. American kids went on picnics all the time, but our parents, coming from poor backgrounds, could not comprehend the idea of spending money for any kind of leisure time activity. However, once a year they would splurge and it was a very special event for all of us. Mama always made the *rawoo* (tomato sauce for the macaroni) on Saturday night, so that on Sunday morning, after church, we could climb into our cars and head for the hills.

All of us kids were so excited to smell the cool, fresh Colorado mountain air and feel the wind on our faces when we stuck our heads out of the back window of the car—that is, if our parents weren't looking.

When we finally got up into the mountains, my father seemed to know exactly where to stop and make camp. A stream had to be nearby. A big watermelon in a burlap sack was immediately put into the cold, rushing stream in a spot sheltered by large rocks near the shore.

Along with my cousins, Genie, Joeie, Helen and Marie Carpinello and Joeie and Gerald Perito, we gathered up some dried-up old branches and twigs from the surrounding pine forest so that we could build a fire in order to boil the water to cook the macaroni. After all, it was Sunday, and in every Italian family, that automatically meant pasta with all the trimmings—no matter where you were. The fact that we were now out in the wilderness made no difference at all.

The women then got busy with dinner preparations. How they managed to set up a table so quickly on that uneven ground, I'll never know. The kids' first priority was always a short hike up the nearest mountain. We never went too far, but it felt like miles. After returning to camp and waiting for the water to boil to cook the pasta, we tried to find spots with natural stepping stones that would allow us to walk across the stream without getting wet—a major accomplishment for any of us. We were not deterred by the angry shouts from our parents like "don't fall in the water" or "get away from there, you're going to hurt yourself." We all pretended not to hear them. If one of us did fall into the stream, we could expect a *shkaf* for disobeying their orders. No big deal.

And then we ate—what a treat! The smell of the burning pine branches in the clean, crisp mountain air, the sound of the rushing stream, the taste of the meat balls, macaroni, vegetable salad, cake, and cold watermelon is a memory I will cherish forever. The joy and laughter we shared was a tonic for all of us. Our annual picnic up into the mountains was my idea of a trip to never-never land.

FEASTS

In the summertime, there were several weekend Catholic feast days that were very special events for every Italian family. The feasts honoring St. Rocco and St. Anthony were the most popular. They were celebrated in the same manner as the one Francis Coppola staged so accurately in the *Godfather II* movie, except on a much smaller scale and with no violence. On a Sunday, in midafternoon, a statue of the saint was gently removed from Mt. Carmel Church. It was then held high up on the shoulders of the local men and paraded down neighborhood streets with dollar bills pinned to its robe. A small marching band played all the traditional Italian music.

After that, the band was set up in Columbus Park on Osage Street, along with many different food stands. Papa's older brother, Gerardo lived across the street, and that was where many of my aunts, uncles, and cousins from both sides of the family met and celebrated the feast day. My cousins Rosie, Annie, and Lucille Perito were always fun to be with. Back in the park, the heavenly smell of sausage and peppers being fried permeated the air. Eggplant and mozzarella sandwiches and homemade Italian cookies seemed to be everywhere. We even had a hot-dog stand, and that was my favorite, because it was something we never had at home. For the adults, there was lots of beer and wine to add to the joy of the celebration. Knowing it was a safe place to be, our parents let us kids play games and run wild—all day long. What fun!

I am delighted to say that this annual celebration still takes place every summer—thanks to the efforts of my dear old friends and family members in Denver. They are dedicated in preserving our old Italian-American heritage. Long live the Potenza lodge. It has just celebrated its 104th anniversary.

I am supportive of all ethnic groups that aim to preserve *their* old-world heritage. Our wonderful country of America is made up of many different cultures, and the great exchange of ideas gives us the inspiration, energy and determination to succeed at whatever we do. We have learned, and we'll continue to learn from each other that education enhances all of our lives. As a result, we live in the greatest democracy in the world. May it always be so.

CHICAUDIA

Weddings and funerals were events that always brought the Italian community together. They loved to laugh and/or cry together. Funerals involved attending the church ceremony and then somehow finding a way to get to the cemetery for the burial. This was the respectful thing to do—honor the family of the deceased. Getting to and from the cemetery on the outskirts of town was a difficult thing to do because not many people owned automobiles. My father did own a car and in the winter and early spring months, when his peddling business was slow, he became a self-appointed taxi driver for those who needed transportation to the cemetery. He charged one-dollar round trip per passenger. He was very popular, because in the early spring, when the dandelions were growing wild in the fields, Rocco would stop the car on the way home and allow his riders to take out their paper bags and kitchen knives and pick this wonderful green plant we called *chicaudia* (dandelions). It was and still is an Italian staple, loved by one and all, and it's free. Years later, my nephew, Geno Ligrani referred to it as a *weed that made good*. My American pals at school didn't have a clue as to what this kind of thing was all about.

I was told that, not too long ago in Denver, an interesting incident took place. Many of those formerly old rural areas where the dandelions used to grow wild, have now become large housing developments inhabited by a mixture of nationalities. One day a group of young Italian-American men stopped their car near a large field filled with chicaudia. They carried large kitchen knives and shopping bags to hold their pickings. Several local residents frantically called 911 thinking they were being invaded by drug-crazed, knife-wielding hippies. The police showed up immediately and fortunately, one of them was of Italian descent. He immediately recognized that the long-haired guys were only carrying out an old Italian custom and he allowed them to complete their harvest, much to everyone's relief. I like to think that many of the residents were happy to learn about this new salad treat.

In the earlier years, Denver was a small city and the surrounding countryside had many lonely roads that were perfect for those of us kids who were excited about learning how to drive an automobile. The verdant open fields rewarded us with plants that grew wild and were also very healthy to eat—like the above mentioned chicaudia. Generally, after Sunday mass, Uncle Jimmie and Papa allowed me to "drive" the car on the country roads while they searched for *funghi* (mushrooms). They grew on old tree stumps in abandoned or not yet cultivated farm lands.

Wild asparagus was another delicious vegetable treat. From acres away, my sister Marian's uncanny eyes could spot them growing amidst all kinds of weeds and other green plants. She and Mama cooked them is such a delicious way that we all looked forward to the spring of every year so that we could go out looking for either chicaudia, funghi or wild asparagus—poor folk food. What great taste treats they were—and still are. Small town living provided us with great natural food supplies and we enjoyed them all—and, they were free.

CHAPTER 3

UNCLE JIMMIE

Although Mama had many brothers and sisters who lived in Denver, we rarely saw them or their families. Two of her sisters, Aunt Ange and Aunt Rosie remained very close to her as did their children. My cousins—Genie, Joey, Helen, and Marie Carpinello; and Joe and Gerald Perito were like brothers and sisters to Marian and me. We all grew up together sharing birthdays, holidays, good times and bad times. Other cousins like Mike, Lucy and John Perito, Roxie Veretta, Gene Maffeo, Virginia, Louie, and Mike Pastore, and Marcella and Dorothy Comnillo were only around on special occasions. We were, and still are, very proud of our ancestors.

Our favorite uncle was Jimmie, one of Mama's younger brothers. He came to visit each of his sisters and their families every Sunday morning after mass, ostensibly to "check the macaroni sauce." After dipping a couple of crusts of bread in the sauce, he gave each of us kids enough money to go to the movies. Unfortunately, he and his wife never had any children of their own and as a result, he was our Santa Claus twelve months a year. What a guy! He also loved music and he became one of my biggest supporters. Every Sunday, after tasting the sauce, he would give me the music of a popular new song that he had purchased at the local dime store. But first, I had to play the tune he had given me the week before. If he liked my rendition, I then received the new song. Improvisation came easy for me and he enjoyed listening to my different interpretations.

He shared my love for baseball and the major leagues. At that time, Denver was considered a hick town with no hope of ever having a big league team of its own (Boy, how times have changed). As much as I admired Uncle Jimmie, we did have one major disagreement. Jackie Robinson had just broken the color barrier in the major leagues and he became an immediate hero to all underprivileged people. I mentioned how wonderful it would be if, one day, I could play shortstop with Jackie who was a second baseman. Uncle Jimmie roared back, "I'd never play on a team with that nigger!" His anger frightened me so bad that I dropped the subject.

I was very confused and depressed for an entire week, because I remembered how my father and all of his Italian friends hated being called *dago* or *wop*. Yet, it was OK for them to refer to the Jews as *kikes*, the Mexicans as *spicks*, and the Negroes as *niggers*. That inequality didn't set well with me because I remembered spending many quiet, solitary moments asking myself "who am I?" and "why am I me—and not somebody else?" Many times I expressed these thoughts to my mother, who would become annoyed and shout back at me, "Why do you always have to ask so damn many questions?"

I had just received my first communion a year or two earlier and the things I learned about Catholicism from the catechism book were still very fresh in my mind.

As usual, Uncle Jimmie came over the following Sunday after mass. He tasted the sauce for the macaroni and after listening to my accordion playing, we started to chat. I mentioned how sad I had been all week just thinking about the injustice of racial intolerance. He angrily answered, "Are you still talking about that nigger, Jackie?" I paused for a moment, and knowing that he was a staunch Catholic, I asked him the first question in catechism— that was "Who made the world?" Before he could answer, I said, "God made the world," and then I quickly asked the second question which was "Who made the people?" and again, I gave the answer, "God made the people!" I went on to explain that I didn't have a request to be born a boy—an Italian with brown eyes—and if we are all truly children of God, as we were taught in the Catholic religion, then why must we discriminate against each other?

He yelled for my mother to come into the room and demanded to know who I had been talking to or hanging around with. Mama responded with her usual, "Don't pay any attention to him. He always asks too damn many questions."

Fortunately, Uncle Jimmie still came over every Sunday after that and went through his usual routine with the macaroni sauce and giving Marian and me money to go see a movie. Although we never discussed Jackie Robinson again, I was certain that I gave him cause to reexamine his feelings. Our entire family knew that deep down in his heart, he was a kind, gentle, and caring man. I am so thankful that he graced my life because he, unknowingly, provoked me to keep thinking, learning, and asking questions.

Sister Marian was 10 years old and I was 3—same twosome 55 years later

MY SISTER, MARIAN

My dear sister, Marian was everything a parent or brother could ever ask for. She was seven years older than me and very protective of my every move. She grew up to be a very attractive young lady and Papa was well aware of that fact. He guarded over her like a prison warden. He, himself was a big flirt, but no young man was allowed to be near his precious daughter, Marianna (Italian spelling). It was another "Italian thing" that I felt was frightfully unjust. Mama and I tried to help Marian live a normal social life, but Papa never relented. In spite of all this, she had many friends, "Having to accompany me" was often her excuse to get out of the house and socialize.

In her early childhood years, she studied piano for a short while but didn't have too much success with it. Her favorite solo piece was "The Rosary," a simple, somber melody that Mama loved. At her first recital, Marian got very nervous. She had a cold, and after walking out on the stage and sitting down at the piano, her nose began to run. My brother Mike entered the hall just as Marian started to play. He stood in the back of the room, while my folks and I were proudly seated in the front row. Unfortunately, Marian did not have a handkerchief and after she began playing, she found it necessary to wipe her nose with her right arm—which she proceeded to do several times. There were large silences in her playing while she tended to her leaky beak. Mike laughed loudly during her entire performance, while my parents were sympathetic and terribly embarrassed for their dear Marianna.

Shortly after that, she happily gave up playing the piano. It just wasn't her thing, but it never interfered with her undying love and devotion to music. Years later, we had lots of laughs watching our brother Mike give his imitation of Marian's performance. She, more than anyone else, always enjoyed his retelling of the story.

As a youngster, in addition to practicing the piano, she spent her time after school learning all the recipes of Italian cooking from Mama. They were both magicians in the kitchen. But one day, Marian brought home an "American surprise." It was a can of creamed corn. We all loved it, including Papa, and it was then that I began to realize that we were slowly adapting to a new American taste.

After her graduation from North Denver High School, Marian got a job down town in the credit department of the Denver Dry Goods store. No girls in our extended family ever went to college in those days. They all had to go out and earn money in order to help pay current household expenses and old family debts. No one had an individual bank account. Mama was our family banker. Whatever money Marian or I earned we gave to Mama for safekeeping. That's the way it was with most Italian families at that time. It was a communal effort on everyone's part to provide, collectively for the entire family. I was allowed to keep maybe three or four dollars in a top drawer in my bedroom just for school books and occasionally, a candy bar. But Mama always knew the amounts spent. That situation existed for me until I came back home from the army, many years later.

Every Tuesday evening for about a year, Marian and I were allowed one luxury. After school, I would take a streetcar downtown, meet her after work and buy an ice cream soda at a local drugstore. Then we would go to see a movie at the Denver Theatre. What excitement we both experienced when we would first walk into that fairyland. It was so beautiful and ornate inside and it had a wonderful smell about it. The anticipation of getting to see the latest Hollywood film was almost more than we could bear. What magic the movies brought to all of our lives.

Besides Hollywood movies, radio was the most important source of entertainment for everyone. After supper, our family would sit around this fantastic device and listen to all sorts of programs. Myrte and Marge, The First Nighter, The Shadow, Amos 'n Andy, Fred Waring and His Orchestra were some of my favorites. But the one show that everyone liked was The Major Bowes Amateur Hour. The musical variety it offered was very appealing. It seemed that every performer, with exceptional talent, was either a graduate or a student of a music school in New York City called Juilliard. This really got my attention and I was hooked on the idea that maybe one day I, too, could go to Juilliard and study music. I was frightened to learn later on that you first had to *pass a test* in order to find out if you even qualified to be admitted as a student.

Brother Mike at age 35—Mike and me in 1990

BIG BROTHER MIKE

My big brother, Mike left for New York City shortly after I was born. He got a job with a local band as a saxophone player and they went off to the "Big Apple" to seek their fortunes. He loved the big city life. After studying with the best teachers like Merle Johnson, he soon began playing with many of the orchestras we heard on the radio. Learning how to arrange music for an orchestra was another of his musical accomplishments. The entire family was very proud of him.

Occasionally, he came home on short vacations and each time, he was impressed by the progress I was making as a young musician. After returning to New York City, he began sending me copies of all the popular songs that he was able to solicit (for free) from the publishers of Tin Pan Alley. He was forever reminding me, "Learn how to read because one day when you get to New York, you will have to play new music perfectly at first sight. If you can't, there will be ten guys behind you who can!" All the while I was growing up, he constantly reminded me of that fact.

When I was ten or eleven years old, his trips back home became more frequent. He was the big man in town because he had made it in New York City. He was very supportive of my playing and the fact that I was interested in all kinds of music. His personal preference was jazz and popular music.

One Saturday afternoon, he took me to the Denham Theatre, in downtown Denver, to hear the Jimmie Lunceford orchestra. I was literally blown away listening to all those fantastic jazz musicians. That experience turned out to be a big turning point in my life. It was then that I decided to seriously study piano. So much more musical literature was also available to me on that instrument.

My first piano teacher was a priest named Father Domenico, who was an instructor at nearby Regis College. In addition to piano, he taught me chorale harmonization. Each week, I had to write out several examples of what we had discussed in the previous lesson. My early studies in *solfeggio* helped me greatly. He took music very seriously and he wanted to make sure that I did also. If I ever appeared to be a little foggy, he would give me a light slap on the back of my head as if to say, "Hello, wake up—*stupido!*" But at the end of each lesson, he always gave me an encouraging pat on the back and a big smile.

Mike now had many saxophone students. Every Saturday they got together in the basement of our house and played arrangements that he had written back in New York City. I had developed a good sense of harmony and I asked him to teach me how to arrange for that group. My first assignment was to write an orchestration for four saxophones on a popular song of the day called "I Don't Want to Set the World on Fire." I can't describe the joy I experienced when one week later, I heard it played back. Mike then asked me to write an arrangement for a big band he was rehearsing at the time. It consisted of three trumpets, two trombones, four saxes, and four rhythm (drums, bass, piano, and guitar). I was frightened to death, but I wasn't going to admit it. I chose to arrange "The Sheik of Araby" as my first big band chart. Hearing it played back two weeks later made me actually tremble with excitement. I was twelve or thirteen years old and all of the older band members were very complimentary and supportive. My brother Mike was also very proud of my writing, but he never ever told me so. It was just his way of making sure I wouldn't become conceited and stop practicing and learning. I tried desperately to get his attention, but each time I came up with an idea I thought was exciting, he would say, "No big deal—all good musicians do it that way." I became accustomed to his way of thinking because I learned later on, from his contemporaries, that he was very proud of his little kid brother—but he *never* admitted it to me.

Rather than pay someone a compliment, it seemed more comfortable to say something almost rude. I know this sounds crazy, but it's an old Italian kind of thing. After a while, I realized that was the way my loving family conveyed their admiration. I now find it very amusing.

Mike, like Papa, had a wonderful gift of gab. He enjoyed telling jokes and stories—all with his own unique comedic twist. Mama, her sisters, and many of their lady friends were quite short and a bit stocky. That prompted Mike to say that they all should have sued the city of Denver because every time they had to step down to walk across a street, they would "bump their asses on the curb."

Mama and Papa's families were both very large. Mike always said that if we ever had a real family reunion, we would have to rent the cavernous Denver City Auditorium or Madison Square Garden.

EARLY TEEN YEARS

Elitch's Gardens and Lakeside Park were two summertime venues that all Denverites loved. In addition to the picnic areas and exciting amusement rides, both parks had beautiful dance pavilions. Swing music was in full bloom and every week or so, different traveling dance bands appeared. Practically every Sunday afternoon, Marian and I, together with many of our young cousins, went out to hear bands like Kay Kyser, Les Brown, Bob Crosby, Dick Jurgens, and Eddie Howard. The orchestra of Ted Weems featured a handsome young Italian singer who immediately captured the hearts of all the ladies, especially those in my family. The rich, warm quality of his voice was very appealing to one and all. We were so happy to know that we now had another Italian hero to root for, Perry Como. Little did I realize then that one day I would become his musical director and have the honor to spend so much of my professional and personal life with this wonderful man.

Berkeley Lake had a large tree-covered picnic area in North Denver where various groups would gather in the summertime to celebrate American holidays like Arbor Day, Flag Day, Labor Day, etc. Two of my cousins, Genie and Joeie Carpinello and I decided that we should have an Italian Day. However, we didn't know what to call it or what we should celebrate. Food was very important in our lives, vegetables in particular. Zucchini was called "Koocoats," and it was humorously referred to in many of Papa's old ethnic stories. Why not celebrate "National Koocoats Day?" What a great idea!

We decided the best way to promote and celebrate our new holiday was to stand up in the back of an open pickup truck, along with several of our friends, and drive through Berkeley Park on a Sunday afternoon where many of the American groups were celebrating. We wanted desperately to get their attention, so we proudly displayed a large sign saying, "National Koocoats Week," and blew the horn loudly several times—then we all proceeded to sing at the top of our lungs, a set of lyrics written to the tune of "Alexander's Ragtime Band." Are you ready? Here are the words:

> We like koocoats, we like koocoats,
> We like koocoats that's fried with eggs.
> We like koocoats, we like koocoats,
> We like koocoats in many ways.

> You can eat them fried, you can eat them baked,
> But if you go and get a stomach ache,
> Don't blame those vitamins "X" and "Z,"
> We're telling you.

> Come on along and try koocoats
> And you'll admit they can't be beat.
> You'll eat 'em hot, you'll eat 'em cold,
> You'll even eat 'em with no meat.

> Although it's true fried peppers are the favorite in North
>   Denver,
> Come on along, and try koocoats,
> 'Cause it's the best food in the land!

> (spoken tag) We're gonna tell you one more time in case you
>   didn't hear—
> (sung) We like koocoats, we *love* koocoats,
> 'Cause it's the best—food—in—the—land!

Try this rendition out on your front-room piano someday, especially when a few drunken friends show up. I think you'll all have a good time. This lyric was written by two of our teenage friends, Ralph Germano and Frankie Mangone, both great baseball players.

Shortly after I entered the seventh grade at Skinner Junior High School, I began studying with a pianist named John Kirkland. He was qualified as both a classical and popular music teacher. We spent several exciting years together and I learned a great deal from him.

About this time, brother Mike brought home a recording made by a jazz accordionist in Chicago named Art Van Damme. What a thrill it was the first time I heard him play. I had never before heard the instrument played like that. He sounded like a great jazz clarinetist. His playing convinced me that the accordion should be taken more seriously and was not just an instrument to play ethnic folk music. There were many great, serious accordion artists at the time like Pietro Diero, Charles Magnante, Gallarini, and others, but the music they played (I felt) was too formal and not as communicative as jazz and popular music. Although I kept on playing the accordion, the piano was now taking up all of my time and energy.

I continued to write arrangements for my brother's big band, all the while learning from him and my cousin, Clyde Comnillo, who played piano beautifully—especially when they improvised together, playing duets in our front room. Mike specialized on alto saxophone and clarinet. I was fascinated by their ability to improvise with such ease and how they would musically communicate with each other by what they were playing on their respective instruments. Listening to them really opened my eyes and ears to what jazz was all about. We would spend hours discussing the many different possibilities of harmonizing a song, which we call "chord changes," in the language of popular music.

One of my first jobs was playing piano with a three-piece combo at a local Italian restaurant. My pay was seventy-five cents per night and a meatball sandwich. While I was still in junior high school, I worked with the local dance bands of Vern Byers, Johnny Hawes, and Stan Koskoff.

A group of string players headed by John Browning, concert master of the Denver Symphony, formed a small orchestra that played Viennese waltzes every Monday night at a local hotel ballroom. Since they couldn't afford the money to pay for three French horns to play the "um-pa-pa" rhythmic parts, I was chosen to play this rhythm on the accordion. My ability to sight-read and improvise stood me in good stead. I still wasn't old enough to drive, so Mr. Henrich (the first clarinetist and father of Val, one of my classmates) drove me to and from the job. It always amazed me to hear these classical musicians play so many notes, at first sight, with such ease. When I expressed my admiration to Mr. Henrich, he said something that I have never forgotten, and that is, "It is more important for you to learn how to play three notes beautifully and soulfully, rather than to play thirty notes fast." How true, how true.

This orchestra became quite popular and we were asked by the Denver City Council to play a Viennese waltz concert at an outdoor area in the foothills outside of Denver. They wanted to test the natural acoustics of a particular location and see if it could be developed into an outdoor concert stage. Imagine all of us musicians in tuxedos, carrying our instruments and climbing up the side of a foothill on a breezy summer night with dust swirling all around us. We were not a group of happy campers. When we finally arrived at a fairly level plateau and reluctantly began to unpack our instruments, we noticed all the members of the city council and their friends seated up on the various rock outcroppings, trying not to slip or fall on the tilted terrain. Large floodlights were set up so that we could see our music and proceed with the concert. But, as luck would have it, as soon as we started to play, a strong gust of wind blew all the music and the stands off the stage! The conductor was in a state of shock. Fortunately, one violinist named Freddie Trahan, and a bass player and I continued playing because we could improvise without the music. While the rest of the orchestra happily packed up their instruments and left the area, our trio continued on for almost an hour playing all the Strauss waltzes we could remember. As a result, the council members and various sound experts were satisfied with the natural acoustics. Consequently, money was allocated to develop the project.

And that's how the world-famous Colorado "Red Rocks Amphitheater" was born.

NATIONAL HONOR SOCIETY

All through school, Mama was very concerned about my grades. Every student was academically judged by 1-2-3-4-5 in elementary school and A-B-C-D-E in junior and high school. She became annoyed if she didn't see all 1's or A's on my report cards. One of her favorite expressions was, "What is—IS!" If I wanted something, I had to study, learn and work hard for it. Praying would not solve the problem, and there was no one to "help me with my homework." She got her message across, and as a result, I worked hard and got straight A's.

My American classmates sometimes boasted about the nickels and dimes they received as *rewards* for getting B's and C's—grades that Mama would have really frowned upon.

I hated to miss one day of school—not because I loved it, but because I realized that I'd have extra homework to do in order to compensate for my absence. Having to catch up never made any sense to me. Snowstorms and freezing cold weather often provided us kids with perfect excuses to stay home. Since there were no buses provided, we all walked to and from school, no matter what the weather was like. An old buddy of mine, Ray Valente, always came by and we placed paper bags over our heads to protect us from the blizzards we had to endure. We cut little peep holes in the bags so we could see where we were going. Mama thought we were crazy, but it was a challenge for us and we had a lot of fun doing it.

In my senior year at Skinner Junior High, I was voted president of the National Honor Society. At the award ceremony, all the mothers of the honorees were expected to be up on the stage with them. Mama became very upset when I told her of this plan. She felt uncomfortable because she didn't know what to wear amidst all those "American ladies." She was also frightened that they might ask her to say something. Hearing her tell me that I should "get out of things like that at school" convinced me that she just didn't understand. Yet, I insisted that she be with me. After much pleading, she finally agreed. All of the teachers and parents in attendance acknowledged her and made her feel important and needed. I will never forget the beautiful smile she had on her face when we got home.

Although Mama was born in Denver, she never had the opportunity to learn or fully understand any other culture but Italian. But I always admired her innate intelligence and understanding of the basic true values of life. The things I had quoted her as saying to me while I was growing up may sound harsh to you, but I knew, then and now, that she loved me with every breath she took. She also knew that I felt the same way about her.

Many times during my early childhood, she found it necessary to punish me for some stupid thing I had done. She would swat me on my behind with a thin wooden slat from a cantaloupe crate. As I grew older and realized that I could run away from her, my physical punishment days were over. After an hour or so, her anger would subside. Then I'd sneak up behind her—put my arms around her so that she could not hit me—and give her lots of kisses. She would yell and still pretend to be angry—but eventually she would start to laugh, because she knew she had already taught me a lesson.

Papa was always interested in learning about new things. Shortly after he arrived in the United States, at the age of fifteen, he began to teach himself to read and write English. Over a period of several years, he attended night classes at a free educational institution in Denver called "Opportunity School." After many months of studying American history and related topics, he finally passed the big test and became an American citizen. A major accomplishment for a man coming from his background.

RICHARD PETERSON

One of my closest buddies all through junior and senior high school was Richard Peterson. He was a very talented artist, and we both hoped that one day we would be able to go to New York City to study our respective crafts. He wanted to attend the Pratt Institute of Art in Brooklyn while I wanted to go to Juilliard. His sense of humor was unique. For example, in our early teens, we both became aware of our respective libidos. Rich managed to find a great book, written by a doctor that very clearly described what should actually take place, sequentially, when a man and a woman had sex. He told me about it on the telephone and promised to come right over to my house and give me a copy. It was a Sunday afternoon and Mama and several of her friends were sitting and chatting in the front room. Just as I finished playing the piano for them, I saw Rich come walking through the front door. He politely greeted Mama and her friends and then loudly said, "Hey, Nick, here's that great book I promised you." I was so embarrassed that I could have smacked him right on the spot. However, on closer examination, I discovered that he had cleverly covered the book with brown paper, and using his great artistic ability, he sketched on the cover (in beautiful old English print) the words "Pilgrim's Progress."

CHAPTER 4

LATE-TEEN YEARS

When I was fifteen years old, I was offered a job at KLZ, a local radio station. Rollie Chestney, a violinist, was the leader of a five-piece group that featured a marvelous pianist named Barclay Allen. I must admit that my brother asked me to lie about my age, because in order to get the job, I had to be a member of the Musician's Union and sixteen was the minimum age to join.

This was a great step up the ladder for me because these players were all professionals. The singers we accompanied rarely had any arrangements for us to play, so we listened to each other and improvised. The daily programs had a casual talk-show format and a good time was had by all. It lasted one whole summer, and then I had to quit in order to go back to school.

I was driving my brother's car and listening to the radio when I first heard the jazz pianist, Art Tatum. I was flabbergasted! His playing actually took my breath away. I had to pull over to the curb and stop the car. I felt my heart was going to leap right out of my body. To this day, I marvel at that man's incredible ability. A true genius who has influenced pianists all over the world.

The music of Glenn Miller, Tommy Dorsey, Harry James, Artie Shaw, and bands like that were dictating the popular songs we sang and danced to. Social hours and proms gave us all a chance to mingle. Jitterbug dancing was very popular, but I preferred to slow dance cheek to cheek. In those days, how else could you hold a beautiful girl in your arms and get away with it? I loved this part of growing up, but I wasn't able to go to many dances like most kids my age because I was playing in a band somewhere almost every Friday and Saturday night.

Even though I had abandoned my desire to one day become the shortstop for the New York Yankees, I still loved to participate in any athletic-type game. My brother, Mike, and cousin, Clyde became interested in playing golf. All of us were avid sports fans. But the thought of having to walk all day in the blistering sun and try to hit a small white ball around seemed stupid to me. However, one day I was persuaded to tag along with the two of them. At the first tee, Mike told me, "Go ahead, try to hit the ball." Since I always had great confidence in my physical coordination and natural athletic ability, I obligingly picked up a club and rather smugly thought I was going to make a big impression upon them. Well, after missing the ball completely on my first five tries and having to suffer their outrageous laughter, I knew I was *hooked* on the game. That day really taught me a lesson. After a lot of practice, I became a fairly good golfer and ended up making the golf team two years later at North Denver High School.

MUSICAL INFLUENCES and KLZ

Senior high school offered more challenges, both scholastically and socially. The Merry Macs, a vocal group on the *Fred Allen Radio Show*, became very popular. They sang pop songs in four-part harmony with a great rhythmic beat. They inspired me to form a similar group in high school, one girl and three boys. We did our best to copy them. Our quartet became very much in demand at all school functions and we had a ball performing many of the hit songs of the day.

Our choirmaster, Mr. Bybee was very supportive of our efforts. This dear man would many times let me have the last five minutes of our choir class to "experiment" with the full chorus, singing jazz harmonies I had learned from listening to the big brass sections of famous dance bands. What fun we all had singing that kind of music after we had just done a Bach chorale. The variety was a blast for all of us. At Mr. Bybee's request, I wrote an a-cappella arrangement on "Summertime." What a joy it was for me to hear all those beautiful voices and also be singing in the tenor section. I loved this man, my quartet, and the entire choir.

Another of my favorite classes was shorthand and dictation. My buddies teased me about this, because I was one of only two boys in a class of thirty girls. The Gregg shorthand method was very challenging, but I managed to pass my one-hundred-twenty-words-per-minute dictation test. If the music business didn't work out for me, I was told that I could always get a job as a court reporter. My three years at North Denver High School were happy ones. I had grown up with many of my fellow students, starting with our kindergarten classes at Columbian grade school.

During my last year of high school, I got another job at radio station KLZ, playing accordion and piano in a trio featuring Capt. Ozzie Waters, a country singer and guitar player. We were on the air every Monday through Friday from 6:30 AM to 8 AM. Bob Freed was the announcer and he delivered a lot of commercials advertising various farm products. The show catered to rural areas and early risers. Ozzie never liked to rehearse, so whenever he sang, the bass player and I just filled in behind him. Occasionally, I would play a piano or accordion solo to add a little variety to the show.

One very sleepy morning, Bob Freed was doing a commercial aimed at the chicken farmers in the area. The product was called "Gooch's Best Starting Feed," good for baby chicks. Somehow, Bob got his tongue twisted and what he said was, "Hurry on down to your local supply store and stock up on Gooch's best FARTING steed!" We all roared laughing. Bob punched his announcer's *off the air* button, which silenced his laughter and embarrassment, and he walked out of the studio. Capt. Ozzie was unable to sing because he couldn't stop laughing. For the next ten to fifteen minutes, I played accordion solos, silently laughing, with tears streaming down my face all the while. Yes, I just happened to be there, except this time, I wasn't able to get any watermelon for my efforts.

RELIGION

In my late teen years, I was having difficulty reconciling my growing differences with the Catholic Church. As a child, I was impressed with the altar proceedings on holidays and Sunday masses, the robes and the celestial music, but as I grew older I started asking too many questions. There I go again. I didn't like phrases like "through my fault, through my fault, through my most grievous fault." I never understood why I should ask forgiveness for something I didn't do. I attended Sunday masses to please my mother, but I was slowly drifting away, particularly when my libido started to make its presence known. Going to confession always gave me a comforting feeling, but shortly after I had my first experience with sexual intercourse, I knew I was in trouble.

One day I went to confession and after telling the priest about having had sex, he said something like, "For your penance say ten 'Our Fathers' and ten 'Hail Marys.'" As I knelt down to say my prayers, I saw two lovely young ladies kneeling in the pew in front of me. I couldn't help but notice their very attractive *derrieres*. It was then I realized that I was definitely not sorry for my *sin*. It would be truly hypocritical to continue on with this charade. How could I possibly have any remorse or feel guilty for doing something that I felt was so natural? If God gave me this wonderful urge, and it happened only with a consenting partner, what was so wrong with it? My brother Mike and his buddies had already made me aware of all the necessary precautions and responsibilities of sexual activity. I took their teachings very seriously.

Knowing that I was getting *to that age*, Mama was concerned that I should speak to somebody older about the boy-girl subject. Papa took for granted that I already knew what sex was all about. When I foolishly expressed to Mama that she was being old-fashioned and worrying unnecessarily, she looked me straight in the eye and said loudly, *"Madonna Mia, comma see stupeedo! Thoo mi peel-ya per fay-sa? Thoo see mio feel-yo. Mai scordar kaa eeo ad-dja fa-tha thay!"* (My god, how stupid you are! Do you take me to be a fool? You are my son. Don't ever forget that I MADE YOU !)

Attending Sunday mass was still important to me, but I now had a different opinion about the Catholic dogma. I felt that if *any religion* gave you comfort and solace, then you should practice it, absolutely! We should all respect each other's concepts and beliefs and live in harmony. Tolerance was, and still is, the main issue. To each his own. "Do unto others as you will have them do unto you" became my motto.

I always knew that my mother had great faith in Catholicism, but she didn't go to mass regularly. She considered Sunday a serious work day. Preparing for the usual big dinner, which generally began around 1 P.M., was a big responsibility for her. But come holidays, she always managed to go to confession and take communion.

Papa, on the other hand, never gave Catholicism or any other religion much credence. He believed in God and the teachings of Christ, but he had bad memories of his childhood days growing up in Italy. He said the priests in his village were selfish and mean. They always had the best food—all donated by poor peasants and they lived in great comfort, as compared to the local folks. At Sunday mass, the priests set up a long wooden pole protruding from the pulpit and if any of the children accidentally dozed off during the ceremony, they got smacked on top of the head with the pole.

One Sunday during mass, a priest was proclaiming that "God will provide for all." Suddenly, a pregnant young lady stood up, and pointing to her extended torso, yelled, "Who is going to provide for this?" The townsfolk, all knowing that the priest was the father of her unborn child, didn't say a word. Every one of them got up and slowly walked out of the church. Firmly believing in the *fear of God*, they never protested anything the priests did or said to them.

Papa never forgot that, and for the rest of his life he had very little regard for religious figures of any faith.

ITALIAN "INSURANCE POLICIES"

At this point, I knew that my parents, like so many of their counterparts, looked upon their offspring as insurance policies. They were totally in agreement with an old Italian peasant concept of family life. And that was, as long as their children lived at home and were able to work and earn money, all was well and life was beautiful. However, if an outsider, be it a husband or a wife came into the family, all hope was lost for Mama and Papa. They felt that their children would then move away from home, concentrate on raising their own families and leave them to die in poverty.

No matter how hard my sister and I tried to convince them that we would care for their every need forever, they still detested the idea of my brother, sister, or me ever getting married.

My brother Mike returned to New York City a couple of years earlier, and Mama was crushed when she learned that he got married. He had sent for his Denver girlfriend, Alice McMillan and they were living in New York City. Sadness and gloom filled our house in those days. I loved Alice, and I secretly wrote letters to the newlyweds, giving them updates on activities within the Perito household. They eventually moved back to Denver and later had two great children, Robert "Bobby" and Carolyn.

Several years later, my sister Marian also got married, much to the dismay of both my father and mother. Even though her dear husband, Mike Ligrani was a full-blooded Italian, he still took a lot of verbal abuse from Papa. They raised two handsome sons, James "Jimmie" and Eugene "Geno."

As the years went by, tensions eased and our enlarged family learned to live together in love and peace. I choose now to think of all the good times we shared—and we certainly had many, many of those.

My North Denver High School graduation photo, June 1942

BACK TO MUSIC

Upon graduating from North Denver High School, I received an academic scholarship to Denver University. I chose to attend the affiliate, Lamont School of Music in order to study piano with Ruth Parisoe. She had been a student of Madame Rosina Lhevinne from the Juilliard School in New York City. I never gave up hope that one day I would have the opportunity to study at that famous institution. The next year was spent with Ruth Parisoe and a harmony teacher named Mr. Hedges. I practiced and studied only heavy duty classical music because I knew that kind of knowledge and ability was what was required to gain entrance to Juilliard.

Because of the fact that I owned a tuxedo and could sight-read music, I was asked by the dean of Lamont School if I would like to be a page turner for the pianist Adolph Baller, who was to accompany the famous violinist Yehudi Menuhin, at a concert the following week. I was ashamed to admit that I had never been to a classical music concert. Ruth Parisoe, however, assured me that I would do just fine. She instructed me to sit at the left of the pianist and turn the pages with my left hand so as not to interfere with his vision and playing. It was going to be a new experience for me, and I was nervous.

I met Mr. Baller backstage a half-hour before the concert and he explained very quickly the music they were going to play. He told me not to be nervous. All I had to do was follow him wherever he went. They opened their program with the "Georges Enesco Violin Concerto." What wizards these two musicians were! They performed the piece magnificently. When they finished, the applause was deafening. They walked off the stage and I followed. After a brief pause to allow Menuhin to wipe the perspiration from his face, he took his violin and beckoned to Baller. They walked back onto the stage and I followed. Just before I got past the curtain to go on stage, the promoter grabbed my arm and spun me around. I was furious until I looked back on to the stage and realized that Baller and Menuhin were only taking a bow. You can imagine the embarrassment I felt for having almost committed a real classical goof. The rest of the concert went perfectly and it will always be a night to remember.

Five nights a week I played piano with Lou Morgan's dance band at the Brown Palace Hotel. A beautiful white grand piano was almost in front of the band, and as a result, I got a lot of attention. Interacting with the dancers on the floor was lots of fun, but sometimes I unknowingly would start to rush the tempo while we were playing. Harry Logan, an old pro dance band drummer, never hesitated to remind me, "Would you mind playing along with the rest of us?" I knew he was my dear friend, but he never spared the rod when it came to correcting me. Thank you, Harry.

Benny Goodman, Duke Ellington, Count Basie, and Charlie Barnett were some of the top jazz bands then, and I loved listening and learning from all the different types of orchestral arrangements they played. At the same time, I was determined to go to New York City and Juilliard. My life was filled with music, classical and popular. However, World War II was roaring and I would soon be drafted into the army.

CHAPTER 5

WORLD WAR II

A written test was given to all new inductees and we were under the assumption that the grade you received would determine whether you became a front-line soldier or a candidate for officers' training school. The war was taking a terrible toll on U.S. servicemen and nobody wanted to be in the infantry. I was happy to learn that one of my aunts was secretly able to get me a copy of that test. I studied it religiously and felt prepared.

On June 1, 1943, I was inducted into the army at Ft. Logan, Colorado. You can imagine my dismay when I discovered that the army gave not just one but five or six different tests. Naturally, the one I was given was not the test that I had prepared for. My hopes plunged! However, knowing that there was a strict time limit to complete the test, I started right in—perspiring all the way—and finished just as the bell rang.

The next stop was the barbershop where we got our GI haircuts. We were treated like a flock of sheep being fleeced. How depressing. You had nothing to say about it. The barracks were stark and cold. Life was grim. My buddies were soon shipped out to various training camps all over the country. Why I also didn't get my orders caused me great concern. Later, I learned that the grade I received on the induction I.Q. test was very good, and that caused the army brass to grant my desire to stay in music via an army band.

HALLORAN HOSPITAL

Staten Island, New York, became my new home for the next

three years. Halloran Hospital was a receiving station for wounded soldiers returning from the European front. The band was unauthorized, which meant we were not listed as musicians but rather as medics. In addition to driving ambulances and doing menial tasks, we were kept busy playing not only for retreat parades and GI functions but also shows and dances for the personnel of the entire post. Our group was made up mostly of musicians from New York City and the surrounding New York state and New Jersey areas. I was the only one from "out of town."

My brother had taught me the fingering on a baritone saxophone because the army recognized that as a *legitimate* military instrument. Piano players were considered *nonessential* and, therefore, perfect infantry material. My first job was playing cymbals in the marching band. I hated that because my ears kept ringing long after our daily retreat parades. When it became known that I could also play a saxophone, piano, and the accordion, my cymbal playing days were over. On strictly military functions, I played tenor saxophone and tried not to make too much noise. I wasn't very good, but nobody seemed to care. When I asked for help from some of the professional reed players in the band, they would always say, "Put the horn back in the case and go write an arrangement for us."

Our group consisted of thirteen Jewish Americans, twelve Italian Americans, and the other six or seven players were regarded as *civilians*. We had a sixteen-piece jazz band, which was not bad. It was part of the over all twenty-eight-piece military marching band. Five or six of us played all of the officers' club dances because we could fake and knew all of the popular tunes of the day. General DeVoe loved that, and he alone was the reason why we were never shipped out. Especially during the time of the "Battle of the Bulge" in Europe when the army was looking for every able-bodied soldier to go to the front.

HELEN KELLER

On March 20, 1945, everyone on the post was required to attend a meeting in the auditorium honoring Helen Keller. In her early childhood years, she became ill with a disease that left her deaf and blind. Thanks to the dedication and perseverance of a wonderful teacher named Annie Sullivan, Helen learned to speak and communicate. Her presence at Halloran that day was to help bolster the morale of not only the wounded soldiers, but also the permanent personnel. We were amazed to see and hear this remarkable woman. She was able to actually converse with anyone. By placing her thumb on the throat, a finger on the lips and a finger on the nose of our commanding officer, Brigadier General Ralph G. DeVoe, she could understand exactly what he had just said to her. She would then respond audibly in a raspy sounding voice, but still understandable. Her mentor and guardian angel Annie Sullivan had taught her this incredible way of communicating. Needless to say, we were all blown away. Her nurse/companion this day was Polly Thomson.

Miss Thomson asked if there was a pianist in the audience. All the band members looked at me and I sunk down in my chair, feeling almost frightened. When I remained silent, they all shouted, "Yes, over here." I was persuaded to come forward and sit at a grand piano in front of the entire group. Miss Thomson then whispered into my ear, "Play something soft and gentle." Frantically, I thought—what should I play? I started to noodle, and all of a sudden, I found myself playing "Smoke Gets in Your Eyes." Why I chose that song, I'll never know. A hush fell over the audience as Helen placed her right hand on the closed lid of the piano. After a moment that seemed like hours, she started to wave her left arm in time to the slow tempo of the music I was playing. The audience erupted with cheers and applause. I continued playing until Miss Thomson again whispered into my ear, "Now change the music to a more rhythmic beat." I immediately segued into an up tempo boogie-woogie blues tune. Helen stopped waving her arm, and my spirits plunged. After a moment, however, she again raised her left arm and started to wave it exactly in time to the faster tempo I was playing. You can imagine the response she received this time. It was thunderous, and rightfully so. Later on, I had the distinct honor to be introduced to her by Polly Thomson and Helen pronounced my name perfectly. It was a day I will never forget. And I am so happy that *I just happened to be there.*

Our band was made up of many different personalities. All essentially good guys. One, in particular, got everybody's attention. Seymour "Zish" Molbegott was his name. He was a very good drummer, but his real talent was comedy. He had played in bands in the Jewish Alps in upstate New York and, as a result, learned a lot from listening to the famous comedians who performed there. Zish was the emcee for many functions and he had a unique approach to comedy that was all his own. He could improvise instantly on the current topics of the day and make everyone laugh, officers and enlisted men alike. He brought a lot of joy to all of us during some very trying times. Little did I realize then that our paths would cross again after we were released from the army.

Our band became authorized after about one year and a new conductor took charge. He was warrant officer Mr. Halloway, a regular army man with a very rigid concept about *everything* in life. He was not a big hit with the band, musically or personally. However, he was our new leader and he did *everything* according to the army way. You've heard the expression, "the right way, the wrong way, and the army way"? Well, this man defied them all.

*Playing for Helen Keller at Halloran Army Hospital—
Staten Island, New York, 1945*

CROCITTO'S

Adolph Tramontana (Dolph Traymon), a very good pianist, and I traded off playing piano in our jazz band. He managed to get a job for five of us every Saturday and Sunday night at a local pizzeria in South Beach, Staten Island, called "Crocitto's." Buddy Katz played tenor saxophone; Benny Caruso, drums; Gaetano Frega, bass ("Gate" became a member of the famous Joe Mooney jazz quartet after the war); Eddie Aversano, trumpet; Dolph Traymon, piano; and me on accordion. We always got weekend passes from Halloran Hospital and that gave us all an opportunity to relax and play whatever kind of music we wanted. And we each made five dollars per night. We were in the chips.

In addition to playing dance music, we also accompanied the various singers, comedians, and other entertainers that were booked for the weekend variety shows. Unfortunately, a large bar and pizza kitchen was right next to the dance floor and the night club area. The chef was an angry old Italian man who didn't give a damn about anything or anybody other than to loudly inform the *entire world* when a pizza order was ready. No matter what was going on in the restaurant, we regulars soon became accustomed to hearing him yell out at the top of his voice, "PORRRRTA VEEEYAH" (Porta Via)—which meant *take it away!*

Many nights just after the show started and the lights were dimmed, an attractive young entertainer would start to sing a soft, sentimental love song that always created a very soothing and romantic atmosphere. But it was only for a minute because suddenly, from out of the kitchen, we would all hear the old man scream, "PORRRRTA VEEEYAH." His timing was terrible and many of the performers wanted to do him in right then and there! It so happened that he was closely related to the owner and there was nothing anyone could do about his loud outbursts. He gave us musicians lots of laughs, and we appreciated his pizzas.

Radio Station WOR in New York City decided to have a weekly show emanating from Halloran Hospital, with Stan Lomax as host and featuring many of the returning, wounded soldiers who could either sing or relate an interesting story. Barry Gray was the associate producer of the show. He would one day become a famous New York City late-night radio talk show host. Dolph Traymon wrote a lovely theme song for the show and I arranged it for the band in the style of Glenn Miller. It started out with a very impressive fanfare and it was a big hit with everyone. After our orchestra played the show every Saturday afternoon from 3 PM to 4 PM, we all got our weekend passes.

Saturday morning was barracks inspection time. Our living quarters had to be immaculate. No wrinkles on the bed covers, shoes shined, and clothing in perfect shape—all according to army code. Our warrant officer loved being "king" at times like this. One Saturday morning, he decided that the windows in our barracks were a little dusty. So just before we started to rehearse the music for our coast-to-coast radio show, he informed us all that our weekend passes were suspended. Talk about doom and gloom. We immediately called Pat Crocitto, the pizzeria owner and he became enraged! I think he may have even threatened to make a call and have the "Jersey Boys" come over to "straighten out the entire situation."

Our spirits were crushed and none of us were enthused about having to play the radio show. Eddie Aversano, our first trumpet player who was the lead trumpeter at the Copacabana in New York City before the war, had a secret up his sleeve. He didn't say a word to anyone. At the dress rehearsal, just before we went on the air, he took it upon himself to get the warrant officer's attention. As soon as the announcer yelled, "This is Halloran," the band started the fanfare and Eddie played so many wrong notes it was difficult for the rest of us not to laugh. His example caught on immediately with every member of the band. You never heard such cacophony in your life. We all stared directly ahead of us—not daring to look at each other. Our warrant-officer leader stopped the orchestra and asked Eddie, "Why so many wrong notes?" Eddie apologetically replied that he had a canker sore on his lip and he thought it was cancerous. Nothing more was said. However, just before the show started and we went on the air, Staff Sergeant De Martino gave us all back our weekend passes. Oh, boy! That old army guy really got the message. When he threw the opening downbeat at the start of the live broadcast, the band played better than it had ever played before. Pat Crocitto served us some great pizzas that entire weekend.

THE "POW"

We had several hundred German prisoners of war on the post. They worked at menial tasks and several of them spoke English. On one occasion, I had a POW as my helper. Our job was to take down all the technical info regarding every soldier returning from the European front who was admitted to the hospital. It was a grim task because so many of them were severely wounded and it broke your heart to see such pain and sorrow in their faces. I angrily remarked about what I thought of Hitler and the entire Nazi regime, using every four-letter word I had ever heard, which was normal for GIs at times like that. I knew my helper understood everything I said, but he remained silent. He kept a pleasant look on his face and did his best to help me with our collective job.

Going to church on Sunday still gave me a chance to meditate and reflect. I remember kneeling down one Sunday morning and not paying too much attention to the priest and the altar boys as they made their entrances onto the altar. When the priest did turn around to give his blessings to the congregation, I almost fell through the floor! He was the same man who had been my helper at the hospital two days earlier. All of the cuss words I had uttered began to haunt me. I was so ashamed of myself and I couldn't wait for the mass to end so that I could go back to the sacristy and apologize to this nice man. He was very kind and gracious. He told me that he understood my anger and frustration. I learned that he, along with several other Catholic priests, were inducted into the German army and sent to the front lines as infantrymen. What a story he had to tell! We became good friends and after that, every time he walked by the band barracks, we played "Lilli Marlene," a very popular German song. His smile always made us feel better. What a dear man.

HORSE PLAY

The permanent personnel of Halloran was made up mostly of doctors, nurses, and young people who were pre-med students before the war. It wasn't a very strict military institution. Except for one adjutant general. He was head of a horse parade group and he got his jollies pretending to be John Wayne. You can imagine what the band members thought of him. At any rate, he decided that our band should practice inside the horse corral so that the horses could get used to the loud music. Then they wouldn't bolt when we had a parade for visiting dignitaries and the horsemen had to pass in review in front of the band, while it was playing loud military music.

On one miserably hot summer day, we were ordered to hold our practice session inside the horse corral. We began playing a Sousa march at a very loud level. It quickly became obvious that the horses did not like all the noise we were making. They reared up and started to charge us. Our conductor at the time, Sergeant De Martino, loved leading the band no matter where it was. He had his back to the horses and did not see their oncoming rush. But all the band members did see them racing toward us and we immediately started to run and climb the corral walls, throwing our army-issued instruments into the air and over the fence. Utter chaos resulted. Some wise guy suggested that before we started, we should have asked the horses if they had any favorite tunes we could have played.

I am forever grateful that I didn't have to go overseas and do combat duty. Those were terribly difficult years for everyone, physically and emotionally. Being with guys all the time was the only big drag for me. I longed to hear soft female voices and smell perfume again. I was tired of writing letters back home to old friends and I was just plain lonely. One of the happiest days of my life was when I got my army discharge on April 1, 1946.

CHAPTER 6

FREEDOM

I felt like I had just been released from prison. What joy! What freedom! Back home again with my family and old friends. Wow! Lady luck was on my side. I resumed studying with Ruth Parisoe and life was beautiful again. I soon got my own fifteen-minute radio show—three times a week playing piano and accordion solos. Papa arranged for me to get my own car. What could be better? I was a big fish in a small pond, but who cared? I was happy.

Although I had dated several different girls during my high school and army years, one young lady named Judy Stone, now had all of my attention. We first met in the a-cappella choir back at North High School and we dated occasionally. But now, we were getting serious. We did have one big difference of opinion and that was religion. She was born and raised as a Christian Scientist and that was a far cry from Catholicism, which I still clung to mostly because I knew my family expected it of me. We skirted the religious issue for several years because we were in love, and that's all that mattered at that time.

The thought of going to New York City and having to audition in order to just gain *entrance* to a school was very intimidating for me. I began to think that maybe Juilliard wasn't so important after all. Who needed that kind of pressure? I was a big deal now, back in my old hometown.

When my brother Mike got wind of my intentions, he really lowered the boom on me. He absolutely refused to hear any of my reasons to stay home and he insisted that I "get my ass back to New York and study music *seriously!*" End of discussion. Now, many years later, I am so grateful to him for not letting me off the hook. After many more piano lessons with Ruth Parisoe, I left for New York City.

JUILLIARD

Although Ruth had prepared me for my piano-playing audition at Juilliard, I was still a nervous wreck. I couldn't begin to describe my feelings the moment I walked into the audition room, knowing all of those professors were staring at me. Somehow I managed to perform fairly well. I spent two agonizing days in a very long line of students, all of us waiting for an opportunity to meet the admissions department executives and find out if we had passed our respective entrance exams and were going to be admitted to the school. It was heartbreaking to see some students leave the building in tears after learning that they had not qualified. Some of them actually had degrees from other universities. You can imagine what was going through my mind all of this time. "What in the hell am I doing here?" was a question I constantly asked myself. In addition to my piano audition, I had also submitted a passacaglia for string quartet as an example of my compositional ability.

When my turn finally came, I felt as though I was going to meet my executioners. A very cordial panel of judges asked me what I hoped to accomplish in the field of music. I answered that I wanted to learn how to compose music for Hollywood films in the style of Victor Young and Max Steiner. The judges were all pureblood classicists and I later realized that my statement didn't go over too well. In spite of that, they kindly informed me that I had passed the piano exam and was accepted as a student, starting classes the following week. I wanted to stand up and scream with happiness, but I kept my cool. One of my childhood dreams was actually coming true. I couldn't believe it!

Mike and Agnes Serao, who were friends of my family, lived in the Bronx with their two children and they invited me to move in with them. Mike, at one time, was a very good guitar player. My brother Mike and he were old pals, and they had worked together in dance bands in New York City many years earlier. Agnes was a fabulous cook and they all made me feel like I was at home. The entire family tolerated my constant practicing and kept assuring me that they actually enjoyed listening to me. They were all very supportive and encouraging and I lived with them for an entire year. How fortunate I was to have such devoted friends.

JEANNE BEHREND

Jeanne Behrend was relegated to be my piano teacher. She was a graduate of the Curtis Institute in Philadelphia and a former student of Josef Hoffman. Samuel Barber had been one of her classmates. Jeanne was a short, thin woman with small hands for a pianist, but her energy and enthusiasm were unlimited. In addition to all the obvious piano composers, she loved the music of Villa Lobos and Louis Moreau Gottschalk. She insisted that my scale passages had to be as smooth as oil pouring out of a bottle.

Walking down the halls, listening to so many wizard students practicing their respective instruments was, sometimes, very intimidating for me. Virtuosi seemed to be everywhere. Jeanne would have nothing to do with my anxiety. She knew I could improvise and she encouraged me to do so, even though there wasn't a big call for that in the classical area. I learned later on that in the days of Mozart and his contemporaries, improvisation was encouraged and appreciated by everyone. All concertos give the performer an opportunity to improvise when the moment comes for the cadenza. I know that Mozart and his contemporaries thrilled audiences with their improvisations on themes previously stated in the concertos. It is sad that classical artists of today do not choose to do that. What a shame.

After a year or so, I was still showing signs of pressure, and Jeanne suggested that I stop practicing for one entire week. She insisted I get a book of essays by Ralph Waldo Emerson and read the one on self-reliance. It seemed odd to me that she would prescribe this as an antidote for my anxiety. But I did as she requested. What a cure! One theory of Emerson's has stuck with me ever since, and that is, in every genius we recognize a little of ourselves—the difference being, while we are thinking about it, he is *doing it*!

Naturally, a great deal of time was spent on practicing technique and studying piano literature. We also discussed many artistic theories. Jeanne felt that music was the subtlest of all the arts. Paintings and printed words could always be appreciated by simply looking at them. Music, however, had to be performed, played, or sung. Otherwise, it was just a lot of small dots on a piece of paper. This opened my mind to the theatricality of every musical performance. If the setting is right, musical emotions can be transmitted so much more effectively.

When I mentioned to her that I had some economic and family problems running around in my head, she suggested that I think of each problem as being in a box, and all of the boxes are in a net hanging over my head. If each day, I would reach up and take one down, open it, and resolve the problem inside, then in a short while, there would be no more boxes. An interesting theory and it did help me.

At one particular lesson, I was criticized for playing Bach too rigidly. Jeanne said, "This music was not written by a robot. Bach was a human being—a real man. He had twenty-four kids. My god, what a man! Now, take a deep breath and play this piece with some feeling." She made her point. I had the good fortune to study with this amazing woman for three years.

THE JUILLIARD SCHOOL of MUSIC
120 Claremont Avenue, New York 27

Jeanne Behrend and her Juilliard piano students

ROBERT SHAW

Once a week, all students were obliged to take part in a big choir rehearsal in the auditorium. We were divided into the usual SATB sections and our collective project was to sight-sing the Bach B Minor Mass. The choir was conducted by the now-famous Robert Shaw. I was a bit shocked by his attire. He wore an old comfortable pair of pants, ordinary slippers, and a sweatshirt—not exactly the acceptable dress code in those days for a person of his stature. However, his passion, energy, and knowledge of the music was a joy to behold. At least for most of us.

One day he became frustrated, because he wasn't getting the type of musical response he expected from a Juilliard group. He finally threw up his hands and yelled, "That's the trouble with this school—it's all FINGERS and NO HEART!" I have never forgotten that statement, because it explains exactly how I feel about many performers that I've heard who are too rigid and classically oriented.

BERNARD WAGENAAR

Besides my wonderful piano teacher, Jeanne Behrend and Robert Shaw, a couple of other professors really showed me the way. Bernard Wagenaar taught composition and orchestration. He always wore a bow tie and smoked cigarettes that smelled exactly like *pot*. He insisted that they were a particular Turkish blend. Hmm?

On several occasions, some of my classmates would try to impress Wagenaar with their classical knowledge by referring to an old melody written by a specific composer. Invariably, after a moment of reflection, Wagenaar would name the *correct* composer and then proceed to play the part of the composition that contained the motif they were referring to. He was not to be fooled by anyone. What a remarkable memory he had.

When he was asked questions like "What does a trombone or a clarinet sound like in the upper register?" he would answer, "My goodness, haven't you ever heard Tommy Dorsey or Benny Goodman play?" If you can imagine someone saying that in a thick German accent, you will understand the charm that this wonderful man exuded. His love, appreciation, and knowledge of all kinds of music were astounding. I was delighted to learn that he was also a big fan of one of my idols, Art Tatum. He was thrilled when I gave him a copy of a trio album Art made with "Slam" Stewart and Tiny Grimes.

While sitting at the piano one day, he played and sight-read the original orchestral score of a composition I had written for a full symphony—all the while, making suggestions like "not good for the bassoon in that register"—or—"you've been listening to *Kostelanetz* lately," referring to a particular string passage I had written. An amazing man.

Arturo Toscanni was at the height of his career with the NBC Symphony in those days and Mr. Wagenaar told us the story of his meeting with the maestro. At the suggestion of his friends, Wagenaar submitted one of his symphonies to Toscanni, hoping to be honored with a performance. At their first meeting and after Wagenaar played each movement on the piano, Toscanni said something like "bravo" or "very poetic." He agreed to perform the symphony on his return from Europe the following September, much to Wagenaar's delight.

Months later, at the first orchestra rehearsal, Wagenaar was seated in the audience with a score copy of his symphony on his lap. Toscanni was conducting the orchestra up on the stage and making corrections—with NO SCORE in front of him. He had memorized the entire symphony. I still remember the look of admiration Mr. Wagenaar had on his face when he related this story to our class.

TEDDY WILSON

What a delightful man. He held classes at Juilliard one summer, and fortunately, I was able to study with him. His gentle, mild manner won everyone over—to say nothing of his enormous talent. We met twice each week for eight weeks. The first weekly class involved all of his ten or twelve students and we discussed jazz harmonies and old standard tunes. Teddy encouraged each of us to get up and play and demonstrate how we felt about certain passages. In addition to this class, each of us had a private piano-playing lesson with him each week. This allowed me to sit side by side with Teddy—at two different pianos—and we alternated playing choruses. Naturally, I was very timid having to play next to this master of improvisation. But he soon made me relax and kick back. One day, he actually stopped me in the middle of a song and said, "How did you finger that run?" I almost fell off the piano stool. I sheepishly told him it was a run that I had learned from an Art Tatum book. The smile on his face told me immediately that he was also an admirer of Tatum. He then proceeded to tell me about the early days in Harlem. On certain nights when many of the jazz pianists in town finished their respective gigs, they would all go uptown to hear Art. It was always in the wee hours of the morning. Each of them would play a tune or two, and then after everyone finished, Art would be coaxed to leave his bottle of Budweiser at the bar and get up to the piano. "It was *then*," Teddy said, "that you really got to hear Tatum play." After an hour or so, everybody would go home with big smiles on their faces, knowing they had just heard the master.

It was very inspiring for me to study and hang out with such a great jazz musician—a kind, gentle, humble man, and to know that he too had his heroes.

IRWIN FREUNDLICH

Here was another teaching giant. The course he taught was called Literature and Materials, L&M for short. It was wonderful because we discussed and analyzed the actual compositions of the masters as opposed to a lot of rules and examples in a textbook.

Freundlich never sat at a desk in front of the class. He preferred to sit in a chair amidst all of us students. Many times he began the class by saying, "What are you all going to teach me today?" This approach really got our attention because he never *held court*. It wasn't a big deal if he asked a question and you didn't know the answer. He felt that his job was to make us aware of our individual weaknesses and, hopefully, after a lot of practice and study, we would be able to seek our own solutions. Whenever students came to class late, he would welcome them and then briefly tell them what we had just discussed. He told us early on, "This school insists that I give you a test at the end of the semester. But if you feel you can pass this course without attending class, it's perfectly OK with me."

Mr. Freundlich was knowledgeable in whatever kind of music we agreed to discuss—anything from Bach to Gershwin. And whatever instrument we chose to play (while expressing our opinions) was acceptable to him. Our performances on those instruments were not judged. The *content* of the music we played was most important. He created a wonderful democratic forum where we all participated and were constantly reminded that there was no such thing as a *stupid question*. Exciting verbal exchanges took place because he created a friendly and safe environment in which we all participated and expressed our innermost thoughts and feelings. He made us aware of the fact that a learning experience could also be very entertaining.

The day before my graduation, I was summoned to his office for a final consultation. He congratulated me and asked, "How do you feel now that you are graduating from Juilliard?" I paused for a moment and then answered, "I finally realize how little I know about music." He sat back in his chair and roared with laughter. Then he added, "I'm so happy to hear you say that, because now I know I have succeeded as a teacher. You have all the necessary talent to make exciting new musical discoveries. Go out and put it to good use!" I gave him a teary hug and did my best to thank him for all the wonderful things he taught me about music—and life itself. What a great man. He was a perfect role model for teachers all over the world.

FERRANTE and TEICHER

These were two younger teachers. Arthur Ferrante taught keyboard harmony and Lou Teicher taught ear training. They both had graduated from Juilliard a few years before and each was an excellent pianist. Their classes were very relaxed and everyone was able to communicate without any tension. They realized that I had a background in popular music and aspired to become more knowledgeable in the classics. Later I learned that they also knew and appreciated the music of Broadway and the movies. They had become a piano team and did a lot of classical concertizing during off-school hours. I had no idea at that time that our lives would one day become so personally and professionally involved.

JOE MALIN (MALIGNAGGI)

Social life at school was nonexistent, except for the student lounge. That was where we all hung out, waiting for a practice room to open up. Thanks to one person named Joe Malignaggi, it was a fun place to be. Joe was the life of the party. He had a great sense of humor and was a fabulous storyteller. Violin was his major and he had attended Juilliard one year before he was drafted into the army. He and I bonded immediately and that was the beginning of a "brother" relationship that would last forever.

Joe had known Arthur and Lou (Ferrante and Teicher, respectively) before the war. Since Joe was also a master cook and a great host, we all began to socialize and we became close friends.

With the exception of the teachers I had singled out, I felt that Juilliard was preparing me for a world that was not for real. After many discussions with several other faculty members, I began to realize that they had no idea what *earning a living* as a musician in the outside world was all about. Trying to become a concert pianist was not one of my aspirations, so I directed my energies to other musical categories. Although I was studying orchestration and had to compose a lot of little pieces, I was never given an opportunity to actually hear a live orchestra play what I had written. This was extremely frustrating because I was convinced that "one listening is worth a thousand words." Therefore, I took it upon myself to attend all of the school orchestra rehearsals. Thanks to my pal, Joe

Malignaggi who was a member of the violin section, I learned beforehand what was going to be played. The orchestra scores were available in the library, so I was able to study them prior to each rehearsal. What a wonderful learning experience it was to be able to *hear* the music, follow along with the score, and listen to the comments of various conductors. One particular young man named Cavalo (from Brazil) really fascinated me. He was a protégé of Serge Kousevitsky. One day while rehearsing the Berlioz "Symphonie Fantastique," he threw a downbeat and then proceeded to walk through the entire ensemble as they continued playing. He finally returned to the podium, stopped the orchestra and chastised them for not playing *in time*. He begged them to *listen* to each other and, if necessary, "tap the fingers in your feet." He couldn't remember the word for toes. What an interesting musician he was.

I concentrated on learning to accompany singers, whether they were classical or popular, and studying how to compose and arrange for orchestras of all sizes and different styles—not just the classical approach that was taught at school. These kinds of job opportunities were what New York City had to offer at that time. What an exciting and challenging place for anyone who was determined to make the necessary sacrifices to succeed in the field of music.

CHAPTER 7

CLUB DATES (1947-50)

A club date was any single function that needed music. Weddings, family reunions, office parties, debutante balls, corporate celebrations, political rallies, and other similar occasions gave us an opportunity to make a living in the music business.

Zish Molbegott, my old army buddy contacted me shortly after my return to New York. He was delighted to learn that I had been accepted at Juilliard. Knowing that I didn't have classes on weekends, he suggested that I play club dates and make some extra money. He recommended me to a man named Joe Rosenthal, an orchestra leader who played for a lot of Jewish weddings and Bar Mitzvahs in Brooklyn. The fact that I played both accordion and piano stood me in good stead. I was very naïve and apprehensive about what types of music I was expected to know and play. Zish assured me that it was the same kind of stuff we had played in the officers' club when we were in the army.

Joe soon called and gave me several dates. My first was at a catering hall somewhere on Euclid Avenue in Brooklyn. I was told that I would have to accompany a cantor. He had no music, but Joe said, "Don't worry—just listen and follow him—he sings in D minor. Oh, and when he says, (what sounded to me like) 'Barook arturo gudoy' (Baruch Atah Adonai), play these three chords very majestically." Not being familiar with the Hebrew language, I took comfort in the fact that I remembered an old Argentinean prizefighter named Arturo Gudoy.

The cantor finally began to sing and I improvised his accompaniment. He was very easy to follow, so Joe and the musicians were all giving me soft verbal encouragement during the performance. At the conclusion of the ceremony, the cantor came over and gave me a big hug and, in Yiddish, began to compliment me. Since I didn't understand one word he said, I modestly tried to inform him that I had never accompanied a cantor before. Finally, Joe yelled at me in a rather exasperated manner, "Schmuck, shut up! Can't you see you're a fucking hit?"

SID JEKOWSKY

Early on in the club date business, I was fortunate to meet a man named Sidney Jekowsky who was a graduate of New York University and had a master's degree in music. Clarinet and saxophone were his major instruments and he had a fantastic memory for songs and their original harmonizations. We immediately became close friends because we both felt similarly about all aspects of music and the business we were in. More about Sid later.

Being a keyboard player, I was expected to know "all the tunes." Learning lots of ethnic music and popular show tunes, old and new, kept me busy constantly.

All the while I was a student at Juilliard, I worked practically every weekend playing with different bands—thanks to the recommendations of my old pal Zish Molbegott and my new friend Sid Jekowsky. I remember studying my sight-singing lessons while sitting in the subway train on the way to my jobs. The train made so much noise that none of the other passengers could hear me humming. It seemed I never had any spare time just to kick back and relax. Juilliard and the music world I lived in outside of school were two distinctively different places.

Commuting by bus and subway became a problem because the Bronx was a long way from school. After one year, I found it necessary to move into Manhattan. The Serao family understood and gave me their blessings. I was fortunate to find a small apartment at 24 West Eighty-third Street. I shared it with my old Denver high school buddy, Richard Peterson who was an art student at Pratt Institute in Brooklyn. Mrs. Costelli, the landlady, had a piano in her downstairs apartment and she allowed me to practice on it in the early mornings.

CAFÉ SOCIETY and LUCIENNE BOYER

The east side of New York City was teeming with many different nightclubs where artists from all over the world performed nightly. Barney Josefson ran such a club. It was called Café Society Uptown. One day I received a call to play accordion for a French artist named Lucienne Boyer. They needed someone who could sight-read and improvise in the French style. Franck Pourcel, a violinist and a graduate of the Paris Conservatory, was her conductor. We hit it off immediately. Since Franck didn't speak English and we both spoke Italian, I was able to translate his instructions to the rest of the musicians. Working so late at night and having to rise early every morning to go to school, took a toll on my energy level. But I was assured that the engagement would last for only two weeks. Between the 8:30 P.M. and midnight shows, Franck and I discussed my Juilliard homework. He wanted desperately to stay in New York City and become a studio musician. I introduced him to several people that I hoped would help him, but to no avail. Little did we realize then that on his return to Paris, he would later become famous as one of France's most popular "easy listening" orchestra leaders. It couldn't have happened to a nicer and more talented man.

Well, the two-week engagement turned into six months. Lucienne was a smash because everyone remembered that she was the lady who introduced "Speak to Me of Love" and made it such an international hit many years before WWII. I was a very happy, but sleepy, guy in those days, and burning the candle at both ends didn't concern me. Several exciting things were happening around this time that changed my professional life forever.

Lucienne Boyer at Café Society Uptown NYC 1947—
Franck Pourcel, violinist-conductor and me on accordion

JOHN HAMMOND

John Hammond was the man who started it all for me. Yes, the same man who discovered Count Basie, Billie Holiday, Bob Dylan, and many others. What an eclectic musical palate he had. He liked the style of easy jazz that I played on the accordion while accompanying Lucienne on a solo number I did with her on stage at Café Society Uptown. He introduced me to Mike Levin, the editor of *Downbeat* magazine. As a result of Mike and John's efforts, the publicity I received was great for my reputation on the New York City music scene. Again, thanks to John, Willard Alexander, a big band promoter and booking agent, offered me a job as the leader of a relief combo at the Commodore Hotel next to Grand Central Station. From 4 PM to 6:30 PM, I played piano in the cocktail lounge, along with a guitarist and a bass player. Then from 8 PM to midnight, we played in the main dining room as a relief group opposite the various popular big name bands that were featured regularly every two or three weeks. Sid Jekowsky, my clarinet-playing buddy, joined the group, and we became a quartet.

Going to school, trying to find a piano to practice on and playing six nights a week kept me very busy. A friendly hotel house detective would always tell me where there was a vacant conference room with a piano so that I could practice, often times from midnight to 2 or 3 AM.

John introduced me to an interesting circle of his friends. Among them were the composer Alec Wilder and an oboist named Mitch Miller, the same man who later became a very successful record producer and television star on "Sing Along with Mitch." John also arranged a recording session for me with Ellis Larkin, a wonderful jazz pianist. Just Ellis, me, and a bass player. We actually met in the studio and then decided to record an Alec Wilder song called "Who Can I Turn To." I was impressed with Larkin's jazz ability and I had never *recorded* before, so you can imagine my anxiety. Anyway, I interpreted the melody as though I were a jazz singer and left all the harmonic playing to Ellis. The flip side was "Beer Barrel Polka"—no, not like a Lawrence Welk version. I still don't know why in the hell we chose that song. Anyway, the record got a lot of play and it was good for my reputation.

My quartet at the Commodore Hotel in 1947: bass, Don Russo; guitar, Don Costa; clarinet, Sid Jekowsky

COMMODORE HOTEL and DON COSTA

Mundell Lowe, my original guitar player, moved on to more popular jazz venues and he was replaced by a young arranger with the Vaughn Monroe band. He came from Boston and his name was Don Costa. Since he wasn't yet a six-month member of Local 802, another guitar wizard, Don Arnone took over until Costa became available. From the very first day Costa and I met, we became brothers. We felt and thought so much alike in almost everything we did. Don was gifted with a natural musical talent for arranging and orchestration. Not having had any official musical training, he still had the ability to write down whatever musical sounds he heard. Sid Jekowsky said he acquired more musical knowledge listening to Don and I argue about certain harmonies and musical theories, than he ever learned as a student at New York University. He likes to remind me about one particular rehearsal when Don disagreed with me regarding a certain musical passage, and he told me politely to "shove Juilliard up my ass!" I can still hear Sid's high laugh along with the guffaws from our bass player, Don Russo. The Commodore Hotel gig was a learning experience and we were all grateful for the rewarding musical moments and ideas we shared together.

Although I kept a very busy schedule, I managed to write daily letters back home to my girlfriend, Judy. Since I was raised as a Catholic and she was raised as a Christian scientist, our religious differences were causing both of us a lot of pain and anguish. I read Mary Baker Eddy's book *Science and Health*—talked to several practitioners as well as Catholic priests and yet, I was still in a quandary. I wasn't convinced about any particular religion. What to do was the big question. As a result of our mutual frustration, Judy and I stopped writing to each other for almost an entire year.

After eleven months, the Commodore job folded. What a relief! I was able to find an apartment two blocks from school on 124th Street (just off Broadway), and I had my very own piano to practice on. For a short while, Don Costa was my roommate. My Juilliard brother, Joe Malignaggi lived upstairs along with two other students.

Being the master cook that he was, he graced us with his gourmet meals every night. The rest of us took turns doing the dishes after dinner. All except Don. He was the only person I ever knew who could leave more of a mess in the kitchen *after* he cleaned up than before he started. We all agreed that after dinner, he would stay out of the kitchen and go downstairs and write arrangements. Juilliard and classical music every day—jazz and pop music every weekend—and delicious food all the time. What a life!

JIM PROCTOR

In the fall of 1948, John Hammond introduced me to a press agent and Broadway publicist named Jim Proctor. His clients and friends were many of the new producers, writers, and actors on Broadway—people like Arthur Miller, Elia Kazan, Jean Stapleton, Alex North, and many other liberal-minded artists.

Jim had taken accordion lessons as a kid and he wanted to learn how to play the popular tunes of the day. He was a devout student of art, literature, and politics. During the following few years, I felt he taught me more about these three areas than I ever taught him about music. I loved his theory that one's lifestyle is determined by—"how you spend your leisure time."

Being a press agent, he was able to provide me with complimentary house seats to practically every Broadway show that was playing at the time. What an incredible learning experience that was for me, musically and theatrically. After every accordion lesson, we would sit around for at least an hour, discussing current artistic and political events and/or the play or musical I had recently seen. I particularly enjoyed Tallulah Bankhead and Noel Coward in *Private Lives*. What theatrical giants they were.

Jim was a true liberal, and he took a dim view of the political scene at that time. Racial and social injustices were everyday occurrences, and we both were activists in the sense that we wanted equality for one and all.

When *Death of a Salesman* opened on Broadway, Jim (being the press agent) asked me to play the opening night party at "21," the famous New York City night spot. These affairs were usually happy and upbeat., All interested parties waited patiently (after the show was over) for the newspaper reviews that so often determined whether the production was going to be a hit or a flop. *Death of a Salesman* was a deep, depressing drama about an American family and I knew it was going to be a rough job to try to keep the party atmosphere light and happy. Arthur Miller, Lee J, Cobb, Mildred Dunnock and all of the other cast members, along with many Broadway celebrities, began to arrive around 11 PM. I started playing the usual upbeat Broadway tunes like "Just One of Those Things" and "I Get a Kick Out of You," but I soon realized that I was fighting an uphill battle. People conversed in soft low tones and the atmosphere was almost like a wake. Everyone was still reflecting on the mood of the play. Alex North, the famous composer, sensed my discomfort and suggested that I take a break and have a drink. In my entire life, I was never so happy to *stop playing*. The reviews finally were read and everyone was relieved and happy to learn that the show was a smash.

I put the accordion back in the case and was privileged to sit back, have a drink, and talk with many of the great talents I have already mentioned. In the history of American theatre, this was truly a memorable night.

THE "TASTY YEAST JESTERS"

The Tasty Yeast Jesters were a trio of middle-aged folk-type singers who had grown up together as kids and they learned to sing practically every popular song in three-part harmony. They also accompanied themselves with a bass, tipple (small guitar), and a minimal drum set. In addition to live performances, they also did a lot of radio commercials and occasionally they added an accordion. I loved hearing them tell stories about their early experiences in radio. My favorite had to do with an engineer they worked with on a daily early morning radio show on WOR. He was grumpy and uncooperative practically all of the time. The Jesters decided on a great way to get his attention. For several days, they rehearsed singing "Easter Parade." However, at certain points during the song, they would suddenly stop making sounds with their voices and instruments but still continue to mime the lyrics and pretend to keep playing. For instance, while singing "Easter Parade" they would likely sound something like this, "In your Easter bon—with—frills up—you'll be—est—the East—ade." They could do the entire song in this manner. A week before Easter, they sang the song exactly like that while they were *on the air.* Naturally, the engineer flipped out! Thinking something had gone terribly wrong with his equipment, he kept making frantic calls to the transmitter operator over in New Jersey. All the while, he kept pushing buttons in and out on the control board in his own studio. The Jesters pretended that nothing was wrong and performed the song like this many times during the ensuing two weeks, driving the audio engineer absolutely crazy every morning. When they finally admitted their prank, he totally changed his attitude and became a real pussy cat. Ah, those early days of radio when everybody and everything was *live.*

My last year at Juilliard was a very intense period of my life, because in addition to doing lots of recording sessions and weekend club dates, I was diligently practicing and preparing for my final exams. My upstairs buddy, Joe Malin (as he would later be called), was also busy preparing for his final violin exam. The beautiful string sounds that came down from his apartment upstairs were very comforting to me. Plus, he still prepared fabulous meals every night for me and two of our other Juilliard friends who lived in adjoining apartments. Joe always provided an environment where we could share our thoughts and opinions about what was happening, not only in the world of music, but also in each of our personal lives. He had a marvelous sense of humor and the ability to always accentuate the brighter side of life.

FINAL PIANO EXAM

On the day of my final piano examination, I was allowed to practice fifteen minutes on the piano that I would actually play later that day. I was full of anxiety and tension because the keys *felt like* they were an inch deeper than any piano I had ever played. At

2 PM that afternoon, I walked out on the stage. The concert hall was empty, except for nine or ten members of the faculty sitting way back in the last row. I couldn't help but smile because behind the seated judges, I saw my dear teacher, Jeanne Behrend. She was waving her arms and making silly faces at me. Praying that my memory would not fail me, I sat down at the piano, took a deep breath, and started a Bach prelude. I got halfway through it when, all of a sudden, my mind went blank and my fingers stopped moving! I paused for what seemed like a full minute. I don't know why I didn't panic. Forcing myself to relax, I slowly felt my confidence return. Knowing then that I was in control again, I figured, "What the hell—go for it!"—and I did. When I finished playing the four pieces I had prepared, the judges politely applauded. I took a short bow and quickly left the stage. What a relief knowing that it was finally over. I found out later that I received a grade of B+ for my performance. Joe helped me drink a lot of wine that night. Now we all looked forward to graduation day, which was two weeks later on May 27, 1949.

Judy and me on our wedding day—May 28, 1949

GETTING MARRIED

After spending a brief vacation in Denver the summer before, Judy and I became involved again. This time quite seriously with daily letters going back and forth, still trying to figure out what our collective religious life might be. Finally, we both agreed to get married and let *nature take its course*. We were both in our early twenties. My mother was not happy about me getting married to *anyone*, particularly an American girl. She felt that they were all *scroves* or *putanas* (loose-moraled women), and they could not be trusted to be a part of any Italian family. I told her she was terribly wrong in her thinking and I was going to marry Judy, in spite of her opinions. I wanted her blessings and attendance at our wedding. Judy's father, a strict Christian scientist, was also skeptical about my Italian Catholicism.

Judy flew back to New York City the day before my Juilliard graduation because I wanted some close family member to be there to help me celebrate the occasion. Unfortunately, I had a terrible cold and I was a physical mess. In spite of that, immediately after the graduation ceremony, we hopped on a plane and arrived in Denver early the next morning. She went to her house and I went to mine. After a short nap to recover from the long plane ride, my mother and sister sat me down and tried to convince me that I was making a big mistake. They insisted that there was still time for me to back out of the wedding. We all shed a few tears, but I was able to convince them that I was not going to change my mind.

We had decided to be married by a judge in the front room of Judy's house at 6 PM that same evening—no priest or no minister. We didn't want to offend either side of our family. Her mom and sister made all of the necessary arrangements. Happily, all members of both immediate families were present. My brother Mike, was my best man and Louise, Judy's sister was her maid of honor. An old friend of mine played "Here Comes the Bride" on the front-room piano. However, the judge got nervous and mixed up our names. He kept referring to me as *Mike* and Judy as *Julie*. Down through the years, I've enjoyed reminding Judy that as a result of this mix-up, we are not *legally married*. I always make sure there is an easy exit close by after I say that.

It was very comforting for Judy and I to see how quickly our families learned to respect and care for each other. In later years, Marian became affectionately known as "Auntie Mimi"—not only to our close family members, but everyone else who had the good fortune to meet her and get to know the kind, loving and caring person she really was.

Shortly after our wedding, we returned to New York City and took up residence in Joe's apartment upstairs at 534 West 124th Street. He went on the road because he got a job playing violin in the Shep Fields Orchestra, along with his beautiful lady friend, Carmel Mancini, who shortly thereafter became his wife. A marriage made in heaven. They have two great children, Mary and Paul and our families remain bonded to this very day.

Judy soon became acquainted with all of my local friends and immediately understood what I had been trying to tell her about the realities of life in the big city. She saw for herself the uplifting things that education, tolerance, and understanding can do for people of all nationalities when they forget their prejudices. She became the champion of every downtrodden group in the vicinity—campaigning, marching, and doing everything she could to help those in need.

My clarinetist buddy, Sid Jekowsky and I worked a lot as a trio playing club dates with a bass player named Lou Simon. He was a well-schooled musician and a member of the CBS radio/TV staff orchestra. In later years, I remembered him complaining about his son, a young high-school student. Lou was frustrated, because instead of studying and doing his homework, "the darn punk just sat around and strummed a guitar all day." Are you ready for this? That *darn punk* turned out to be Paul Simon, the famous contemporary rock-and-roll singer-composer!

DOMINIC CORTESE and THE ACCORDION

One afternoon, I had to leave a club date early in order to get to a recording session that I had previously booked with Hugo

Winterhalter. While packing up my instrument, I heard the substitute accordionist and his great playing really got my attention. His name was Dominic Cortese, a master of the instrument. He was born in Italy and came to New York City when he was still in his early teens. Baseball became an obsession with him, as it was for me when I was a youngster back in Denver, Colorado. We really had a lot in common.

Dom had a very ingratiating personality, and he was admired and loved by everyone. His technique on the accordion was impeccable and he understood all the many styles that this instrument was identified with. He played everything from club dates and recordings up to the Metropolitan Opera. In later years, his lovely wife, Sandy, and their two sons, Richie and Tommy, all became a part of our extended family.

Carrying an accordion all over the New York City area was exhausting and sometimes very painful. My fingers became sore and it was difficult to play when I finally arrived at my destination. In order to limber up my fingers, I had to soak my hands in warm water.

Dominic suffered with the same problem, but he did some research and assured me that having wheels put on my carrying case would not disturb the reeds inside the instrument. Hallelujah!

My apartment on 124th Street, just off Broadway, was still a long way from the Lennox Avenue subway station in Harlem. Thanks to the new wheels on my accordion case, I now didn't mind the long walk. *Plus,* many of the little neighborhood African-American kids thought it was great fun to ride on top of the case as I wheeled it down the street. What was initially a great chore suddenly became a lot of fun. Some of the bigger kids eventually took over for me and I just walked along beside the entire troop. When we arrived at either my apartment or the subway station, I always managed to have enough loose change in my pocket so that my helpers could buy themselves some candy. What a fond memory that is for me.

Soon, arranging and playing the piano took up most of my time and I could see my accordion playing days coming to an end, except for very special occasions. As a result, I recommended Dominic for everything I could not do, and he soon inherited the No. 1 accordion position in town.

LESTER LANIN

He was a terrible drummer and one of the cheapest men in the world—but he enjoyed a great reputation as the best "society" club date leader in New York City. His client list read like the Fortune 500 club. One very wealthy client hired Lester to fly a fifteen-piece orchestra to Cincinnati, Ohio to play his daughter's coming-out debutante party. As usual, the music stands were set up on the bandstand, but to my surprise, there was no music on them! I soon learned that these great musicians were able to play, by ear, almost any popular song. Hearing fifteen *different* players make their collective performance sounded like a well-rehearsed orchestra was really a major artistic accomplishment.

Almost all of Lanin's jobs were continuous, which meant that each musician was allowed only one short five-minute break every hour. Lester always had to be reminded of that fact. He insisted that the music never stop. Therefore, we were forced to take our breaks in shifts. He was very disliked by all of us musicians, but his jobs still paid more than many others in the business. Down through the years, I think practically every good musician who could fake and improvise, worked with or for Lester at one time or another. Among them were David Raksin, Doc Severinsen, Dick Hyman, Bob Rosengarden, Sid Jekowsky, Dominic Cortese, Phil Bodner, Urbie Green, Bob Alberti, Johnny Parker—and the list goes on and on.

On one occasion, I was playing accordion with a stand-up trio—me, a saxophonist, and a bassist. It was for an outdoor party at the home of a very wealthy family in South Hampton, Long Island, New York. It was a typical society party, in the sense that we musicians were able to watch the behavioral patterns of all the lovely, dignified ladies from the moment they arrived until the party was over. They made their initial appearances, dressed to the nines and beautifully made up. But after many hours of dancing, eating, and drinking champagne or hard liquor, many of them ended up looking like hell—their makeup smeared and hairdos all messed up. Gene Tierney (famous movie actress) met up with Oleg Cassini (famous designer) at this party and I could see the immediate attraction they had for each other. In the middle of the evening, they wandered off down the beach and returned an hour or so later, both looking very disheveled and not giving a damn what anybody thought. They were still having a good time, as was everyone else.

Our trio played from 8 PM until 3 AM continuously! We deserved the Charles Atlas award for stamina. When I finally got home a couple of hours later, I had to awaken my wife so that she could help me take off my jacket. Standing up and playing the accordion for all of that time made my shoulders numb.

JERRY JEROME

Jerry was a featured jazz-tenor saxophone player in Benny Goodman's band for many years and later became a successful leader with his own band on NBC. Television was really in its embryonic stage when Jerry hired me to play piano on a new weekly variety show called "Versatile Varieties." It featured various solo singers, dancers, acrobats, etc., and we were on the air for a half hour—live—every Friday night from 9 to 9:30 PM. Definitely prime time! Anne Francis and Carole Ohmart were the beautiful poster girls dressed in skimpy little sexy Scotch kilt outfits advertising the sponsor's product, "Bonnie Maid Linoleum." (Years later, they both became featured actresses in Hollywood.) Our show was seen only as far as Chicago because coast-to-coast television was not possible yet. George Givot, an old vaudevillian, was the original emcee and the show became very popular. Phil Krause played drums and percussion; Jerry played tenor saxophone and clarinet; I played piano and, occasionally, the accordion. That was it—a three-piece band. Jerry was a good jazz player but he was not a good sight reader. Whenever the music got fast or technical, Jerry stopped playing and conducted Phil and me. Nobody seemed to notice or mind that only two musicians were playing, so we just did our best and laughed about it later on. The show stayed on the air for almost a year and we were presented with a lot of musical challenges during that time.

HARRY BELAFONTE

Art Ford was a popular disc jockey and every Saturday night, he had a show on television station WPIX. The guest stars were mostly singers who wanted to plug their new record releases. Jerry was again the leader of a trio that consisted of himself on tenor sax and clarinet, Jack Zimmerman on bass, and me on piano.

A handsome young singer named Harry Belafonte appeared on the show one night. He was seated alone in what appeared to be a French café and was miming the lyrics to a lovely ballad that he had just recorded. All of a sudden the record got stuck and it kept repeating "I love you, I love you, I love you" in a very erratic pattern. Harry tried to mime the situation so that it would appear to be normal—but he was fighting a losing battle. The audio engineer finally stopped the record from playing, much to everyone's relief. However, after an embarrassing moment or two, the engineer again dropped the needle at another spot on the record. Although he was taken by surprise, Harry immediately started miming and made a valiant effort to make the whole thing seem real. Finally, Art Ford mercifully came to his rescue and put an end to the entire charade. Everyone started to laugh and we all gave Harry lots of support for his "show must go on" attitude. It was one of those priceless moments when live television was at its best, depending on how you looked at it. Shortly after that, Harry changed his style of singing and as we all know, he became very popular and eventually achieved worldwide fame as a folk artist and social activist. Our paths would cross again later.

CHAPTER 8

FREELANCE MUSICIAN (1950-53)

Freelance musician was a perfect definition for my activities during these years. I played piano and/or accordion on endless recording dates with many different artists and conductor-arrangers. Never a dull moment. A new musical challenge every day.

Jerome got us another job on television station WPIX. It was called the *Ted Steele Show* and we were on the air every day from 2:30 PM to 5:30 PM, Monday through Friday. We had a five-piece combo that featured Jerry, myself (accordion), Dick Carey (piano), Don Costa (guitar), and Jack Zimmerman (bass). The host, Ted Steele played the piano and interviewed guests and lots of singers or entertainers. The show was totally impromptu and we never knew who we would be accompanying the following day. It lasted for one whole year. Ted was very frugal, money-wise (a real cheap skate), and at Christmastime it came back to haunt him. When the stagehands realized they were not going to get a gift from him, they devised a plan to get even. You can imagine Ted's surprise when he tried to demonstrate, on camera, the great suction power of a brand new vacuum cleaner. The stagehands had secretly rigged it so that instead of sucking up the dust, it blew it out—all over the studio!

CORAL RECORDS

Coral Records contacted me to record an album of Italian songs, to be done in typical ethnic style. It featured a lot of *show off* accordion playing accompanied by bass (Jack Zimmerman), guitar (Don Arnone), and mandolin (Dick Dia). What great players! The album was called "Neapolitan Favorites." I have to squirm now when I think that Judy and I actually drove across the country, promoting this album to DJs from coast-to-coast. They were all very cordial, but I hate to think of what they were really thinking—that being the age of early rock and roll.

We purchased a brand-new Mercury convertible for our trip across country. The day I picked up the car, we decided to drive out to Elmont, Long Island to show it to our dear newlywed friends, Joe and Carmel Malin.

The car only had nine miles on it and it was beautiful. On the way across Harlem from our apartment on West 124th Street, we stopped for a red light behind many other cars. All of a sudden, a junk man in a horse and wagon decided to pull out from the curb, apparently not knowing that we were already in the lane he was about to enter. I will never forget the sound of crunching metal and the pain in my stomach, as I felt the protruding axle of his wagon totally chew up the right front fender of my brand-new car. Rather than create an international incident (since he didn't speak English), I chose to bite my tongue and move on. That was a day when "I just happened to be there" took on a totally different meaning.

PHIL MOORE

In my opinion, the lyrics of a song dictate the treatment that it should get. As a frustrated singer myself, I know that I helped many performers better understand what they were trying to say in a song by the manner in which I accompanied them.

Early in 1952, a popular singer named Bert Taylor asked me to accompany him at an audition for Monte Proser's La Vie en Rose, a famous east side nitery. We met at Phil Moore's studio apartment in Carnegie Hall. Phil had a great reputation as a vocal coach for many big performers, especially Lena Horne.

After Bert sang, Phil excused him but asked me to stay on for a chat. I was flattered to learn that he was impressed with my accompaniment and asked if I would be available to work with him while he coached some of his students. I gladly accepted and spent many happy hours accompanying and listening to him tell his singers all the same things I felt about how to interpret a lyric.

He always sat in a big "Don Ho"-type Polynesian chair at the back of his studio. Then he would ask the singer to tell him the *story* of the song he or she was about to sing. It would upset him if they used a portion of the lyrics to explain their feelings. His response was always something like, "I already know the words the lyricist wrote. I want to hear how *you* feel about what *you* are going to transmit to me." Often times after only a few bars of a bluesy ballad, he would yell out, "I don't believe you! What the hell is that smile doing on your face? You don't seem to understand the essence of this song! You just got screwed over!" He insisted that his students live and breathe every word and musical nuance of a song. Phil and I were of the same opinion that a singer is first, an actor and secondly, a vocalist. I am convinced that it is such a fabulous gift for any singer-performer to have a musical instrument (his or her voice) that *speaks words*. (I am saddened that so many of today's vocalists aren't aware of that fact).

With Dorothy Dandridge backstage at La Vie en Rose night club, 1952

DOROTHY DANDRIDGE

At this same time, Phil was personally accompanying a new singer named Dorothy Dandridge at the La Vie en Rose nitery. She was getting rave reviews and Phil was very happy and proud because she was one of his prize pupils. Plus, they were also romantically involved. At the end of her stay at La Vie en Rose, Dorothy was offered several jobs out of town and Phil asked me to be her pianist-conductor. He was too involved with other artists and could not break away from New York City. All of my friends advised me to refuse the offer and stay home, because I was now getting very busy as a sideman in the recording and commercial jingle field. To leave town at that time would not be a wise move. After a lot of thought, I figured, "What the hell, take a chance. I really want to be a conductor," I met Dorothy and, after a brief rehearsal with Phil, we were off to St. Louis and the Chase Hotel.

At the first orchestra rehearsal, she whispered in my ear that none of the musicians "had any balls." That cracked me up. I also agreed with her, but I still had to work with them. She had become accustomed to some great New York City musicians who played with lots of energy and passion (which she called "balls"). She often used the term "no balls" to describe any man or woman who performed or behaved in a blasé or lackluster manner.

Dorothy was a big smash at the Chase Hotel, playing to packed houses and always getting standing ovations. On the third evening after her performance and before returning to my hotel down the street, I said good night to her backstage and then noticed that she was heading through the kitchen for the waiters' service elevator to return to her room. I stopped her and insisted that she go up the front elevator in the main lobby like everyone else who lived at the hotel. She reminded me that St. Louis was still *down south* and in those days, blacks only used service elevators. I flipped out! She had just received a standing ovation and now she was *not allowed* to go up the front elevator. I insisted she take my arm because I was going to walk her through the hotel to the elevator in the front lobby. She reluctantly accepted and kept muttering to me under her breath, "You are out of your mind." I told her to relax, keep smiling and everything would be just fine—and it was. I was aware that some people were staring at this gorgeous black woman on my arm, but I just smiled back and marched on. The manager of the hotel met us by the time we got to the lobby. He was very cordial but I could sense his uneasiness. Dorothy and I made this grand exit every night after each show and by the time the engagement ended, people actually waited to see her walk through the lobby. That was the real beginning for me of a long fight for equal rights. I related this story to Harry Belafonte many years later and he laughingly referred to the Chase (at that time) as an upholstered sewer. The racial issue was red hot in those days and I welcomed any opportunity to help solve it whenever an occasion arose.

In spite of her beauty and talent, Dorothy was constantly reminded that she was *different*. This would cause her a lot of emotional stress, pain, and sorrow in years to come. She felt that she didn't belong anywhere. She was not really accepted by her own race, because they felt her behavioral patterns were too white and, on the other hand, the whites regarded her as a Negro— therefore, she was subject to all of their racial discrimination— except when she was performing on stage. We spent many hours discussing the great injustices that were being taken for granted at that time. This was before Rosa Parks and the civil rights movement really got rolling.

The Chase Hotel engagement was followed by one and two-week stands in Cleveland and Pittsburgh (Jackie Heller's). We also had Sunday off, so Dorothy took a quick trip to New York City to see Phil Moore. She returned on Monday night just before the show, looking very distraught. My gut feeling was that things had not gone well for her on her visit. In the middle of her act, she actually fainted on stage. I learned, the next day, that she and Phil had broken up. She recovered very quickly and the following week, we were off to Sahati's, a gambling casino on the south shore of Lake Tahoe. It was on this engagement that I first met her manager, Earl Mills. He liked to refer to himself as her manager, but he was more like a male servant who took care of her business affairs. He was madly in love with her, but he tried to pretend that she was just his client. Dorothy treated him very rudely at times and that always saddened me. It is interesting that years later, he wrote a book stating that in Dorothy's final days, he became her lover. That, I find impossible to believe.

Jose Ferrer, actor/singer; bass, Chubby Jackson; guitar, Don Costa; me on accordion

JOSE FERRER

Back in New York, my friend, Jim Proctor asked me to form a trio to accompany Jose Ferrer, who wanted to sing some songs in between each viewing at the premier of a new film of his that was opening in Washington, DC, in the fall of 1952. Jose had just won the Oscar for his performance in *Cyrano de Bergerac,* and now he was also a big star on Broadway. I persuaded Don Costa to play guitar and Chubby Jackson, from the Woody Herman band, played bass. Jose had a pleasant voice and the audience loved his renditions. His girlfriend was the beautiful and talented Rosemary Clooney. But they were not supposed to be seen together for familial reasons. Therefore, my wife, Judy became the "beard" for Rosemary. We had a wonderful dinner celebration after the last show—just six or seven of us—and then we all returned to New York City the next morning. Jose became smitten with his short singing career and he insisted we record all of the songs he had sung in Washington. We did make a recording one week later. He and Rosemary were married shortly after that. Their lives took many twists down through the years, but they did raise a lovely family together. Jose possessed natural musical talent and enormous ability as an actor. He was a great guy and we had a good time together.

MARTHA RAYE

Shortly thereafter, I got a job on a television show *acting* in a comedy skit with Martha Raye. The part I played demanded that off stage, I take a big puff on a cigarette—then hold my breath, walk on stage in front of the camera and begin to play the accordion as Martha made her entrance down a long gangplank. Just as she reached me, she was to take a puff on her cigarette and then blow the smoke into my face. At which time I was supposed to blow the smoke (that I was holding in my mouth) back into her face. Very funny, yes? Not really, because when I started to concentrate on playing the accordion, the smoke I had taken in my mouth slowly escaped out of my nose, and tears began to roll down my cheeks. I couldn't figure out why that happened every time. When the close-up moment came for me to return the smoke back into Martha's face, only hot air came out of my mouth—no smoke! Martha really cracked up every time we rehearsed the scene, but the director became very annoyed. After several takes, I managed to control my breath so that I was able to do what the skit called for. Martha understood my predicament and was an absolute doll the entire week that we worked together. What should have been fun for me was actually physically traumatic at times.

STUDIO ONE TV SHOW

In the early days of television, all the dramatic and variety shows were broadcast live. Tony Mottola, a phenomenal guitarist was playing original guitar music underscoring the scenes of a weekly dramatic television show called *Danger*. A producer named Stan Margolies, called me to do the same thing on accordion for a CBS TV drama on Studio 1 called *Stan the Killer*! It starred Eli Wallach and the setting was Paris—thus, the need for an accordion. This had never been done before on live television. I composed and played the entire score using *musette* reeds on the accordion in order to achieve the *French sound*. What a challenge that was. Especially since everything—actors, director, technicians and me were all *live*! No retakes.

HELLO, JENNIE! (1953)

January 18, 1953 was one of the most glorious days of my life. Judy gave birth to our beautiful daughter, Jennifer Lynn. I couldn't begin to describe the joy that filled my heart, knowing that I was now the father of a little baby girl. Life took on an entirely new meaning. I loved the feeling of being elevated to another emotional plateau. Judy's parents were also thrilled because "Jennie" became their very first grandchild. I stayed close to home those days in order to learn my new role as a "daddy." Judy and Jennie both taught me well . . . I think.

DANDRIDGE IN RIO and HOLLYWOOD

Meanwhile, Dorothy was off to Rio Di Janeiro. She confided in me about a lot of things in her personal life, but this episode she kept to herself. I learned, years later, that it was a very emotionally disturbing engagement for her because she fell in love with a handsome, rich Brazilian, and after a very short, torrid love affair, they broke up. Fortunately, she managed to get over it, in a month or so, before returning to Hollywood.

I joined her there to do a television show for the General Electric Co., honoring Thomas Edison. One of my composer heroes, Victor Young was the orchestra leader and I was asked to write the arrangement for Dorothy's solo spot. I was very excited, yet a bit nervous because I was told that while Dorothy and I were performing on camera, the orchestra would be in another studio down the hall. We'd be able to hear each other via microphones and playback speakers but, even so, it was difficult for me to play and improvise with an orchestra that was that far away from me. Fortunately, it all turned out OK and Victor was very complimentary, which really made me happy. He was one of my favorite motion-picture composers.

LA VIE EN ROSE

Cleveland and Pittsburgh were next on the agenda. Again, Dorothy played to full houses and very appreciative audiences. La Vie en Rose in New York City was the next stop and we were there for one whole month. Ray Gilbert had put together a new act for Dorothy that I had orchestrated for a large stage orchestra. It was difficult to play with just a trio—piano, bass, and drums. But that was all that this engagement provided. The nightclub was not very large. A small stage was at one end and you had to walk through the audience to get there. On one particular Saturday night, we started to perform and on the second song, the entire pedal structure of the piano became unhinged and fell on the floor. Naturally, this was a disaster for any pianist, but I had no choice but to keep on playing. My fellow musicians (the famous Milt Hinton on bass) immediately understood my plight, but they couldn't help me because they had their own parts to play. Dorothy also sensed that something was wrong with my playing, but she was also concentrating on her own performance. I was a real "basket case," because much of the act called for lots of dramatic piano accompaniment, and I had no sustaining pedal. A real nightmare for me. Dorothy was such a smash that night that the audience would not let her off the stage. Encore after encore—until the small curtain was finally pulled—and the show was over. She immediately turned to me and very worriedly said, "What's the matter with you? Are you OK?" With sweat pouring out of every pore in my body, I pointed to the pedal structure on the floor. She gave a big sigh of relief and then began to laugh like crazy. She said, "Thank God! I thought you had flipped out!"

After drying my wet brow and calming down as best I could, I started to make my exit through the audience. Now, get this—I was stopped by at least six different tables of guests, complimenting me on my "brilliant piano playing." There have been many times in my life when, after a performance, I felt that I had played quite well, but people seldom commented. This night was the *worst I ever played* and yet, I was cheered! You figure that one out.

EDDIE FISHER

Thank goodness, the calls kept coming in for more recording dates. Again, Hugo Winterhalter hired me for a date at Manhattan Center with a big string orchestra for Eddie Fisher. It was a known fact that Eddie had a very poor sense of rhythm and often skipped beats, which made him difficult to follow, especially with a large orchestra. Hugo had written a solo accordion intro on one of the songs, but he wasn't fond of it. When I offered my own flashy interpretation, he said, "Great! Do that every time." I felt as though I had painted myself into a corner because I got nervous standing up in front of that large orchestra with every string wizard in the recording business listening to my solo intros. Plus, whenever I felt that I had played it OK, Eddie made a mistake and we would have to start all over again. All my heroes were in that orchestra and I wanted to make a good impression upon them. What an emotional evening that was for me. Back then, it was the norm for musicians in the recording industry because, as I said before, we did not have the luxury of overdubbing. These kinds of challenges made us all better craftsmen.

BACK TO VEGAS WITH DOROTHY

Dorothy called and we were off to Philadelphia and then on to The Last Frontier in Las Vegas, again. This time she really tore it up and the whole town was hers. However, she still was not allowed to go down to the pool or eat in the downstairs restaurant. She was literally confined to her room. The Mills Brothers were appearing across the street at the Desert Inn and she commiserated with them and Sammy Davis, Jr., all of whom had to live on the other side of town. I protested loudly and vigorously to anyone and everyone who cared to listen. She kept reminding me that we were again "down south." I still seized every opportunity to walk her through the lobby, stroll by the pool area, and then stop for a snack at a restaurant in the lobby. We were never stopped, but I was aware of the management's dislike for my behavior. Screw them, was my motto.

There were very few major hotels in Vegas then and it was really a desert oasis. Across the street, the Desert Inn had a bar over the main lobby called the "Sky Room." It was on the third floor and we could all watch the planes land at the airport miles away. Appearing in the showroom was a Cuban girls trio known as the "De Castro Sisters." I became friendly with Bob Lilley, who was their manager and husband of Peggy, the lead singer. He loved the arrangements I had written for Dorothy and hired me to write some for his trio. In the process, I was introduced to a friend of theirs who was a wonderful songwriter named Gene DePaul. Gene already had several hits to his credit and he loved telling this story about how one particular song of his became popular. Bob and Peggy were at his house in Northridge, California, one night for dinner. Gene's daughter, April, who was then a very little girl, insisted upon singing a song before she had to go to bed. Sammy Cahn and Gene had written the song months before and they couldn't get *anyone* interested in performing or publishing it. Peggy and Bob were thrilled when they heard April sing it. Skip Martin wrote the recording arrangement for the De Castro Sisters and it became an overnight smash. The song was "Teach Me Tonight."

The city of Las Vegas was not far from the A-bomb testing cites in Central Nevada. One night, several of us musicians and fellow performers stayed up after the last show and had a party until the wee hours of the morning. Then, we drove far out into the desert where, we were told we could get a great view of the expected atomic test explosion. That is exactly what we did. We were all a little high and having lots of laughs. About 5 AM, we pulled over to the side of the road and got out of our cars so that we could better observe the atomic blast, which was actually going to occur miles away to the north. It was pitch black outside. The silence was ominous and there was hardly a breeze blowing. It seemed the earth was actually standing still. After several minutes, we were startled to see the entire sky suddenly explode into a brilliant red, as though it was on fire! But there was no sound. After a minute or so, several blasts of hot air hit us from out of nowhere. We held on to each other, so as not to be blown away as we watched the fiery madness going on overhead. We were all stunned and speechless. It finally faded after several minutes and we slowly got back into our cars. Not a single word was spoken as we drove back to town. When we got back to the hotel, we nodded good night to each other and then went our respective ways. What a frightening experience that was for all of us.

Walter Winchell saw Dorothy's show one night at the Last Frontier and wrote a glowing review of her performance. He also added some very complimentary comments about my playing and presence on stage. This was a giant plus for me, because everybody read Winchell's column. Now MCA, Dorothy's booking agency started to entice me to get my own band and go on the road playing at different hotel ballrooms all over the country.

Back in New York City, I discussed this with Neal Hefti, the great jazz arranger-composer. He was also being encouraged to go on the road with a "society-type band"—can you imagine that? Anyway, Neal advised me to stay in New York City, except for my outings with Dorothy, because I was making more money as a studio musician than I would ever make out on the road as a hotel bandleader.

JOEL GREY

In August of 1953, Joel asked me to be his piano-conductor for a two-week engagement at Bill Miller's Riviera nightclub on the New Jersey side of the George Washington Bridge. Harry Belafonte shared the bill with him, but Joel got star billing, which meant he closed the show. Joel, the son of an old vaudevillian named Mickey Katz, was a young, energetic performer. Harry had become very popular as a calypso singer who performed with just guitar accompaniment. He had great sex appeal and his career was really beginning to take off.

A large portion of Joel's act consisted of his imitations of old-time singer-performers like Eddie Cantor and it soon became apparent that he was getting clobbered having to follow Harry's act. Several old pro comics went backstage after an early performance and advised him to *open* the show, because "this Belafonte guy is killing you." Because he had star billing, Joel turned a deaf ear to them and proceeded to close the show every night. He loved imitating Billy Daniels singing "That Old Black Magic," but I didn't enjoy yelling at him from the piano, "Sing the song, man!" a la Benny Paine. Two young white guys trying to imitate two giant black entertainers was very embarrassing for me. Joel and I worked together several times after that, but then our respective schedules took us down different paths. Later on, Joel's career really took off. He is a great guy and a very talented performer. We all know that he became a big star and won a Tony *and* an Oscar for his role in the musical *Cabaret*. Quite an accomplishment!

CHAPTER 9

RAY CHARLES (1954-56)

As a result of working together on various recording dates, I became good friends with Ray Charles, the multitalented choral director, arranger of all of Perry Como's early hits. We had a mutual admiration society going right from the first day we met. He became a recording artist in his own right, as a result of many beautiful albums he arranged for his choir—all great singers and brilliant sight-readers. I was privileged to be a part of a group of musical giants who accompanied them on all of their early albums: Dick Hyman, piano; Bob Haggart, bass; Tony Mottola, guitar; Bob Rosengarden, drums; me on accordion; and occasionally, a harpist named Janet Putnum. On every song, Ray provided each of us with a lead sheet containing all of the chord cymbals and the melody the choir would be singing. After one rundown of a song, it was like magic—we musicians, all seemed to know when and where an improvised fill-in should be played and *who* should play it. Occasionally, Ray indicated what specific instrumental lines he wanted, but for the most part, we were all on our own. In the space of three hours, we always recorded four songs—never going overtime. I still marvel at the ability of those amazing singers who came in for rehearsal just one hour before the session began and sight-read and sang with such accuracy and perfect intonation. I just happened to be there, and what happy times we all shared.

I am grateful to Milton De Lugg for writing a song in the early fifties called "Hoop-De-Doo." It was a polka with a catchy lyric and it became very popular. The *Perry Como* television show used it as an opening number several times. Thanks to Ray Charles and

111

the contractor Hank Ross, I was called to play the accordion part. Thus, began my association with the *Perry Como Show*. Mitch Ayres and all the members of the band were very supportive, particularly the great reed players like Bernie Kaufman and Stanley Webb— also Bob Haggart (bassist) and Tony Mottola (guitarist). Perry was always very pleasant and appreciative of whatever I improvised, especially when we appeared on camera together.

RAYMOND SCOTT

"Your Hit Parade" was a popular weekly coast-to-coast radio/ TV show in the late '50s and early '60s. Raymond Scott, the musical director, was a knowledgeable musician and a very demanding conductor. When the song "Autumn Leaves" became a hit, I was hired to play the accordion and provide the "French sound." At the orchestra rehearsal the day before the show, I asked to see the music of what I was expected to play, but the contractor told me to sit quietly until my song was called. I waited patiently for a long time, and fifteen minutes before the rehearsal ended, I was given a copy of the conductor part and summoned to the recording/ rehearsal stage. After quickly looking over my music, I realized that every open spot or "fill in" had already been allocated to various other instruments in the orchestra.

Raymond was in a darkened control room and all we heard was his booming voice coming out over the loud speakers. I sheepishly asked what he would like me to play since there was no specific accordion part. He answered, "You figure something out. But now, let me hear only you and Arnold Eidus (the violin concertmaster) play the song as though you were performing it in a night club." Arnold and I were both very surprised at this request because it had *nothing* to do with the actual rendition the orchestra was all set to rehearse. Raymond then insisted that we play the song in the key of F sharp minor—a different key than the arrangement indicated. He was just "testing" me—and Arnold. I played a little intro and we began. The rest of the orchestra sat there and just listened—all of them happy that they weren't being asked to do the same thing. I gained confidence as we went along and we played it very well. After we finished, the band members applauded enthusiastically and I was greatly relieved.

After a moment of silence, Raymond's voice boomed out again and he said, "Now, play the same thing in the key of B minor." The sympathetic groans from the orchestra members echoed my feelings exactly, but Arnold and I did as we were told and we received another roar of approval from our fellow musicians when we finished.

Realizing that there was only four minutes left in the rehearsal period, Raymond quickly tapped off the tempo of the arrangement that was written for "Falling Leaves." The orchestra played it once and the rehearsal was over. That song was on the "Hit Parade" for the next seven weeks and I managed to improvise something different on each show. I was happy to have the job.

In order to exert their power and authority, some of the older conductors enjoyed putting their musicians under that kind of unnecessary pressure—a very masochistic thrill for some of them. I obviously passed Raymond's "test" because after that I worked for him many times and on each occasion, he was a gentleman and very respectful. Interesting?

That was New York in those days, and I was so grateful for the warnings and teachings my brother Mike had given me when I was a little kid back in Denver—aspiring to one day "make it" in the big city. "Name that Tune" and "Stop the Music" were two very popular television programs and I was the pianist in the orchestra for both shows. Harry Salter received musical credit, but thanks to a man named Ted Raph, his arranger, we were able to function as a musical unit.

BROADWAY (CAN-CAN)

Broadway was truly a magical place. I became a bit player when I was hired as a substitute piano-accordionist in the pit orchestra of the Cole Porter show, Can-Can. A French lady named Lilo, was the dynamic star. Carol Haney was also in the show, as were several later-to-be-discovered stars. Milton Rosenstock was the conductor and a typical New York *realist*. A talented, no-bullshit kind of guy with a great sense of humor. It was funny hearing him yell up at the beautiful chorus girls on stage, "Shake your asses, kids, they love it!"

After doing the show for one week, practically everybody memorized their parts. Unless you could relax and have fun, the job became a giant bore. I loved hearing Milton tell the story about an evening in New Haven, Connecticut, prior to the New York City opening of another show. A lot of new music was inserted at the last minute, without any previous rehearsal for the orchestra. It was a common occurrence because, according to Milton, many producers felt that if things were not going right, it was always the fault of the music and not the script or other facets of the production. Anyway, when they got to the part of the show that had been altered, the conductor (Milton) and all the musicians were reading and playing this new music for the first time. It was a difficult ballet piece and Milton accidentally turned two pages at once of his conductor part. He soon realized he was in the wrong place. To add to his panic, the producer was in the audience, sitting in the first row right behind him. He kept waving his arms but repeatedly told the orchestra, "Don't follow me! Don't follow me!"

Even after the regular pianist returned to play *Can-Can* I was retained to play the auditions for substitute performers on Tuesday and Thursday afternoons. Singers would lean over the edge of the stage, look down into the orchestra pit, hand me a lead sheet or piano copy of a song, and often times ask if I would play it in a different key. While they were answering questions from the producers sitting away back in the darkened theatre, I would figure out the transpositions and then proceed to accompany them. One day, I became strangely aware that someone was staring at me. I looked up to see the face of Cy Feuer, one of the producers, peering down at me and asking, "What's your name?" Before I could answer, he quickly added, "I knew it was somebody new, because the other guy never played those kinds of chords." We met later over a cup of coffee and became good friends. He was not only a producer but had also been an orchestral arranger in Hollywood.

Silk Stockings was his next Broadway production and I was hired as the pianist to play the new Cole Porter songs for the backers' auditions. These were events where people were asked to put up money to sponsor a new production. I played many Park Avenue parties where people like George F. Kaufman, and his ilk made their presentations. Then I would accompany various singers who performed the songs Cole Porter had written for the show. Cy Feuer kept cautioning me not to improvise, because if Porter suddenly appeared, he would expect to hear exactly what he had indicated on the piano parts. I did as I was told and was soon offered the job as assistant conductor for *Silk Stockings*. I turned it down, because I told Cy that I didn't want to sit in the pit, night after night, hoping the conductor would get sick or fail to show up, so that I would have an opportunity to conduct. I felt the need to move on. He totally understood my position. Cy and I remained good friends for many years afterward. My only regret was that I never got the opportunity to meet Cole Porter in person.

While we are still in a Broadway mood, I can't resist telling you about Frank Loesser, a wonderful composer. He wrote many classic American musicals. Unfortunately, he was married to a woman who was very difficult to deal with. All the musicians who had the misfortune to know or work with her, loved referring to her as "the evil of two Loessers." Sorry, but I couldn't resist including this bit of showbiz info.

CARMEN JONES
(1955)

Dorothy had just completed filming *Carmen Jones* in which she played the starring role. This was quite an achievement for her and it was the first time a black artist had been cast as a leading lady in a major motion picture. The movie created a lot of noise, all to her benefit, and we were booked on a tour that included Vegas, Miami, and my hometown, Denver, Colorado. I was summoned to Hollywood to orchestrate the arrangements for her new act. Every day I showed up at Dorothy's apartment off Sunset Boulevard and rehearsed with her the new arrangements I was orchestrating. Otto Preminger didn't know me and was not convinced that I was the right man for the job. One afternoon, he brought over the famous composer, David Raksin to check me out. Ostensibly, they were there to hear Dorothy's new act but I knew differently. As soon as David made his entrance in the front door, which was downstairs from where I was working, I started playing the love theme from "Bad and the Beautiful," a gorgeous melody that Raksin had composed for the movie of the same name. Naturally, that got his attention. We exchanged pleasantries and I mentioned I had heard that in his early years back in New York City, he also had played for Lester Lanin, the popular society bandleader. He burst out with, "Oh, that prick!" I immediately knew we were talking about the same person.

All the while he was supposedly listening to Dorothy's new act, David scanned through several orchestral score pages that I had just written. After a short while, he said to Preminger, "Let's get out of here. This guy's got everything under control." Otto was relieved and they left. Thank you, David.

DENVER and "THE GREENS"

Food was an often-discussed subject between Dorothy and me. She was never convinced that I, too, had grown up eating poor-folk food like greens, all kinds of vegetables that we grew in our backyard garden and cheap cuts of meat like neck bones and hammocks. I mentioned this to my mother and she couldn't believe that this famous, beautiful performer ever even heard of that kind of food.

In February of 1955, Dorothy was booked for a two-week engagement at the Park Lane Hotel in Denver, Colorado. After the first week, Mama insisted upon making a large pot of greens (minastra) and neck bones, which I delivered to Dorothy at the hotel. I still remember the strange looks I got from the bedecked patrons who just happened to be in the same elevator car with me on their way up to the top floor of the hotel to see Dorothy's show. The garlic smell from the pan I was carrying permeated the area. I stopped at Dorothy's floor to drop off these goodies just before show time. As the door of her suite was opened, I yelled out that I had a surprise package for her. Otto Preminger and a couple of his friends were nervously waiting for her in the parlor. When she came out of her bedroom and smelled the garlic, she knew exactly what was in the pot. Off came the lid and she dove right in like a little kid at a candy store. Her lipstick and makeup got all smeared— and she had a ball! Large towels were wrapped around her neck so she wouldn't soil her beautiful gown. Everyone else, except me, got annoyed because she was going to be late for her show. When she finally did get on stage, she apologized to the audience and explained the reason for her tardiness. Mama was present that night along with my sister, Marian and several of our relatives. Dorothy insisted that Mama stand up and take a bow. The audience's response was terrific. Many patrons wanted to know if they, too, could have an order of greens. Lots of laughs and a good time was had by all.

A few nights later, the academy award nominations were broadcast on television just before show time. Joel Fluellen, a handsome black actor friend of Dorothy, was there and we were all anxiously waiting in her hotel suite to hear the nominations. You can imagine the tension in the room at that moment. When Dorothy's name was finally announced for her role in *Carmen Jones*, we were all overcome with joy and happiness! I remember Joel stuck his head out of the window and just yelled at the top of his voice. Showbiz and social history were made that night.

MIAMI and NEW YORK CITY

Next came dates in Vegas and then Miami, Florida. The Fountainbleau Hotel, where Dorothy was going to perform, had a policy stating that black performers could not live at the hotel. They were forced to stay at another hotel on the *other side of town*.

Again, I flipped out and again, I was reminded by Dorothy that we were *down south*. However, I was determined to change that stupid policy. In the absence of her manager, I insisted upon having a lengthy discussion with the hotel manager. Fortunately, I was able to convince him of this frightful injustice, and Dorothy *was* allowed to stay at the Fountainbleau. Most of the residents of the hotel were Jewish and I knew they supported my opinion and my actions 100 percent. The rest of the engagement went very smoothly.

SULLIVAN SHOW—EMPIRE ROOM

The Ed Sullivan Show in New York City was next on the agenda. The press and the media, in general, were all hot after Dorothy because of her Academy Award nomination. The following eight weeks were spent appearing at the Empire Room of the Waldorf-Astoria Hotel. This was a crucial time in Dorothy's career.

Otto Preminger was on the scene a lot now. He was solely concerned with her sexy image and, frankly, didn't give a damn about how she really felt inside. He was convinced she should shake her buns and become a sex goddess—period. I disagreed with his concept, as did Dorothy. He was what I considered a real *pain in the ass*. Although he was a very successful director of motion pictures, he didn't have any sensitivity or appreciation of "live" entertainment—which was what New York City and Broadway was all about.

True, her sensuous figure and dramatic performance in *Carmen Jones* really got everyone's attention and her fame spread like wildfire. But in spite of all this notoriety, she still felt inadequate as a singer. In the movie, she had to lip-synch to another person's voice. She had grown up in the shadow of Lena Horne and Ella Fitzgerald, and while she admired both artists very much, she had great difficulty dealing emotionally with the comparisons that were inevitably made by so many reviewers. I tried to convince her that first, she was an actress, and secondly, she was a singer. Each song should be *worn* like a dress and she should actually *become* the person she was singing about. That theory made a lot of sense to her, because she wanted people to recognize her as not just a sexpot singer but a woman of intelligence and well-versed in all aspects of life—someone who was concerned with more than just her own career. She loved champagne—and also neck bones and greens. The Empire Room was filled with celebrities every night and the press was interviewing her constantly. She did an extensive interview with *Time* magazine, but what they actually published destroyed Dorothy emotionally. After reading the article, she tearfully yelled, "Why can't those bastards quote me correctly? What they've printed is a bunch of goddamn lies!" Many artists have echoed those words down through the years. Nonetheless, she went on stage night after night and still knocked everybody out.

A famous lawyer became a big fan of hers. He was a very intelligent man and I enjoyed talking with him. What great conversations we had while waiting for Dorothy to remove her makeup and get into her comfortable togs. He was a champion of civil rights and we both saw racial issues in the same manner. He was the one who made me understand that justice and morality really had nothing to do with solving the world's problems. He insisted it was all about money and power. Hello, world!

BELAFONTE—WALDORF

Shortly after Dorothy appeared at the Waldorf-Astoria Empire Room, Harry Belafonte, her costar in *Carmen Jones*, started a lengthy engagement there. My wife and I attended his dinner show one evening and it was wonderful. Knowing the headwaiter naturally gained us a great table just off ringside. The audience greeted Harry with lots of applause and cheering. After his first few songs, he recognized me sitting there surrounded by the rich and famous of Hollywood and Broadway. When it came time, in the middle of his performance, to say "hello" to the audience, he said all the correct things. But instead of introducing any one of the many stars who were present, he chose to say some flattering things about *me*. I stood up and took a bow, and I was positive that very few people knew or cared about who I was or what I did. At the end of his singing performance, he got a well-deserved standing ovation.

After the show, we were invited up to his dressing room. When I thanked him for all the kind words, he just smiled and gave Judy and me big hugs. Harry and I have always shared the same feelings about human rights, the trials and tribulations of performing artists in the music business, and the racial injustices all over the world.

At this point, my career was causing me to make some difficult decisions. I was doing a lot of arranging for various other artists and was also quite active in the commercial jingle business as a player, arranger, and conductor. Having to leave town so often was not the wise thing to do. Dorothy was sad, but yet, she understood my predicament when I explained that I could not go on the road anymore and this would be my last engagement with her. Her manager, Earl Mills insisted that I do one final engagement—Lake Tahoe—this time on the north shore. Just before leaving for Nevada, I got an offer to play, with my own trio, a radio show starring Dick Van Dyke. I felt obliged to fulfill my obligation to Dorothy and was forced to say no to this offer. I think that Mort Lindsay, a good studio pianist, took the job. Fate deals with all of our lives in strange ways. I sometimes wonder what might have been had I taken the job with Dick Van Dyke.

TAHOE and "THE BOYS"

Tahoe was fun because, after the late show, many of us musicians and chorus line singer-dancers would return to the empty showroom where we could just sit around and sing and play our favorite tunes. Our jam sessions got a bit noisy one night and a pit boss bolted into the room and angrily told us all to "get the hell out!" I tried to explain that I was the conductor for Dorothy and we were all in the regular show. He would hear none of it and stood there fuming, until we all left the building. I managed to bum a ride home from one of the musicians, because I was living in a motel about a mile down the road. That was common in those days.

Before the engagement ended, Dorothy's lawyer-friend stopped by to see her on his way across the country from San Francisco. We met at the bar one afternoon for one of our lengthy chats and I mentioned that one of the pit bosses was very angry with me for having been part of a noisy, late-night jam session in the main showroom. My friend just smiled and then started chatting with the bartender about having represented some of "the boys" in legal battles back east. They both referred to these men using only their first names like Tony, from Cleveland or Angelo, from Chicago, etc. I thought it was strange when we were immediately offered a drink *on the house*. Then the bartender took a short break. When he returned, I noticed the angry pit boss was walking toward us from the gambling tables. He pulled up a bar stool and sat down next to me. I have never seen such an *about-face* transformation in my entire life. Our conversation was friendly and lighthearted. He even apologized to me for throwing us out of the showroom a couple of nights before. When he learned that I was staying at a motel down the road, he arranged to have me picked up and dropped off every night before and after the show. How about that! I couldn't help but notice the big smile on my lawyer-friend's face all the while we were drinking and chatting with our newly made friends.

Here was proof of the old adage, "It's not what you know, but who you know that will help you get along in life." No argument from me.

DANDRIDGE AFTERTHOUGHTS

Although I never worked again with Dorothy, we remained close friends until the day she died. I felt so privileged to have been able to know and work with this incredible lady, particularly during a period in our history when dynamic social changes were being made. She loved my family and came to our house several times. I got the feeling that we were a sane, safe group for her to be associated with in the midst of the sometimes-crazy life she lived.

I was probably the only male in her life that she really trusted with her innermost thoughts. Yes, I knew about her various love affairs, but I don't think that is really for public discussion. The stories about her and Otto Preminger being lovers, I will never be able to figure out. Here were two people who I always felt were planets apart in every human sense. But apparently Dorothy felt that he was her only ticket to real stardom, and she chose to take it. Sad, but true.

We often discussed her early life as a child and the problems she encountered growing up. Her mother, her sister, her failed marriages, and her daughter were people and events that filled her life with more heartache and sorrow than with joy and happiness. A weaker individual would have given up and sunk into oblivion, but not Dorothy. She overcame a lot of hurdles and had the determination to succeed at all cost—and she did!

Several books have been written about Dorothy's life, but only one really got all the facts straight. It's called *Dorothy Dandridge (a biography)*, written by Donald Bogle, a great writer and an honest man.

CHAPTER 10

JULIE STEIN (1956)

All of the agents at MCA knew Dorothy and I became friends with many of them. I got a lot of jobs playing cocktail piano at very sophisticated parties because I knew *all the popular songs.* Dave Baumgarten, an agent and an old friend, called me to play an after-theatre party starting at 11:15 PM honoring Julie Stein. It was to be held in the posh corporate party room on the top floor at MCA headquarters on Fifty-seventh and Madison Avenue. I managed to brush up on every Julie Stein song I knew or ever heard of. On the night of the party, I was met at the elevator by a very nice man who said, "Nice to see you. I'm Julie and I know all about you. Have a drink, be comfortable and the piano is over there in the corner—you know what to do." I proceeded to play as people started to come in, all stars of Broadway and/or Hollywood. I played every Julie Stein song I could think of, but I couldn't get any reaction from the man himself. He walked by me several times and smiled but never said a damn word. Other people were very complimentary, and after a couple of hours, the party ended as I was appropriately playing "The Party's Over."

Dave Baumgarten called me the next day to tell me what a big smash I was the night before, but I interrupted him saying something like, "I don't give a damn if I ever play for that character again. I played every song he ever wrote and he never once acknowledged what I was doing." Dave roared with laughter and couldn't talk, so he hung up. I didn't see what the hell was so funny. He called me back later and said, "Calm down your hot Italian temper and let me tell you something.

Last night, you played a party honoring *Jules* Stein, the owner/
CEO of MCA—*not* Jule Styne, the composer." Hearing that also
made me laugh at my own stupidity. Dave admitted that all of
the agents in the office referred to Mr. Stein as Julie, but that's
where the similarity ended.

MARILYN MONROE

I subsequently played many late-night parties at MCA for no
specific person or reason, just their clients and guests. One
particular night, the room was jammed with celebrities—Edward
G. Robinson, Kirk Douglas, William Faulkner, Jack Benny, and
many more. Marilyn had just finished filming *Gentlemen Prefer
Blondes*. It was very interesting to sit there quietly, play the piano,
and observe the byplay between various guests. Marilyn was doing
her best to get William Faulkner interested in something she was
quietly talking to him about. But I knew, from the expression on
his face, he couldn't have cared less. The party finally narrowed
down to a precious few and Marilyn was persuaded to sing "Bye,
Bye, Baby" from her recent movie. We were both at a piano in a
corner of the room up against a wall. Pretending to be very shy,
she finally started to sing, and just eight bars before the end of
the song, she suddenly stopped. She said she forgot the lyrics.
This same routine was repeated several more times and it became
a little embarrassing for all concerned. I started to noodle on the
piano in order to fill in the uncomfortable silences. Since no one
could see the keyboard of the piano and she was standing up
beside me, she pressed her hands down on mine, which made it
impossible for me to play. She knew the spotlight was on her—
and nobody was going to take it away from her.

Out of embarrassment for her, people began to talk amongst
themselves. On her final rendition, she was about to stop again,
when suddenly Jean Stapleton yelled out, "For Christ sake,
Marilyn—Bye, Bye, Baby—Bye, Bye." The party ended shortly
thereafter. What a beautiful, confused lady Miss Monroe was.

LILO, THE FRENCH BOMBSHELL

I wrote many arrangements for Lilo after the show *Can-Can* closed. She was a bombastic performer with a great body and a great Broadway voice that needed no amplification. Lilo was the darling of the east side of New York City and often performed at private parties on Park Avenue. At one such occasion, I played piano and accordion for her. The honored guests were the Duke and Duchess of Windsor—yes, Wally Simpson and Edward himself. Lilo was a big hit and after the performance, the Duke came over to me and explained that, as a youngster, he also played the accordion. He was very cordial and a real down-to-earth kind of guy. We had a very pleasant conversation.

On the way home, Lilo was happy to hear about my chat with Edward. However, she had had a very different experience with Wally in the ladies' room. Lilo said, "I was seated in front of a mirror, fixing my makeup and suddenly *that beetch* came up behind me, reached down into my strapless gown, and squeezed my teets." I laughed like mad, but Lilo didn't see any humor at all in the experience.

JACQUELINE FRANCOIS and JACK ELLIOTT

This famous French chanteuse came from Paris to appear at the Persian Room of the Hotel Plaza. She brought along her own guitarist, Jacque Tilche. I was called to play piano for her, but my schedule was so crowded that I recommended a friend of mine named Jack Elliott. He played good jazz piano and had studied in Paris with Nadia Boulanger. Jack also spoke French and I thought he would be perfect for the engagement. Her music called for only a piano, guitar, accordion, bass, and drums accompaniment. After their first rehearsal, I received a frantic phone call from Dave Baumgarten at MCA who had booked Jacqueline. He told me she didn't like Jack or anything about the job and was returning to

Paris on the next boat. I was soon informed by Jack that neither the bass player nor the drummer showed up for the rehearsal. Michel Legrand had written all of her arrangements and the accordionist couldn't read a note of music. Now I knew something was definitely wrong, so I volunteered to play the accordion for the next day's rehearsal—and I brought Jack back with me to play piano. Dave pleaded with me to get another pianist, but I refused.

Jack was also reluctant to return, but I insisted. He and I got to the Plaza early for the rehearsal. When Jacqueline and her guitarist walked into the room and saw Jack again, she started to swear in French, all of which Jack understood. Again the drummer and the bass player didn't show up, because as I later found out, they were not going to get paid for rehearsals since they were part of the Ted Straeter band that played nightly in the Persian Room.

So it shouldn't be a total loss, I suggested that we try playing some of her arrangements, even if we were shy of a couple of players. She reluctantly agreed and we started off—guitar, piano, and accordion. Since her arrangements were written for only five men, the accordion part was very important. I charged right in, along with Jack and Jacque, and within five minutes, she was thrilled. All of a sudden, she loved both Jack and me, and I got the feeling she didn't care if the other two guys ever showed up. When I informed her, through a translator, that I could not play the engagement and I was only there to convince her about my friend Jack, she paused for a moment—and then made me a financial offer I couldn't refuse. At that time, I was subbing for my friend Dick Hyman, who was the leader of a small orchestra on the daily Arthur Godfrey radio morning show. Well, I figured for the next several weeks I wouldn't get much sleep, which is exactly what happened. During the course of the engagement, we developed great friendships. Jacques "Gui Gui" Tilche, Jacqueline, Jack, and I really had a good time working together. At the end of the job, she took Jack back to Paris with her and he became her arranger as well as her pianist. The fact that he also spoke French convinced me that this was really a bonding of talents. It proved to be the beginning of a great career for my friend, Jack Elliott.

Alfred Hitchcock made a movie in 1956 called *The Wrong Man*. It was the story of Manny Balestrero, a bass player in the orchestra at the famous Stork Club who was wrongly accused of a crime. Jack Elliott was the pianist in that same orchestra. When the movie was filmed, Jack made it possible for me to appear as the accordion player in the band, along with himself and several of the original musicians. Henry Fonda was the star of the movie and he played the role of Manny, the bass player.

We were all called to show up at 3 AM after the Stork Club had officially closed, and for the following three hours, Hitchcock shot our musical sequence for the film, along with many beautifully attired extras who were hired to simulate an actual weekend crowd—lots of dancing and drinking, etc. It was great fun for me being up there on the bandstand next to Henry Fonda, who pretended to play but, actually, didn't make a sound on the bass. We chatted a lot, and when I asked him why Hitchcock didn't come up and make any suggestions to him, he smiled and answered, "I guess I must be doing it right." What a great actor and a true gentleman.

HELEN TRAUBEL

This great Wagnerian soprano was at the peak of her career and she was a grand diva all over the world. Somehow she was talked into doing a comedy skit on a television show with Jimmy Durante. Ms. Traubel had a great sense of humor, and this skit gave her a new image in the eyes of the entertainment world. Unbelievable as it may sound, she was booked into the Latin Quarter nightclub just off Times Square. The classical reviewers thought she had lost her mind, but she was just going to have a good time and probably make a lot of money in the process.

I was hired to do some arrangements for her night club appearance. Knowing she was a giant in the opera field gave me cause to wonder how she was going to make the transition into popular music. But shortly after we met, I realized she was going to be a joy to work with. I explained to her what to expect performing in a noisy nightclub and often times, for a lot of drunks, particularly on Saturday and Sunday nights. She smiled at me and said, "Don't you worry, my dear. Those poor people have been working hard all week long, and those are the nights they can go out and have a good time. Besides, they are only coming to see me to get what they think is their *pound of culture.*" What a wonderful line. I have quoted her many times since then.

We had several conversations regarding her classical operatic life. One story involved the maestro, Arturo Toscanini, who had a reputation for being very difficult at times. Helen admired him greatly but said she locked horns with him once over the interpretation of a particular Wagnerian aria. He begged her not to hold certain notes so long and even got down on his knees, in front of the entire orchestra, to make his point. She smiled and told him that she would sing it his way on the radio broadcast, *but* when they made the recording the following week, she sang it *her* way. I was so happy to have had the pleasure of working with this great artist. What a warm, dignified, classy woman she was.

BING CROSBY and "TRUE LOVE"

This was the hit song from the movie, *High Society,* starring Bing Crosby, Frank Sinatra, and Grace Kelly. Bing had a smash record on this song that featured a solo cadenza played by a concertina. Many other artists also recorded the song and they all wanted the same sound that was on Bing's rendition. As a result, I was busy imitating the concertina on their recordings.

The *Ed Sullivan Show* was very popular and I appeared on it many times playing either accordion or piano in the orchestra, while accompanying artists like Dorothy Dandridge, Jacqueline Francois, and Steve and Eydie. Ray Bloch, the conductor, was a very brusque individual. He sometimes treated the performing artists, as well as the members of his orchestra, in a very rude manner. One day a musician said to him, "I think I have a wrong note in bar twenty-seven." In a very annoyed voice, Ray yelled back, "Fix it!" That was it—no more discussion. Plus, he would never let any other conductor direct the orchestra, even if the performing artist wanted it. He was a rough individual to deal with.

In preparation for an appearance by Bing Crosby singing "True Love," he decided that a small cabaret orchestra would play up on the stage, but off camera, while accompanying Bing. We had our music taped to the floor so that just in case the camera did pan over and see us playing, it would all appear to be very casual. During the rehearsals, we found it extremely difficult to watch Ray, who was conducting us and at the same time, read our music that was taped on the floor. He would not listen to our problem. The plan was that Bing and Ed would have a little chat out in front of the curtain and on a certain cue, we would start the musical intro of the song. Then the curtain would rise and Bing would sing. Good idea?—Not really. When we got on the air, we started the intro as we had rehearsed, but when the curtain was supposed to rise, it got stuck! And that was just as I started the solo cadenza. Ray Bloch was in a dither. All of us backstage could hear Ed and Bing adlibbing and trying to make light of this unexpected hang up. All the while, I just kept on playing and improvising while chaos was going on all around me. Finally the curtain did rise, and just before Bing started to sing, he paused for a moment, turned to me and said, "Thank you, Mr. Paganini of the accordion." Ray Bloch was much more cordial to me in our subsequent meetings. Little did I realize at the time that years later, Bing and I would meet again and work together many more times.

THE HOME SHOW WITH HUGH DOWNS

My friend Stan Freeman, the great pianist, recommended me to take his place for one week on a late-morning television show that starred Hugh Downs and Arlene Francis. My job was to accompany any vocalists that might show up and, occasionally, do some adlib noodling under little speeches that Arlene or Hugh would be asked to make. I was informed that Arlene wanted me to play a piano solo on the song "You'd Be So Nice to Come Home To." It would be performed on the show the following morning. I tried to suggest another song that I was more familiar with, but the director refused my request. I went home and practiced like a demon.

The next morning, I was told that prior to my solo, I had to improvise some humorous little piano punctuations (ala Victor Borge) while Arlene made a silly speech about cooking. In order to hear Arlene speak, I naturally had to keep my earphones on. The director would not allow me to remove them for my piano solo, which followed immediately. I felt strange playing a piano solo, on camera, with earphones on my head. But he insisted we do it his way. OK? I was seated at a beautiful, grand piano with a mirrored keyboard, and shortly after I started to play my solo, I was aware that the cameras were photographing my hands, my face, my entire body from every imaginable angle. The only distraction for me was that I could also hear, in my earphones, all of the conversation that was going on in the control room—camera directions, etc. Suddenly I heard the director say to me, "Nick, I never realized you played so beautifully. We now have a great shot looking down on you from high above—but I think you should know that *your fly is wide open!*" Panic registered on my face immediately and, in the earphones, I heard a roar of laughter coming from the control room. The noise was deafening and I couldn't hear what I was playing. I continued on, not knowing where in the hell I was musically. Just as I ended the song, I heard Hugh Downs sign the show off the air. I was emotionally disturbed, but I managed to calm down, and after a few minutes, I walked into the control room. Everybody was quiet and pretending to be deep into their work. I couldn't hold back any longer and I yelled, "You dirty rotten bastards!" Then the whole room exploded with laughter. Everyone came over for a hug and thanked me for being such a good sport. They had really set me up. It was a moment I will never forget. P.S. My fly was *not open.*

CHAPTER 11

HELLO, DANNY!

Mama and Papa with our newborn son, Danny, in 1956

The most magnificent thing that happened all year occurred on October 28, 1956. Judy gave birth to our first son, Danny (Daniel Martin). I couldn't believe that I was the daddy of another beautiful child. We had just moved into a new house in Bayside, Long Island. My mother and father were there from Denver. Jennie was delighted with her new little brother, and life was truly worth living. We ended the year with lots of family celebrations.

THE FRENCH LADIES (1957-60)

The year started off with an engagement at the Pierre Hotel, playing and conducting for the "French Bombshell," Lilo. The music of France was very popular, particularly on the east side of Manhattan, and Lilo was charming the audiences nightly.

In early March, Jacqueline Francois returned to the Plaza. Again, I did my balancing act of playing two jobs at once—playing for Jacqueline in the evening and also subbing for Dick Hyman on the Arthur Godfrey early morning radio show on CBS. Never a dull moment.

The fact that I could play the accordion with the French "musette" sound stood me in good stead with all of the European singers. Juliette Greco, a gorgeous actress and singer from Paris, took up the next several weeks on my schedule, appearing in the Imperial Room at the Waldorf-Astoria.

Miles Davis, the legendary jazz trumpeter, was very enamored of this lovely lady. Juliette allowed me to leave my tuxedo in the guest closet of her big suite at the hotel. Many of my days were filled with recording dates all over town, so I was grateful for Juliette's hospitality. But Miles and his buddies took a dim view of this "white cat" coming in nightly to change in and out of his tuxedo. And to make matters worse, he played the *accordion*, which was definitely not a *hip* instrument to play. It was then that I experienced the true meaning of the phrase "you got two strikes against you."

Lilo, the star of *Can Can,* and her husband, a dashing French marquis named Gui Dela Passardiere, called me to do an album of French songs with her. This started a friendship that lasted for many years. Two energetic, dynamic people that helped to broaden my life in many ways.

Lilo kept me busy for the next several months writing arrangements for two record albums and a one-month live engagement at the Hotel Plaza. During this time, I got to really know her handsome husband, Gui. He was a real charmer with the ladies and also a great storyteller. While attending prep school in Paris, he became friends with two fellow students, Ali Kahn and

"Bebe" Rebosa. Later on, both of them acquired big reputations as lovers and men about town. Gui enjoyed telling me how they had achieved such fame.

According to Gui, the two most important rules in a man/woman relationship were (1) *never* allow your love to find you asleep and (2) *never* admit you achieve orgasm. That way, your lady partner will keep trying to—ah—well, you get the idea. I have reason to believe that Gui also cut a mean swath through the Park Avenue ladies club. He proudly bore the title of Marquis de La Passardiere. His father had long before squandered the family fortune, but Gui still loved flaunting his title.

PAUL ANKA

Don Costa, who had just become the A&R man for Paramount Records, was very busy arranging for many different kinds of singers. One in particular drove him crazy. I remember meeting Don for lunch one day and he was very annoyed because some little jerk was up in his office pounding on the piano. After lunch, I walked Don back up to the office and I met the *little jerk*. I think he was about fifteen or sixteen years old and very hyper. He played the piano badly and the harmonies he used would drive you nuts. Don insisted that he record (on a little walkman tape recorder) the song he wanted to sing and then "Get the hell out of here! I'll see you at the recording session tomorrow." Don fixed the rhythmic meter so that there was the same number of beats in each measure. He also changed many of the harmonies and wrote out the arrangement for the orchestra. The next day, they recorded the song. It was "Diana," and that little punk was Paul Anka. Don repeated this procedure with Paul for several years (I know because I conducted many of the dates), and as a result, Paul had a string of hits that made him tons of money. His father was very aware of the publishing situation in those days and he managed to get all of the rights for his son. Don was only getting one hundred twenty-five dollars per arrangement, while Anka was making tens of thousands of dollars.

My buddy, Jerry Bruno, the bassist on practically all of Don's recordings, liked to tell the story about a night when Paul's father approached Costa at a recording company party, and thanked him profusely for the many hit records he had arranged for his son. Several musicians witnessed this scene, and when Mr. Anka shook Don's hand, they could sense that he was quietly giving him some money as a thankful gift. After Mr. Anka left, everyone was stunned to learn that he had only given Don ten dollars.

Years later, Paul was interviewed by one of the famous magazines, and he unashamedly lied that he always wrote all of his own arrangements. This really hurt Don's feelings. Anka should give thanks to some deity every morning and every night for the good fortune of having had a Don Costa in his life. Ah, showbiz—isn't it wonderful?

GEORGE SANDERS

George Sanders, the famous English actor, wanted to record an album singing many of the great classic American pop tunes. I agreed to help Don by writing the arrangements on six of the twelve songs. George had just split up with Zsa Zsa Gabor and the newspapers were filled with lots of gossip. She called him at the studio one night, just after we finished recording. I'll never forget watching all of the secretaries running to their respective phones so that they could eavesdrop on the romantic (?) banter between George and Zsa Zsa.

Don decided that we all go out to dinner after the final recording session. George was not too comfortable with the idea. I sensed a big cultural gap between him and the rest of us musicians. In the crowded taxi going to the restaurant, I asked George several friendly questions, hoping to relax him a bit. He gave me one-syllable answers and then finally said, in a very annoyed manner, "Would you like to see my passport?" Don, sitting up in the front seat of the cab, almost had a seizure trying to stop from laughing at my embarrassment and frustration.

A month or so later, I met George again when he was a guest star on the *Perry Como Show*. I just happened to be there that week playing some polka tune with the orchestra. This time he approached me with open arms and a big smile and insisted on telling Perry, Mitch Ayres, and anyone who would listen, what a great conductor and arranger I was. Talk about an *about-face*!

DON COSTA

Early on, Don chose me to conduct all of his recording sessions, which I did with great pleasure. He preferred to sit inside the studio control rooms and advise the engineers about the sounds he wanted accentuated and also the interpretations he expected from the soloists. Remember, we only had two or three tracks to record on at that time, and it was essential to walk out of the studio with a finished record. It was amazing what the singers, musicians, and engineers were able to artistically accomplish in such short periods of time. All real artists!

Our personal and professional lives became intertwined the very first day we met back in 1949. Don had a magnetic personality, and everybody loved him. He had a great sense of humor and a very special way of telling a story. But more than that, his very persona created a musical atmosphere that was exciting and educational, but not intimidating. Musicians of all kinds loved to hang out with him just to shoot the breeze and always have laughs.

We constantly talked about music, melodies, chord changes, rhythmic patterns—you name it. But most of all, we would exchange ideas regarding various orchestral voicings. What a wonderful learning experience this was, because most of the time, we were in a recording studio listening to the very things we had discussed the night before. Don was born with a gigantic, natural musical talent that he took for granted, while the rest of us just sat back and admired his genius.

MARION EVANS

A new musical energy came onto the scene about this time. His name is Marion Evans. He came from Alabama and he had studied engineering at Auburn University. Marion is a natural mathematics wizard, but he never gave up his first love, music. He had played the trumpet earlier in life, but now he only enjoyed writing arrangements for bands and singers. What he lacked in technique on the piano, he made up for with his great knowledge of harmony and orchestration. He, Don, Jerry Bruno, and I spent a lot of time together when they all lived on West Forty-fifth Street at the old Whitby Hotel. We constantly discussed, besides girls and local gossip, a new musical sound or idea that one of us had recently read or heard about. Marion enjoyed "holding court," while Don generally roamed around the room making statements like, "Are you kidding? That sounds like a bunch of shit to me!" Jerry and I were constantly cracking up, listening to their sometimes-heated discussions. I often managed to be the referee, but most of the time I just listened and learned. Occasionally, I played the piano in order to demonstrate the points they were trying to make. Those encounters with Marion and Don taught me more about orchestration and harmony than I ever learned at Juilliard. Although neither Don nor Marion would never openly admit it, the rest of us knew that they had great musical respect for each other.

Marion had composed and orchestrated for several symphony orchestras, Broadway shows, and contemporary pop and jazz bands. The Tex Beneke band kept him busy in the beginning, but then he, like Don and the rest of us arrangers at that time, began writing for all kinds of singers and bands. The recording business was flourishing. Marion's reputation as a teacher spread quickly, and he was soon inundated with people asking for his musical advice. He moved into Costa's former apartment, just off Seventh Avenue on Forty-ninth Street, which, many years before, had been a whorehouse. It soon became the local meeting place for many of us who wanted to just hang out and talk about or listen to the latest recordings that were being made at that time. Jazz artists like Al Cohn and Quincy Jones, often stopped by to pick his brain. Night after night we gathered, put on the Koss earphones, and listened to the compositions and arrangements of people like Neal

Hefti and the Count Basie band, Nelson Riddle and Billy May from Los Angeles, and all the famous classical motion-picture composers. The orchestrations of Conrad Salinger always took up a lot of discussion. Billy Byers came around Marion's place quite frequently, but I always got the feeling that Billy was going to write it *his way*, no matter what anybody said. And his way was always very good.

For a short while, I showed Marion whatever arrangements I was working on, before my recording dates. It seemed he was always able to find a way to re-voice certain sections so that the emotional or dramatic effect I was trying to achieve would come off more effectively. He was a big influence on my early arranging efforts, as was Costa. However, there were times later on, when I think we all learned from each other. What wonderful years.

Two of Marion's most talented younger *students* were Torrie Zito and Pat Williams. Both of them have gone on to achieve great success and recognition in the world of music. Pat and Torrie are dear friends of mine and I am certain that they agree with all I have said and will say about Costa, Evans, and Robert Farnon.

After several years of arranging and conducting for people like Helen O'Connell, Steve and Eydie, and Tony Bennett, Marion decided to change his occupation. This came about as a result of one particular arrangement of "Blame It on the Bossa Nova" that he wrote for Eydie Gorme. When it was nominated for a Grammy as one of the best vocal arrangements of the year, Marion said, "If this industry thinks that is one of the best arrangements of the year, I am getting out of the business." And he did. He resigned from the musician's union and became a computer wizard. Because of his natural mathematical genius, his software programs were an immediate hit with several brokerage firms. He soon became a very successful businessman.

Years later, I stayed with Marion at his apartment on East Sixty-fourth Street whenever I went back to New York City. Again, we would sit for hours and talk, only these times we discussed mathematics, the stock market, and world wide economic trends.

Early on in our relationship, he shared many Easter holidays with me and my young family. The kids loved having him over for the annual egg hunts. Even now, they still refer to him affectionately as the "real" Easter Bunny.

ROBERT FARNON

Thanks to Tony Tamburello, a dear friend and excellent pianist, we were introduced to the arranging and compositional genius of Robert Farnon. This man in England really got everyone's attention. He soon was lovingly nicknamed "The Governor," a title he justly deserved. We were, and still are, in awe of his unique writing talent. On one of his early visits to New York City, Marion Evans threw a party for him. It started about 11 PM, and all the "cats" showed up. The apartment was filled with great jazz and studio players. Dizzy Gillespie, an old friend of Farnon's, came by to pay his respects and Farnon felt obliged to make a little speech saying something like, "Many years ago, I played trumpet in an orchestra up in Canada. One night, after hearing Dizzy play just thirty-two bars, I realized that my trumpet-playing days were over and I had better find a new musical vocation." The room roared with laughter and we all silently agreed that it was a *happening* where everybody won.

In those days, a piano was generally the place where musicians gathered to discuss various melodies and different harmonic structures. But on the night Farnon was honored, the piano was the loneliest spot in the room. However, somebody brought a girlfriend along—and you guessed it—she insisted on singing a song. No one volunteered to play for her. After a while, Marion persuaded me to do so. She sang "Just One of Those Things." In my entire life, that was the longest chorus I have ever had to play.

Several years later, Joe Soldo hired me to play celeste on a recording session that Farnon arranged for Tony Bennett. During an orchestra break, I asked Bob who inspired him the most, as far as composition and orchestration were concerned. He mentioned several names but emphasized Delius, the great English composer.

He modestly went on to say, "It's all floating around up there (meaning musical thoughts and inspiration), and occasionally, we get a chance to reach up and grab a handful." I liked what he said, but I didn't fully understand the truth of it until years later.

One night in the early sixties, I had dinner with my friends Pat Williams and Torrie Zito. We went to my nearby office-apartment for a nightcap after dinner and, as usual, we listened to Farnon records. I mentioned that I was having trouble getting started on a particular arrangement that I still had to write for a recording session with Perry Como the following day. The song was "How to Handle a Woman."

I improvised an introduction on the piano that I had been thinking about, and both Torrie and Pat said, "Why don't you orchestrate what you just played?" Realizing that I still had an arrangement to write, they both left about 11:30 PM. My copyist, Bill Forman picked up the arrangement at 7 AM the next morning and I fell asleep on the couch until around noon. Knowing that I had had a lot to drink the night before, I began to worry that Perry might not like some of the liberties I took with the harmonies of the song. After the first rundown, I was so relieved to hear all of the orchestra members tap their music stands as an expression of approval. I thought that would automatically turn off Como, but instead, he sneaked up behind me and whispered into my ear, "That was gorgeous—you don't need me to sing and cover it up." Before I could comment about that, he said, "But I would like to know who the pretty lady was that you were thinking about when you wrote that arrangement."

I sent a copy of the recording to Farnon and a letter telling him how his music had inspired me and, if he didn't like the record, he could use it as a coaster for a tall gin and tonic. A week later, I received a note back from him that simply read, "Dear Nick, you reached up and grabbed *several handfuls.*" He made my day.

Bob is a very kind, gentle, and courteous human being. He has been a guiding light to many of us who know what it's like to face a blank orchestral score page. His arrangements and compositions will forever be a great source of inspiration for me.

JULIUS LA ROSA

Julius La Rosa had become a household name as a result of his early appearances on the *Arthur Godfrey Show*. He was very popular with people of all ages. However, after the terrible way he was fired by Godfrey, while *they were on the air,* the audience loved him even more. He has a beautiful voice inspired by his idols, Frank Sinatra and Perry Como, and he sings with lots of feeling.

Artie Malvin asked me to help him put together an album for Julius who had a smash record at the time. I arranged and conducted the follow-up ballad album and then conducted his out-of-town dates for the next couple of years. The audience loved his singing and chatter, but they always insisted that he sing his big hit "Eh Cumpari." Sometimes, he refused to do so, and that didn't sit too well with many of his fans.

I remember one engagement in particular, when Julie appeared at the Sands Hotel in Las Vegas. You can imagine Julie's excitement, and also mine, when we learned that Frank Sinatra was in the audience waiting for our show to begin. Julie gave a great performance that night and, in the process, told the audience of his love and admiration for Frank. After the show, Sinatra graciously invited us to the lounge to have a drink with him. It was my first meeting with the man and I was excited having the opportunity to sit, talk, and laugh with this magnificent entertainer. Before we parted, Frank asked me if I would play for him and Keeley Smith the next afternoon. They were about to make a recording together and it was necessary to select the right keys for the songs they would be singing. I eagerly accepted the invitation. The following afternoon, I met Frank in the lounge again and we took up right where we left off the night before with lots of yakking and joking around. Someone gave me a lead sheet of the music he wanted to rehearse, and when Frank was called away to answer an important phone call, I hurried into the abandoned showroom and learned the song in all twelve keys. I was prepared!—But guess what?— Keeley never showed up. What a disappointment that was for me. Years later, Frank and I would meet up again.

TONI ARDEN

She is one of the greatest girl singers I have ever recorded with. Toni was around long before Streisand and some of the other pop divas. Bing Crosby loved her voice and featured her on many of his broadcasts, as did Como and Dinah Shore. She had a couple of minor hits but never achieved the stardom she justly deserved. We recorded an Italian album for Decca that is still one of my favorites. Toni had a way of interpreting a lyric that really touched your heart. I remember she actually brought tears to my eyes while I was conducting the orchestra during some of the recording sessions.

Besame Mucho was the name of another album I did with Toni, and it was an absolute delight for me. My orchestra consisted of all star studio players. The trumpet magic provided by Doc Severinsen, Bernie Glow, and Mel Davis was something I will never forget. Toni was in great voice and again, she spread joy amongst all of us who were fortunate to be there.

CHAPTER 12

LILO and ARAMCO (1959)

The American Arabian Oil Co. (ARAMCO) hired Lilo and a couple of other entertainers to perform for their American personnel in Dhahran, Saudi Arabia. Each of us had to go through many personal interviews and extensive examinations, not only regarding our health but also our ethnic and religious heritages. Since we were going to perform in Arabia, the oil company wanted to make sure the Arabian nationals would not object to any of us. We were to be flown on a company plane that would depart from a gate behind the TWA terminal at Idlewild (JFK) airport.

I was on a real high after recording the *Toni Arden* album, but now I was filled with uncertainty and anxiety. Having to leave my young family at that time caused me a lot of emotional stress. As Judy drove me to the airport, I kept complaining, "Am I crazy? I don't need this trip." However, she persuaded me to board the plane. I sat nervously staring out of the window as we roared down the runway for takeoff. We were taxiing down the runway for an unusually long time. Suddenly, the plane came to a screeching halt at what seemed like inches away from Jamaica Bay. The pilot quickly informed us that "due to the faulty firing in engine No.4," we were returning to the hanger and would have a four-hour delay before our next attempted departure. You got the picture? I was an emotional wreck and Lilo immediately sensed my problem. We went straight to a bar in the terminal, and she ordered me a double scotch on the rocks. She should have been a doctor because her prescription worked miracles. After a lovely dinner in the airport restaurant, hosted by ARAMCO, we re-boarded the plane and took off. Shortly after we were airborne, the twenty-five or so of us on board were served champagne and more delicious food. I soon discovered that the entire ARAMCO air fleet was manned by the best pilots and personnel in the industry. They were all recruited from the major airlines. For the first time in twenty-four hours, I had a big smile on my face and I was happily *bombed!*

After two pleasant layovers in Copenhagen and Rome, we were off to Beirut. The pilots were now my pals and I found myself up in the cockpit with them at 6 AM one morning, flying over the Aegean Sea and discussing what were the major causes of airplane crashes. They both agreed that 95 percent were a result of human error and only 5 percent were due to mechanical failures. Talking to these experts did wonders to lessen my fears about flying.

BEIRUT, LEBANON

After deplaning at the Beirut airport, I got the feeling we were on another planet There was a strange smell in the air and all the people were dressed in what looked like shabby, dirty robes. We soon learned that our connecting flight to Dhahran, Saudi Arabia had been canceled. We were taken to a very modern downtown hotel and later informed that our trip would continue in a day or two.

ARAMCO suddenly became overly cautious because they had recently learned that some lovely, blonde female European entertainers mysteriously disappeared after entertaining several Arab dignitaries in Dhahran. Since Lilo and another American entertainer with our show filled that description, we were never granted our Arabian visas, and as a result, we spent the next seven days vacationing in Beirut. I had a ball!

The hotel was beautiful with a large pool and all the trimmings. The continental cuisine in the dining room was superb, always served by waiters in tuxedos. A five-piece band from Rome entertained nightly and I had a great time playing piano with them.

Every afternoon, vendors walked on the streets selling what looked like large pretzels. I purchased one and it was delicious. When I asked what it was called, the vendor said, "Koche"— pronounced as "cock." I thought he was putting me on, so I tried to repeat the name to him using a slightly different pronunciation. He became annoyed and began repeating loudly, "Cock—cock— cock!" I was embarrassed as I laughingly walked away. I told this story to my American friends when I returned to the hotel, and they all enjoyed hearing about my experience with the pretzel vendor.

Lilo, however, thought I made up the entire story. Consequently, that night at dinner in the main dinning room, she asked the maitre d', "By the way, Monsieur, what do you call those pretzel-like things vendors sell out on the streets every afternoon?" He smiled at her and loudly exclaimed, "Cock, Madame!" We all burst into laughter. He seemed to take offense and came back seriously with, "Ah, but they eat a lot of cock here in Beirut!" After another roar of laughter, Lilo quickly responded with, "That's done all over the world, Charley!"

On our return to New York City, Lilo and Gui had previously arranged for us to stop over for a week in Paris. What a wonderful experience that was for me to see the real "Follies Bergere" and all of the famous Parisian landmarks, say nothing of the delicious food we enjoyed at every meal. After having seen *Paree*, I knew that I could never "go back on the farm." OK—I'm sorry, but I just couldn't resist throwing that in.

The first piece of mail I opened when I returned home was a check from ARAMCO. No deductions—paid in full. Another time when I must happily admit that I just happened to be there.

YVES MONTAND

Norman Granz, a great jazz entrepreneur, was the producer of a new one-man show from Paris starring Yves Montand, the famous actor and cabaret singer. The production called for a small orchestra and they needed an accordionist who could play the French style music. I was hired along with several well-known jazz musicians. Yves brought along his own French piano-conductor who, unfortunately, could not speak English. Thus, it was difficult for him to communicate with us. When Yves accidentally found out that I spoke Italian, he was delighted because he also spoke the language. Now I became the interpreter for the group. He and I got along very well, but he was unhappy about some of the other musicians. Although they were all great jazz players, they were not too sensitive about his musical demands. The job really called for a group of "club-date type" musicians who could play and improvise in several different styles. Norman Granz didn't seem to understand Yves's frustration, so I was chosen to keep everybody happy with whatever tact and diplomacy I could muster up in order to resolve various musical problems that arose from time to time.

We rehearsed for an entire week before the show opened. The orchestral group (piano, bass, drums, guitar, clarinet, trombone, and accordion) was on stage for the entire performance. During certain dramatic numbers, Yves insisted that our music stand lights had to be turned off—he wanted the band to be invisible. Thus, everything we wore had to be black, and since we sometimes had to play in complete darkness, we were forced to memorize three of the arrangements. The trombonist, Billy Byers sat up on a high stool next to me on stage. One night, he absentmindedly forgot about our dress attire and he wore white socks. Well, you can imagine the effect that was created when the dramatic blackouts came. The audience and Yves saw only those two white blotches in the back of the stage. War almost broke out after that show, but I managed to help keep the peace.

Before each performance, I practiced my accordion in the musician's room upstairs. After a couple of days, Yves asked me to come down and do my practicing in his dressing room. That way, while he was getting made up for the show, he could vocalize on the tunes I was playing and we both could warm up together. It was fun.

Everyone knew that Yves enjoyed a reputation as a big ladies' man. He had just finished starring in a film with Marilyn Monroe.

Unfortunately, both she and Yves's wife, Simone Signoret, an internationally famous French actress, happened to be in New York City at that same time and Simone often came backstage before a performance. One night, while Yves and I were warming up in his dressing room, Simone made a very stormy entrance, yelling at him in French. He continued applying his makeup and humming along with me—occasionally giving her a short, curt answer. Not knowing exactly what to do, I kept right on playing while standing beside him. Suddenly I felt an object hurl past the side of my face, hit the mirror, fall on the dressing table, and scatter all of the jars and bottles of Yves's stage makeup. Simone had thrown her shoe at him and was enraged because she had just learned about his affair with Marilyn Monroe. Thank goodness, she had bad aim and missed both of us. I continued playing, as though nothing had happened and while they continued yelling and arguing, I slowly sidled out of the room still playing "Parlez Moi d'Amour" (Speak to Me of Love).

MOOSE CHARLAP and EDDIE LAWRENCE

Don Costa introduced me to an energetic young composer friend of his named Moose Charlap. He was small in stature but he had the energy of an entire army. He accompanied himself at the piano, and with his raspy voice, he could deliver a lyric that always captured the true essence of a song. I fondly remember him sitting at my piano in our front room, singing his score to *Peter Pan* before the show opened on Broadway. Nobody will ever sing "I Gotta Crow" as well as he did. What humor and talent he exuded. It was always a delight to be in a room with Moose.

He introduced me to another very special talent, Eddy Lawrence, better known as "The Old Philosopher." His special kind of humor kept us all in stitches while we were recording a couple of his comedy albums. My accompanying orchestra consisted of four instruments—trombone, tuba, drums, and accordion. We did our best to imitate a street corner Salvation Army band. Eddy used material that everyone knew, but the comedic twists he came up with were hilarious. In later years, he became a wonderful artist with a painting style all his own. Eddy also appeared as a comedian in several shows on Broadway, but he will always be "The Old Philosopher" to me.

MADISON AVENUE
(1960)

Madison Avenue was synonymous with radio and television commercials. I was very busy writing music for products like Lipton Tea, Noxzema facial products, Instant Maxwell House Coffee, S&H Green Stamps, Parliament and Viceroy cigarettes, and Texaco Gasoline. In the process, I met a lot of interesting people. They were totally different from those who worked in the recording or club date businesses. I found that many of them really danced to the tune of a different drummer. Each individual's opinion always seemed to be the result of a committee's decision. Occasionally, I was fortunate to meet a true individualist.

Almost all of the recording sessions were attended by the entire ad agency's committee that was representing a particular product. Trying to get a unanimous decision on a specific reading given by a singer or announcer would sometimes take hours. Irv Kaufman, an old pro-audio engineer, told me that an announcer once had to make 154 separate takes before the committee from the agency agreed on the way he said "Maxwell House Coffee—good to the last drop." Each of the members had a different opinion on exactly what word they personally felt should be accentuated. After great deliberation and several pots of coffee, they selected take number four.

When music and singers were involved, it sometimes became very difficult to reach a final decision. Each agency executive seemed to want a little more of a particular instrument or a word of a jingle. Irv and I always knew when the orchestra had performed perfectly—the singer or singers were in correct perspective and the recording could not be improved. At that point, he would reach up to a certain dial on his recording board during a playback and take suggestions from the committee by twisting a dial to the right for more volume or to the left for less, depending on what they thought was absolutely essential. That maneuver seemed to satisfy those who felt obliged to make some kind of a statement—and it would happen over and over again. When they finally exhausted what they knew their budget could tolerate, they all walked out of the studio smiling and thinking they had each made a contribution. What they did not know was—the dial that Irv was moving was *not hooked up to anything.* It was only an "editing placebo."

Very often the music for a thirty-second or a one-minute commercial could be recorded in just a few minutes, but we had to *create* stumbling blocks or time consuming "make believes" in order to justify the enormous budgets that the advertising agency had received from their sponsors.

Bill Fredricks and I did all of the commercials for Texaco Gasoline. I was lucky to make friends with two other great guys, Rod Albright and Don Harrington who worked for the SSC&B ad agency. Ray Charles and I also worked on many advertising projects together. I didn't realize then that this wonderful creative artist would be so instrumental in promoting me for bigger and better projects later on in my musical career.

Ferrante and Teicher on the cover of Cash Box, *May 5, 1962*

FERRANTE and TEICHER

My two former Juilliard teachers, both great pianists, stopped teaching and began playing concerts all over the East Coast. I recommended them to Don Costa, who was then an A&R man for ABC Paramount Records. They recorded a couple of flashy two-piano albums, but not much happened. When Don moved over to United Artists, he asked me to contact Arthur and Lou again, because he had an idea about using two pianos on a new recording of the main title from the movie *The Apartment*. I couldn't imagine why he needed two pianos instead of just one. At any rate, we all assembled at the Bell Sound Studio and it was a great feeling for me to stand up in front of a rather large orchestra, many of whom were older Juilliard grads. The players and I had lots of fun teasing and joking with our two former professors who both, fortunately, had a great sense of humor. The recording we made that day became a smash hit and it launched a career for Ferrante and Teicher that lasted for forty years. A couple of months later, Don wrote another arrangement featuring F&T on the theme from *Exodus*. It also became No. 1 on the record charts. These two hits were followed in the next couple of years by "The One-Eyed Jacks," "Goodbye Again," "Tonight" (from *West Side Story*), and "Midnight Cowboy." Arthur and Lou were on their way to recording stardom.

I conducted all of their recording sessions for at least fifteen years, and it was always exciting and challenging. After their early record smashes, Don became too busy arranging for many other artists and he left the arranging chores to Arthur, Lou and me. Don, of course, always sat in the recording booth so that he could tell the engineer what to expect and get the correct balances from the various instruments in the orchestra. We only had three or four tracks to record on in those days and the performances had to be perfect. We didn't have the luxury of being able to punch in the correct notes later on. *And* we were expected to record four sides in three hours—less twenty or thirty minutes for coffee breaks. The artistry displayed by both the musicians and the engineers was truly remarkable. It was all taken for granted.

At the end of one particular recording session, there was only five minutes left and we still had one more song to record. For economic reasons, we were not allowed to go overtime. Arthur had written a lovely but orchestrally ambitious arrangement on "Claire de Lune," and I knew it was going to be a chore for all of us. Because of the time element, we had no chance to rehearse. Therefore, I suggested we go ahead and record our first reading. We finished playing just as the clock ran out of time. It was a very satisfying moment for all of us because nobody had goofed. That version is the one you will hear on their album. In later years, George Foster took over for Don as producer of the last few F&T albums.

My close buddy, Joe Malin, and me after a recording session

HELLO, TERRY!

Judy created another baby-boy miracle! On May 14, 1960, I became the very proud father of our third child, Terry Michael.

The entire family was deliriously happy with our new member. He was a very welcome addition to our close-knit group and he quickly became the source of great joy for all of us.

FRANKIE AVALON

My musician friend, Pete De Angelis, had just produced a couple of hit single pop records for a young artist in Philadelphia named Frankie Avalon. Although he was very popular singing the contemporary tunes of the day, Pete decided that Frankie should do an album in the style of Sinatra. I got the job, and during the next six months we did two albums together. We had a ball making music together, but unfortunately, neither album was very successful. Frankie's forte was in the contemporary style of singing and he was an entertainer unto himself. He, like Perry Como, was also a great golfer and we enjoyed sharing our mutual enthusiasm for sports and music. He went on to achieve great success in Hollywood as an actor-singer, along with Annette Funicello

STEVE and EYDIE

Eydie and I first met at a Jewish center in Jamaica, Long Island performing at a wedding celebration. She was hired as the girl singer with our club date band. We immediately became friends because I could transpose and play in all the keys she sang in. I immediately fell in love with her beautiful voice, and at that time, neither of us, realized that one day we would work together in recording studios and night clubs all over the country.

Costa was arranging for both Steve and Eydie and I had the pleasure of conducting all of their early recordings—both as individuals and as a team. Steve and Eydie achieved a great deal of fame appearing with Steve Allen on his NBC late-night television shows.

After several years, I became their arranger and conductor *on the road.* In one of their early engagements at Caesar's Palace in Las Vegas, I conducted a medley of pop tunes that I had

arranged and it contained a lot of tempo changes. Before the
show began, we agreed that if either Steve or Eydie—while they
were singing—wanted a particular tempo to be slower, they
could motion to me (behind their backs) by pointing their
hands downward. By the same token, if they wanted the tempo
to be faster, they could point their hands upward. What a great
solution, we thought. Since I was conducting the orchestra on
stage behind them, Tommy Check, the drummer, had his eyes
glued on whatever moves they might make. All was going well
until Tommy started laughing so hard he could barely play.
When I turned around, I saw Steve's hand pointing *up*—and
Eydie's hand pointing *down*.

Steve is a great natural comedian and he never missed an
opportunity to do something unexpected. The adlib banter on
stage between the two of them often took bizarre twists, all to the
delight of the band and the entire audience. Several nights, he
would say that Eydie was going to sing a brand-new song—and
then he would make up some corny country-music title. Everyone
laughed because they knew he was joking. Eydie, however,
remembered all the silly titles he came up with and later, she wrote
very clever lyrics to all of them. I composed the music and we
made a demo recording. Knowing the folks in Nashville would
not accept Eydie as an authentic country-girl singer, she listed her
name as, "Penny Swirth." I loved it.

THE GERSHWIN MEDLEY

We spent many years together playing in Las Vegas, Lake
Tahoe, Miami Beach, and the New York City area. Our crowning
moment occurred around 1974 when I arranged and orchestrated
a lengthy George Gershwin medley that Steve, Eydie, Artie
Malvin, and I put together. It was in honor of Gershwin's seventy-
fifth birthday.

We first performed it in Las Vegas and it was an immediate
smash. Caesar's Palace provided a forty-four-piece orchestra for
the occasion, and needless to say, it was a musical joy for everyone.

Terry Trotter and I sat at twin pianos facing each other. We opened the medley with a six-minute version of the "Rhapsody in Blue," which allowed Steve and Eydie to go off stage, change costumes, and then return singing the fabulous music and lyrics of George and Ira Gershwin. The long medley ended with both of them standing on top of the pianos singing "Of Thee I Sing." It was an artistic and theatrical success. I'll never forget Jule Styne's comment after he saw a performance. He shook my hand and said, "George would have been very proud of you." I was flattered to receive such a compliment from Jule since he was a friend and a contemporary of Gershwin, and also a marvelous composer himself.

Many nights between shows, Terry Trotter and I had dinner together. One evening, we decided to celebrate our Gershwin success with a cocktail and a bottle of wine during dinner. I felt a little woozy when we returned to the showroom, but nothing to worry about. The opening numbers went very well. Terry opened the rhapsody in his usual brilliant manner, but when I sat down to play my part, my fingers felt like they belonged to King Kong. What came out of the piano was awful. The booze obviously kicked in, and I was making mistakes galore. To make matters worse, I couldn't help hearing Terry snickering under his breath all the while I was pounding away. The orchestra members also enjoyed hearing me goof because I was known as a task master. After the show, I was teased by everyone in attendance. I never drank between shows after that night.

Gary Smith and Dwight Hemion called us to London, England in 1975, and we filmed a television special called *Our Love Is Here to Stay*. It starred S&E along with Gene Kelly and the program ended with our Gershwin medley. We used the Jack Parnell orchestra. After the television special was aired here in the United States, the show was nominated for several Emmys. I was flattered when some of my fellow arranger-conductor friends called and told me, "You just walked away with the Emmy." However, I was never told that first, one had to nominate himself in order to qualify for the award. Everyone else connected with the show knew that, and as a result, many of them walked away with honors. As a result of my own ignorance, I was left out in the cold. When you least expect it, life can indeed, be a learning experience.

I was paid the basic union scale by S&E for the concert arrangement, and then I received another customary fee from the production company in London for arranging and orchestrating the Gershwin medley for television. Months later, S&E decided to also release a record album of the medley, plus six or seven more songs that we recorded in Los Angeles. The accompanying quartet consisted of Ray Brown on bass, Shelley Manne on drums, Tommy Tedesco on guitar, and me on piano. S&E gave their usual magnificent vocal renditions of the extra songs included in the album package.

While appearing as a guest on the *Johnny Carson* television show, Eydie proudly promoted the new record album. As a result of that, Steve was informed by the Musician's Union Local 47 that I had to be paid a "new use" fee since the medley was now also a record album. This was a well-established fact and everyone in the music business was aware of it. However, Steve became enraged and our wonderful relationship came to a painful halt. It was a very sad day for me.

After several years, the tension finally eased between us. S&E have performed the Gershwin medley all over the country for many, many years, and it has proven to be not only a great artistic achievement for them, but also a wise economic investment.

In 1995 they were honored, and rightfully so, by the Society of Singers who presented them with the coveted "Ella" award. Everyone attending the affair that night received a gift from S&E— a CD of the Gershwin record album. Although the package included extensive liner notes—*nowhere* was there any mention of me, the English orchestra, or the great jazz instrumental artists who accompanied them on the additional songs in the album. It seems to me that a simple acknowledgement would have been the courteous and professional thing to do. I repeat again, "Ah, showbiz—isn't it wonderful?"

"NEVER ON SUNDAY"

Melina Mercouri was the star of this movie, and United Artists insisted that Don Costa record her singing the hit song from the film. Somehow, he was able to find out what key she sang it in, and a recording date was scheduled. Don had never met Melina prior to the moment she walked into the control room thirty minutes late, with Jules Dassin, the producer of the film. I was out in the studio rehearsing the orchestra when Don summoned me into the control room. I soon realized why his voice had sounded so strange over the loud speaker.

Melina and Jules had been partying very heavily the night before, and now they both still had serious hangovers. Smashed would probably be a better word. When I heard her say hello to me, she sounded like a bass foghorn. There was no way in hell she was going to be able to sing three notes in tune, let alone an entire song. She apologized profusely, and then she and Jules mumbled their goodbyes and faded out of the room. I will never forget the pained look on Don's face. After a moment of uttering every Sicilian curse word he knew, he looked at me and said, "Grab a pencil. We got a lot of changes to make." I told the band to take a ten-minute break and together, we decided which instruments would play the melody now that the arrangement was going to be an instrumental—and not a vocal. Fortunately, there were various printing machines close by and we were able to supply the entire string section with new parts. But for the rest of the band it was a "spit and chewing gum" adventure. The special Greek musicians that had been hired didn't know what in the hell was going on, when we started making all the necessary changes. I kept stopping the orchestra when it didn't sound right to me. Finally, Don angrily told me to "Keep going. Don't stop!" It was later I found out that he and Al Weintraub, the engineer, had the Greek musicians' microphones turned off, except for the sections where they were needed. Miraculously, we managed to come out with a pretty interesting record.

Don was famous for having written hit records for practically every singer in the business, but his own instrumental albums never got the acclaim they justly deserved. You can imagine his surprise when "Never on Sunday" became a smash single. It was an unbelievable happening, and it ended up being the only hit instrumental record Don ever made for himself.

CHAPTER 13

TITO RODRIGUEZ (1961-62)

The next few years found me doing lots of recordings with many different kinds of artists. A young Puerto Rican bandleader named Tito Rodriguez was getting a lot of attention and I was called to arrange two albums for his orchestra. The "Twist" became a new dance craze and one of the albums we made was called the *Latin Twist*. Tito, a good-looking percussionist, also had a very special singing voice that exuded energy. It was very sexy-sounding to all of the ladies who came to the Palladium Ballroom to see and hear him. He was a joy to work with.

Because of his very demanding schedule, Don Costa left his job as A&R man for United Artists Records, and I took over his position. Having a nine-to-five job was a new experience for me. I still continued all of my outside freelance work, but I soon found that I was again burning the candle at both ends.

PAT WINDSOR (MITCHELL)

Charles Reader, a percussionist and bandleader-entrepreneur from the Pierre Hotel, had a very elegant manner and a great sense of humor. He called me to arrange and conduct an album for his beautiful wife, Pat Windsor. The album was conceived by her vocal coach, Bobby Kroll. Pat was a fabulous entertainer, and she performed in cabarets and nightclubs all over the country. In addition to her lovely singing voice, she was a master baton twirler and had a gorgeous figure. She thrilled audiences from coast to coast. We assembled a great orchestra for her album, which included all of the heavyweight studio players in town. Ray Charles got the vocal background singers and we had a musical experience that many of us still talk about. It was a delight.

Pat, Charles, and their son, David became a part of our family. As a result, we shared many wonderful experiences together down through the years. Although Charles sadly passed away many years ago, Pat and David are still a very important part of our lives.

"SNOWBOUND"

Meanwhile, back at UA Records, we decided to record a winter-holiday type album featuring Ferrante and Teicher called *Snowbound*. I composed the title song of the album and Ray Charles wrote the lyrics. Arthur and Lou were playing concerts on the West Coast at that time, so we decided to record the album in Hollywood. It was a last-minute project (as so many were then) and Ray didn't have time to finish writing the lyrics before I left New York City. I stopped over in Denver to see my family on the way out to Los Angeles. Ray called and gave me a lyric that I didn't think was exactly right for the mood that I was trying to create. While I was in Denver, I wrote the orchestral and choir arrangements of the song. Ray was unhappy about my comments, but he reluctantly promised to give it another try. Mind you, in just a couple of hours, he called me back with a set of entirely new lyrics that were absolutely perfect. Here they are:

> Snowbound together, we're snowbound together.
> Thankful the weather locked us in,
> Cheek to cheek with the fireplace aglow thru the night,
> So thru the night our love keeps glowing, growing,
> Knowing the blisses of whispers and kisses,
> Cozy and comfortable and warm,
> Just a peaceful pair, happy to be stranded there,
> Two together snowbound, blessing the storm.

This is an excellent example of this man's genius. In later years, I would have the good fortune to see him do this on countless other occasions. Yo, Ray!

"SHE LOVES ME"

A new Broadway show called *She Loves Me* became very popular, and two of my very good friends were a part of it. John Berkman, a brilliant pianist, was the conductor, and Bob Creash was the accordionist in the orchestra. The setting of the show was Paris and the accordion provided a very important sound for the overall ambience of the production. Judy and I saw the show and we were very impressed with the wonderful work of both John and Bob, who had many accordion solos to play throughout the performance.

A couple of months later, I received a frantic early-morning phone call from Bob asking me to sub for him at the matinee performance that day. An emergency had arisen in his family. I, of course, agreed to take his place that day. He had arranged for me to have access to the backstage area of the theatre around 10:30 AM so that I could study and practice the accordion parts. A very nervous and distraught John Berkman called me a few minutes later. He knew me as a pianist, but he had never heard me play the accordion, so naturally, he was quite concerned about my ability on that instrument. Anyway, he agreed to meet me backstage at twelve noon so that we could talk about the music and be prepared for the 2 PM performance. I got there at 10:30 and practiced the music over and over. The overture included a long, impressive accordion cadenza.

John did not show up at twelve noon, but many of the other musicians, all old friends of mine, began to drift in. They all knew that I had been there early, diligently practicing the music. Finally about 1:15 PM, I put my accordion back into the case and asked the orchestra members to help me with a little "prank" that I wanted to play on John. We all loved and respected him, but we also knew that he was sometimes preoccupied and a bit nervous. I didn't want him to know that I had already studied and practiced the music. At about 1:25 PM, he made a frantic entrance. He breathlessly apologized for being late and I said something like,

"Relax man, calm down, because I just got here myself. I also got hung up this morning." I know he didn't want to hear what I was saying. Alarm was written all over his face. The musicians had to turn away to keep from laughing. I told him that I hadn't played the accordion in quite a while. He nervously opened my book and tried to explain what had to be done. I faked a terrible cadenza with mistakes galore. I also told him I didn't sight-read very well, but—not to worry—I could fake my way through anything. Everyone could see now that he was a real basket case. The warning bell sounded and we all walked into the orchestra pit. To make matters worse, I intentionally knocked over my music stand and that only added to his agony. The players were silently enjoying all of the madness that was going on. I played the part of a real klutz. Finally, John reluctantly threw the opening downbeat, and after a few big orchestral chords, I began to play the solo cadenza. I played it quite well, not forgetting to add my own little trills and flourishes. I could feel John's eyes glaring at me, but I kept my head down pretending not to sense the *death rays* he was sending me. After the overture and opening number were over, I innocently looked up and saw his lips form the words "You miserable son-of-a-bitch!" He kept hissing that at me throughout the entire performance, all the while with a big, relieved grin on his face. The orchestra members loved the caper and we all, including John, shared a lot of laughs after the show.

To this very day, John and I are still the best of friends and now, I think he actually enjoys hearing me retell this story whenever some of our old pals are around.

JANE MORGAN

Dave Kapp, originally an A&R man for RCA, started his own record label, Kapp Records. He always liked the way I played the accordion and when he later found out that I was also an arranger, he hired me to arrange and conduct a couple of albums for his favorite singer, Jane Morgan.

In the meantime, Marty Gold called me to play accordion on

an album he had arranged for Kapp Records featuring continental music like that which was played in the movie *Love in the Afternoon*, featuring two violins, accordion, bass, drums, guitar, and marimba.

We had already completed the first tune of the recording session and after finishing a take on the second song, we all went into the control room to hear a playback. At that moment, Dave Kapp and Jane Morgan walked in. They had just been out to dinner. Dave asked to hear the first song we had already recorded. He loved the melody and insisted that Jane try to sing it. When Marty told him that the arrangement was not in her key, Dave said, "Don't worry, Nick can fix it." Marty smiled and gave me a big "be my guest" gesture. In addition to being a successful singer, Jane was also a good musician. After one quick rehearsal at the piano, I informed the musicians that we would have to transpose the arrangement into Jane's key. After a little grumbling, they played it perfectly. We did just one take and she sang it beautifully. It became her biggest selling record ever. The song?—"Fascination."

Cover for my album, Blazing Latin Brass Goes to Italy

STEREO RECORDING (1963-64)

Stereo recordings were becoming the rage about this time. Hi-fi was what everyone expected because it was a new innovation in the recording industry. As the A&R man for United Artists, I was given the opportunity to record a stereo instrumental album of my own. It was called *Blazing Latin Brass*. Al Weintraub, the gifted engineer at Bell Sound, invented a process whereby a listener could hear various sections of the orchestra through different speakers at opposite sides of any room. *And* we could switch these instrumental sections from side to side during a single performance *while* we were recording.

All of the musicians were top-caliber players, and I wrote arrangements that gave them many chances to show off their respective talents. Bernie Glow, Doc Severinsen, and Mel Davis were the mainstays in the trumpet section. Other famous instrumentalists included trombonists Urbie Green, Chauncey Welsh, and Bill Watrous; guitarists Tony Mottola, Al Caiola, and Bucky Pizzarelli; bassist Jerry Bruno; percussionists Bob Rosengarden, Willie Rodriguez, and Phil Krause; reed players Joe Soldo, Sid Jekowsky, and Phil Bodner.

The album was a big success and UA insisted that I record another one. It was called *Latin Brass Goes to Italy*. We all had a lot of fun, because I used many old Italian folk and opera melodies and treated them in a humorous Latin rhythmic manner. The same orchestra was present, except I hired my friend, Dom Cortese, on accordion to add the authentic Italian flavor. Foolishly, I did not record any more personal albums. I was too busy recording albums for many other artists. The immediate money I earned and the popularity I experienced caused me to neglect my own orchestral pursuits. In the next life, I will definitely do things a little differently.

I finally abandoned my A&R job at United Artists Records. Sitting behind a desk answering telephone calls was not *my cup of tea*. Being a freelance musician was exciting and I enjoyed the daily new challenges.

Lee Cooley, one of the original producers of the Como show, directed a big gala variety show at Carnegie Hall for the benefit of the Fight for Sight Organization. At the insistence of my friend, Ray Charles, I was hired to conduct the orchestra. Lee was wary at first, but after the performance he threw a big party at Lindy's Restaurant and I was toasted and feted. What a surprise that was for me! He became my No. 1 supporter.

ARRANGING FOR COMO

In the fall of 1963, Mitchell Ayres, conductor of the *Perry Como* television show, felt he had to have new arrangers for the program. Why, I didn't know. I had great respect for both Joe Lipman and Jack Andrews and I couldn't understand why they were going to be replaced. Thanks to Ray Charles, I was offered, along with Ralph Burns, Kermit Levinsky and two others, an opportunity to audition for the job. Mitch gave each of us a variety of things to arrange for the opening television special, which came from Pittsburgh, Pennsylvania. Several days after the show was televised, Mitch informed me that I was selected to be the new arranger for the Como orchestra. What good news that was for me. They allowed me to have an assistant and I immediately called Torrie Zito. When I saw that we didn't get "Orchestral Arrangers" television screen credit after the following show, I called Mitch and quit the job. I was tired of writing arrangements for television shows, recording artists, and others and not getting credit. Mitch pleaded with me to stay on and said he would do everything he could to rectify the situation. On the next show, Torrie and I did get screen credit and thus, we became the arrangers for the 1963-1964 television season.

At the end of every television season, Perry, for some unknown reason, always took a great deal of time before he rehired his former television staff. That was exactly the situation at the end of June 1964. At this point, Mitch felt it was time to make a change, so he moved to Los Angeles and became the orchestra conductor of *The Hollywood Palace*, a new television show produced by Nick Vanoff, another old Como alumnus. As a result, I got the call to *conduct* the Como show for the next season. Thanks again, to the efforts of my friend, Ray Charles.

CONDUCTING FOR COMO IN DETROIT

Our first show in September of 1964 came from Detroit, Michigan. Dwight Hemion was the television director and we took a nucleus of musicians and technicians from New York City with us. I brought Doc Severinsen, Dick Hyman, and Bobby Rosengarden, who was my orchestra contractor at the time. The rest of the orchestra consisted of local Detroit musicians. Anne Bancroft and Victor Borge were the guest stars on the show. I was a bit apprehensive since this was to be my first live television show as a *conductor* for Perry Como.

The opening rehearsal was going quite well until Perry started to sing the song "People." At the end of the arrangement, the orchestra and I got a bit out of sync with Perry. We continued on with the rehearsal, but suddenly I realized someone was lifting the earphone off my right ear. I was surprised to see that it was Perry. I told him that I was sorry about the mix-up at the end of his solo and added, "But now I know what you are going to do, so don't worry." He paused for a moment and then, with a strange smile on his face, he said, "How in the hell do you know what I'm going to do when I don't even know what I'm going to do?" It was then I realized that Como was a man of impulse. The kind of interpretation he gave a song would be determined by how he felt *at that particular moment*. I found that interesting, and at the same time, quite challenging.

COMO CHRISTMAS SPECIAL IN ROME, ITALY

The next show was recorded and televised in Rome. Roberta Peters and Kukla, Fran and Ollie were the guest stars on the show. I was lucky to get the name of a great Italian-American musician named Ralph Ferraro, who was living in Rome at that time, working as a composer and arranger. He was a graduate of the Manhattan School of Music in N.Y.C. and had originally gone to Italy on his honeymoon. Ralph spoke Italian perfectly, as did his lovely wife, Manuelita. We immediately became close friends, as we are to this very day. How exciting it was to be in my father's homeland and making music with a great Italian orchestra that Ralph assembled for me. The musicians enjoyed listening to me speak Italian, because my accent was *old-fashioned*.

Late one afternoon, Marlo Lewis (the producer), Ray Charles and his wife, Bernice, and I had a meeting with Monsignor Bartolucci, head of the Vatican Choir. I was chosen to be the interpreter. The monsignor greeted us at the door of his little Vatican apartment and we soon realized that he was a character. His hair was mussed and cigarette ashes were all over the front of his sweater, which was incorrectly buttoned. He insisted upon serving us a drink and promptly produced a bottle of Grant's whiskey, which he proceeded to pour into little jelly jars for each of us. Not being able to find his own glass, he poured his drink into a half-pint mason jar. He was very charming but a little absentminded.

My job was to tell him that the following day we were going to film his choir's performance near a little grotto in the Vatican gardens. When the monsignor asked what specific grotto, I remembered that this one had a statue of a large eagle peering over it. Not knowing the correct word in Italian for eagle, I answered, *"Dove il grande uciello,"* which meant, "where the big bird is." I thought it was strange that he laughed when I said that. He paused for a moment and then told us that his choir members would only be available for three hours the following day starting at 1 PM. They were all volunteers (doctors, lawyers, craftsmen, students, etc.), and it was necessary for them to return to their regular jobs by 4 PM. Later that night, I told the *grande uciello* story to my friend Ralph Ferraro and he really broke up. "Hey, man," he said, "you shouldn't have said that at the Vatican, because here in Italy, big bird means a guy has a big—uh—" He didn't have to go any further. I reminded him that the same term was also popular in the United States.

Dwight Hemion was the television director. The next day, all the members of the choir arrived by bus directly on time at the "big bird" location in the Vatican garden and the rehearsal began. As was his custom, Dwight didn't pay too much attention to the time clock. Rightfully so, he wanted everything to be perfect. After a lot of rehearsing and staging, all of us (except Dwight) were aware that time was running out. Finally, after one video take with Perry and the choir singing "Christ Is Born," the choir made their proper exit through the garden and proceeded out to the bus. Almost as though it had been staged, the door of the bus opened and all of the singers got on board. The door closed and off they went—it was 4 PM. We didn't even have a chance to say goodbye. Still oblivious to the clock and not realizing what was happening out in the garden, Dwight said through the loud speaker, "That was great—now let's do one more take!" It was funny to most of us, but to this day, I'm sure Dwight doesn't see the humor in the entire incident.

On the same show, we did an entire day's filming at the ancient Roman seaside village of Ostia Antica. We were there to film Perry's classic *Nativity, The Story of the Birth of Christ*. It was a miserably cold, rainy day and many Italian extras were there dressed in costumes of ancient Bethlehem. They all huddled together trying to keep warm. Someone managed to sneak a bottle of brandy to the "Three Wise Men" who were all very ornately dressed. It was a great way to keep warm, but unfortunately, one of the wise men got a bit tipsy. Whenever the moment came for him to kneel at the crib of the Christ child, he would lose his balance, his crown would fall off, and he'd topple over. Eventually, we managed to keep him propped up for one complete take.

Another old lady extra in one of the mob scenes kept turning and looking directly into the camera. Then she would wave as it passed over her head. We tried to explain to her that that was not acceptable, but she insisted, "How else will my family recognize me on television if they don't see my face?" Good point.

Ostia Antica is located very near the Rome airport. It was almost 1 AM, and we were all exhausted, but we still had to film the closing scene of Perry singing "Ave Maria." The scene opened with a long camera shot, so the first part of Perry's vocal was prerecorded. As he got closer to the crib, he started to sing live, which meant all of the microphones were open. The scene started beautifully, but when Perry began to sing live, none of us in the control van wanted to admit what was happening. Off in a distance, we could hear the engine noise of an incoming flight about to land at the airport. Perry continued singing, hoping that the oncoming plane noise would not be picked up by the microphones. Finally, Dwight jokingly said to all of us in the control van, "I don't hear anything, do you?" Naturally, we stopped taping and after a moment or two of venting our frustration, we all cracked up laughing, including Perry. The airport control tower informed us that in twenty minutes another plane would be landing. Everyone rallied to the cause and I think that was the fastest television take Dwight Hemion ever made.

MOVE TO NEW CITY

In late 1964, Joe Malin and I both moved our families to New City, New York, as a result of the constant coaxing of Don and Helen Costa. They had moved there a couple of years earlier. The commute between New York City and Rockland County was sometimes rough in the wintertime, but Don always advised us to turn on the radio, listen to some good music and enjoy the ride. He was right. In the following years, the Malin kids, Mary and Paul; the Costa kids, Nancy and Tano; and the Perito offspring shared many memorable times together, as did we, their parents.

CHAPTER 14

COMO HOLLYWOOD TV SPECIALS (1965-66)

Hollywood was the next venue for the Como television specials. A terrific studio orchestra was assembled and Ray Charles had a great choir that included the wives of both Henry Mancini and Dave Grusin. I must admit I was a bit uptight when both of those talented musicians showed up at the taping. Carol Burnett and Dean Martin were the guest stars. Perry was slated to sing one song with just me playing the piano accompaniment and I had practiced several pretty chord changes hoping to get the attention of Mancini and Grusin. But when we got on the air, Perry raced like hell through the entire piece and my fancy prepared accompaniment went up in smoke. I learned the hard way that the best-laid plans often go awry.

PETER NERO

On returning to New York City, I received a last-minute call to conduct a recording session for Peter Nero. Since I was the conductor for all of the Ferrante and Teicher recordings, rumor had it that Peter didn't want me to do his sessions. However, this was obviously an emergency. Shortly after the first song was recorded, Peter and I both realized we were going to be great friends. He was a delight to work with—a fabulous pianist with a great understanding of both classical and jazz music—and a perfectionist. My kind of guy. I had the good fortune to record many more albums with him down through the years. Peter has a great career now, not only as a pianist but also as a conductor of several symphonic orchestras—namely the Philadelphia Pops.

BILLY GOLDENBERG

St. Louis was the next stop on the Como television schedule. Again, I brought my lead players with me—Doc Severinsen, Dick Hyman, Bob Haggart, Bob Rosengarden, and Joe Soldo on lead alto. The rest of the orchestra were all local musicians, which would be the case for years to come.

This was also the show that first made me aware of the great talent of a young musician named Billy Goldenberg. Billy was the pianist for the choreographer on the show and he asked me if he could write his first big-band orchestral arrangement for guest star, Shirley Jones's solo spot. Of course, I said yes. He showed me his score before it went to the copyist and I noticed that he had written some very high notes for the trumpet section. I brought that to his attention, but since we had Doc Severinsen on lead trumpet, I assured him it would be OK. After our first orchestra rehearsal, I will always remember the expression on Billy's face as he tugged on my sleeve, looked up at me, and said, "Thanks. *Now I know* what you were trying to tell me." One listening is worth a thousand words—and Billy got the idea *immediately*. He went on to compose beautiful musical scores for television, movies and the Broadway stage. He soon became one of Hollywood's most popular motion-picture composers. The *Kojak* television theme and series were one of the many he wrote for television. My favorite is the Emmy winner, *Queen of the Stardust Ballroom,* which he composed with lyrics by Marilyn and Alan Bergman.

Danny Thomas was also a guest performer on that show. At that time, all variety television shows were live performances and it was mandatory for each performer to adhere to a strict time schedule. Danny knew that he had six minutes to do his solo act. But when we got on the air, he started to get more laughs than he apparently had expected. Then he forgot about the clock and just kept on going. He also chose to ignore all the frantic hand signals that were being thrown at him by the stage manager. Finally Perry, himself, became annoyed and jokingly told the director, Dwight Hemion, to "get the hook and pull Danny the hell off the stage!" Since we were *live* on the air, it was very difficult for the entire crew to make the necessary cuts, because of Danny's selfish overlong performance. While I was conducting Billy Goldenberg's exciting arrangement for Shirley Jones, I heard Dwight saying to me in my earphones, "Hey, pal, we gotta cut four minutes—talk to me!" After a lot of hand signals, we decided to cut two of Perry's songs at the end of the show. Being unfamiliar with live television, the members of the string section didn't understand what I was silently trying to communicate to them. I finally walked over to the concert master removed the two songs from his music stand and tore them in half. Then the rest of the section understood what was happening.

It's amazing what an audience's reaction can do to the egos of certain entertainers. They suddenly lose all respect and concern for other performers and *their* time in the spotlight.

BOSTON ("BOMB" SCARE)

Boston was the city for our next Como television special. Lena Horne, Peter Nero, and Johnny Paleo and the Harmonicats were the guest stars. Nat "King" Cole, whom Perry had great admiration for, had passed away a few weeks earlier. Ray Charles and I put together a medley of Nat's hit recordings for Perry and Lena to sing. Lennie Hayton, her famous musician husband, attended the first orchestra rehearsal with her in Boston, and we all got along beautifully. Apparently, there were several other live musical events going on in Boston at that time, because I ended up with a string section that was not of concert caliber. Since we had many ballads to play, I insisted that they put mutes on their instruments during the entire show. Lennie, sensing my frustration during the rehearsal, tipped his hat, gave me a big smile and waved as he walked out of the room and shouted, "Meet you in the bar later."

At the dress rehearsal the next day, the auditorium was filled with Como fans. Perry was in the middle of his opening monologue, when suddenly a man walked up from the audience on to the stage and gave him a hug. We were all taken by surprise and annoyed because we were timing the rehearsal. The audience got a big kick out of it. What they fortunately did not hear was that the man told Perry that he had a bomb in the paper sack he was carrying under his arm. Those of us with headsets on heard what he said and we were frightened to death! Perry handled the situation like a master magician. He made jokes with the man and summoned a stagehand to come out and meet his "friend." They both were able to miraculously waltz that nut off the stage. Thank goodness, the bag only contained paper scraps. The police were summoned and the man was taken to jail. We were all given an hour break after the dress rehearsal. I went outside to get some fresh air and clear my head. After a cup of coffee and a short walk around the block, I returned to the theatre. Now, policemen were everywhere. Somebody forgot to give me a pass to allow me to reenter the hall. The guard at the stage door was adamant. I could not convince him that I was the orchestra leader, and we were going on the air "live" in about five minutes. Fortunately, Mickey Glass, Perry's manager, happened to walk by the door, and from inside, he was able to convince the officer that I really was the orchestra leader.

MIAMI (WOODY ALLEN)

Our next Como show originated in Miami and the guest stars were Woody Allen, Al Hirt, and Connie Stevens. Ray Charles created a skit for Woody that put him in the midst of many beautiful chorus girls and he sang "Girls to the left of me, girls to right of me". However, when we got on the air—remember we were *live* and not on tape—Woody apparently couldn't hear the orchestra, because he sang the entire song a fourth away from the correct pitch, in spite of the fact that Dick Hyman was pounding the melody on the piano. Ray and I tried to console Woody after the show, but his dressing room door was locked. Woody is a good musician, so you can imagine his pain. We both understood his frustration, but we were unable to give him any comfort.

NYC BLACKOUT

November 9, 1965, was a memorable day for all New Yorkers. I had just finished a recording session at a studio on Forty-second Street near Times Square at 5:15 PM. I knew that trying to find a taxi to take me up to the garage where my car was parked on Fifty-third Street at that rush-hour time of day was practically impossible, so I boarded an IRT subway train to take me uptown. It was jammed with passengers, all anxious to get home. We had traveled the equivalent of only a few city blocks, when suddenly the subway train came to a screeching halt. The lights went out and we were in total darkness. The silence was eerie and frightening. We were all scared to death, but no one panicked. After a short while, little emergency lights began to flicker in the train. Nobody wanted to admit it, but I sensed that we were all thinking the same thing—maybe the Russians had dropped a bomb on New York City? World politics at that time made this thought very possible. Still everyone remained calm. Almost an hour later, we got word that a massive power failure in Niagara Falls had caused a blackout of the entire East Coast. What a relief! Everybody began to cheer. People started chatting with each other, and we all wondered how much longer we would be stuck in the tunnel. Eventually, workmen appeared with flashlights and helped all the passengers off the train. They safely guided us over the tracks back to Times Square. It was so gratifying to see people of all races, colors, creeds, and age groups helping each other, paying special attention to the older folks. It was pitch black out, except for some flares and lanterns that emergency crews had set up. Walking up Times Square that night was an experience I will never forget. The love and camaraderie I witnessed still warms my heart. It was positive proof that people *can* bond together and live in peace. The sad thing is that we always seem to need an emergency to make us aware of that fact.

JUDY GARLAND
(VEGAS—"THUNDERBIRD")

In 1967, Mort Lindsay, the conductor for Judy Garland, called and asked me to sub for him on an upcoming engagement at the Thunderbird Hotel in Las Vegas. I accepted immediately. The infamous David Begelman, Judy's agent, contacted me shortly thereafter, and we agreed upon a fee. I insisted I get paid before I left New York City, because it was a well-known fact that Judy and her business associates were having money problems. He assured me that I would receive a check *before* I left town. I heard from no one for the next ten days. I was quite concerned because I wanted to study the scores I would be playing and conducting for Judy. Mort and I were both very busy, so we finally agreed to meet at the airport an hour or so before my flight to Las Vegas to discuss the music. Begelman assured me that his aide would also meet me there with my check and airline ticket.

My flight was to leave Newark at midnight on Sunday, November 7. I was scheduled to arrive in Los Angeles, Monday morning at 6 AM, then catch a flight to Vegas, and arrive there about 11 AM—plenty of time to prepare for the 2 PM orchestra rehearsal.

On Sunday night, Newark airport was teeming with passengers. After patiently waiting for almost an hour, both Mort and Begelman's aide showed up at the same time. At the check-in counter, the aide gave me my airline ticket and stuffed the paycheck into my shirt pocket. I noticed that the amount was correct—then Mort and I hurried to the departure gate. We sat for just a few minutes and he began to explain an opening orchestral overture that I had not anticipated. I really wanted to know more about Judy's solo numbers, but we never got to discuss that music, because the flight attendant suddenly appeared and told me to board the plane. Mort assured me *not to worry*, because Paul Ditmas, Judy's young nineteen-year-old drummer would be there and it was going to be a breeze for all concerned.

After boarding, I realized I was only one of two passengers on the plane. There would be a short stopover in Cleveland on our way to Los Angeles. Sitting in first class was comforting but I was very concerned about all the new music I had to learn. After cramming as much as I could into my brain, I paused for a moment, closed the conductor book, and decided to look at the paycheck in my pocket. It was then that I noticed *the check was not signed!*

I got off the plane in Cleveland and angrily phoned David Begelman. I threatened to take the next plane back to New York City, but he pleaded with me and said that his partner, Freddie Fields would sign the check the next evening in Las Vegas. I reluctantly re-boarded the plane and was told that I was now the only passenger on it. Obviously, TWA needed that aircraft on the West Coast. As I returned to my seat, a stewardess served me a glass of brandy and handed me a local Cleveland newspaper. I took several deep breaths and tried to calm down. As I turned over the first page of the paper, I was flabbergasted to read "Judy Garland has been admitted to the UCLA Medical Center this evening and is expected to remain there for two weeks undergoing medical tests."

Here I was going to Las Vegas to conduct an orchestra for a giant star whom I'd never met, and *now* she was in the hospital! This entire thing was like a nightmare for me. Jumping out of the plane was not an option—so I sat back, sipped the brandy, looked over the music some more and dozed off.

When I arrived at the Thunderbird Hotel in Vegas around 11 AM, the desk clerk politely reminded me, "Miss Garland is in the hospital." As I turned to go to my room, I met Nat Brandwyne, the hotel bandleader whom I already knew from back in New York City. He said, "How in the hell did you ever get mixed up in this mess? Don't you know she is in the hospital?" He then informed me that the orchestra could not be canceled at that late date, so they were going to assemble at 2 PM for the first rehearsal—except that they had not yet received the arrangements from Judy's husband,

Mark Herron. They were expected to arrive from Los Angeles that day (Monday) at 2:30 PM.

Mort had given me several LPs of Judy's performances, but since the hotel had no equipment available for me to play and listen to them, Nat drove me to a local music shop and I rented a record player. I went directly to my room and started to listen to the various tempos, etc., so I would be prepared for the rehearsal— if it ever happened. At 2 PM, I was informed that the music was going to arrive at the airport at 3 PM, and would I please go out and pick it up since Mark Herron had put my name on it. Can you believe all these snafus? I did as I was told and the rehearsal started around 3:30 PM. I told the orchestra that I would be one bar ahead of them and to bear with me. Being the great pros that they were, we got along fine. It all seemed so senseless rehearsing for someone who wasn't even going to appear. She was scheduled to open the following night (Tuesday).

After many phone calls to Begelman back in New York City, I was told that I should meet Freddie Fields at the Sahara Hotel, later that night, and he would sign my check. After I met Freddie, he said something like, "Nick, chickie baby—don't worry." He was very hospitable, but he refused to sign my check, telling me that I would be paid in cash the next day at the rehearsal. I asked why we were rehearsing for something that was not going to happen—but he ignored my query and kept pouring drinks for everybody.

Rehearsal started again the next day at 1 PM. After an hour or so, we were surprised to learn that Judy had just checked into the hotel, accompanied by a nurse and a couple of friends. We were all happy but somewhat confused by this new turn of events. After another hour, we were told that Judy would be coming down to rehearse at 4:30 PM. At that point, Shep Fields, Freddie's brother and a famous bandleader himself, asked me to join him out in the theatre. I knew Shep from a recording session I had done for him years before. He was a gentleman. As soon as I sat down, he started to pay me off in one-hundred-dollar bills, all the while enjoying the big smile on my face.

Everyone waited patiently for Judy to show up, but around 6 PM, I was told that she was not going to appear and "how well did I know Dean Martin's act?" He was going to sub for her that night. Give me a break! I had never worked for Dean before, and I couldn't believe all of this madness. My pocket was full of money, and I didn't know who I was going to be conducting for come show time that night.

I returned to my room, called room service and ordered a big steak and a double scotch. Then, I sat in the tub, took a nice, warm bath and waited for the phone to ring. Mark Herron called and told me Judy was going to perform after all and that I could meet her backstage at 9:30 PM. I hurried to get dressed only to be informed moments later that our meeting would now occur at 10 PM in her dressing room. Having never met Judy, let alone accompany or conduct for her, I was a bit nervous. Judy showed up at 10:15 PM, and I could not believe my eyes. They practically carried this poor dear into the room and she looked like she was in shock—hair straight, no makeup, red-eyed! My heart sank. Still, she was very gracious and she apologized for not getting to the rehearsal. She thanked me for coming and asked if I had any questions. I answered, "Yes, about a million of them," which brought a smile to her face. I continued, "How fast do you sing the song 'Smile'?" She hummed a few bars in a very raspy voice. Knowing she still had to get dressed and made up, I thanked her and hurried down to the stage. Peter Allen and his brother had opened the show at 10 PM. The audience was very rude and unhappy with them because they were waiting to see and hear Judy. Minutes later, I was told to get on stage with the orchestra and be ready to start the overture. I tried to delay as much as possible, knowing what must have been going on upstairs trying to get Judy ready to perform.

I finally threw the opening downbeat and we were off. Several minutes later, I couldn't believe my eyes as I looked over to the side of the stage. There was Judy in her red pants suit behind a little curtain. When we started to play "Over the Rainbow" and she walked out from behind the curtain, the audience's reaction was something I had never experienced before. They were ecstatic! After a minute or two, she started her opening song a cappella. She was not in a good voice. But with each succeeding song, she got all the frogs out of her throat and by the time she sang "Over the Rainbow" at the end of the show, her voice was in top form, much to the delight of everybody on and off the stage. She graciously took me by the arm up to the microphone and tried to tell the audience, "You don't understand, we never rehearsed together!" But they didn't care and didn't want to know about that. They were in seventh heaven—and so was I. After the show, I peeked into her dressing room to say good night. She was almost crying as she climbed over many famous Hollywoodites to give me a hug and explain to them that we actually met *on the stage!* This was truly a night to remember.

For the next two weeks, we had a chance to get to know each other. It was a joy for me to be able to sit and talk to this woman, who was one of my idols. Accompanying and conducting for her was one of the most natural things I have ever done in my life. It was a dream come true for me. She was the epitome of what I still feel every performer should try to emulate. Her timing and instinctive knowledge of what to do on stage was a thrill for me to behold at every performance. The basic program consisted of nine or ten songs, after which she would do whatever encores the audience might request. It was "hang loose" time and always a lot of fun for us. She had a perfect sense of when *to leave the stage.* When her instinct told her that she really *had the audience,* sometimes after only two or three encores, she would turn to me and say, "Rainbow." That was my cue to sit at the piano, play a little arpeggio, and begin to accompany her on her final song.

My wife flew out from New York to see for herself the magic that was occurring nightly in the showroom when this marvelous lady walked on to the stage. Many afternoons, we all sat in a corner near the pool and just yakked and had laughs. I remember asking her about the exact tempo of a song and she said it might change from time to time. She suggested that I just *watch her foot.* That I did, and "Rock-a-bye My Baby" took on a whole new energy every night.

SAN CARLOS, CALIFORNIA

The Circle Star Theatre in San Carlos, California, was our next engagement. Charley Manna was the opening act. The engagement started off very smoothly until the third night. I had just put on my tuxedo and was about to leave my dressing room when two of Judy's children, Lorna and Joey Luft, came in and said that their mother was crying and there were two men in her dressing room. I dashed over in time to see David Begelman and Freddie Fields coming out. They hurried past me as the comedian, Charley Manna, was just finishing his opening act. When I entered the dressing room and saw Judy sitting in front of the mirror with no makeup on and tears streaming down her face, it really broke my heart. I tried my best to cheer her up, but all she kept saying was, "Those dirty bastards." She wouldn't tell me what had transpired. Through her tears, she moaned that she wanted to cancel the show because her voice was shot. Knowing that time was of the essence because she was supposed to go on in twenty minutes, I pleaded with her to put on her red pants suit and just *walk out on the stage*. The audience would understand because all they really wanted was to see "Dorothy." She yelled back at me, "I'm tired of being Dorothy fucking adorable!" I kept encouraging her by saying that the best way to get even with her two managers was to do the show, no matter what—collect the check and then tell *them* to go to hell. I continued talking nonstop saying things like, "Don't let me down, please. I can't sing—I don't know any of the words— and the audience will kill me if you don't show up." She interrupted, saying, "Don't you understand, my voice is shot." I quickly replied that I would put mutes on all the brass and we would play very softly. I kept babbling on, still not giving her a chance to speak. As I walked out of the room, I again shouted back to her, "Please, baby, don't let me down—just walk out there!" The stage manager ushered me into the orchestra pit and I started the overture, hoping all the time that she would rally to my plea.

When the overture was almost over, I looked up and there, standing at the back of the theatre, all dressed up, was Judy. I was so happy that I wanted to cheer. As usual, the audience went crazy when they saw her walk down the aisle to the stage. It was exactly like our first meeting in Las Vegas two months earlier. Again, she started out all alone singing, "He's got the whole world in his hands," and her voice was almost a groan. The audience couldn't have cared less. Their angel was on the stage and that was all that mattered. It was wonderful to watch and hear her transformation from misery in the dressing room to ecstasy on stage. This is where she belonged. After a couple of more songs, her voice was back in full glory and the rest of the show was heaven for all her fans. I kept shouting words of encouragement up to her during the entire show and that brought a big smile to her face. When she took her final bow and the audience went crazy, she looked down at me in the pit and yelled, "You Italian bastard—I love you!"

Conducting for Judy Garland at the Diplomat Hotel in Florida, 1965

HOLLYWOOD, FLORIDA

The Diplomat Hotel was our next engagement starting February 1, 1966. The audience, as usual, loved her and she had a good time with all of the old retirees that jammed the room nightly. One evening, she unexpectedly turned to me and said, "Come on,

Nick, let's jitterbug." I loved to dance, but jitterbugging was definitely not my forte. The audience loved her teasing me. The band started to improvise an old jazz tune and Paul Cohen, the lead trumpeter, came down from the brass section. He and Judy had a ball dancing all over the stage. Now, several of the older Jewish men in the audience started to line up, because they, too, wanted to dance with Judy. It was all an impromptu happy occasion and Judy seemed to have more fun than anyone.

JUDY and PERRY (NYC)

Shortly after that, Mickey Glass informed me that Judy was going to be a guest on one of Perry's television specials, emanating from the NBC studio in Brooklyn. A week before the actual filming, Judy came to Perry's office for our first rehearsal. Perry, Mickey, and Ray Charles immediately fell in love with her. It was late in the afternoon, definitely cocktail time, and Perry asked her if she would like a little Tanqueray Gin on the rocks (his favorite drink at that time). She gracefully declined and then opened up her black briefcase. It contained two glasses and a bottle of vodka—she said shyly, "I brought my own." Perry almost fell on the floor laughing, as did the rest of us. I was seated at the piano, ready to rehearse— but that wasn't going to happen for at least another hour or so. We, New Yorkers, were delighted to hear Judy's Hollywood stories. Perry, particularly, was fascinated by her forthright candidness. She spared no words to describe certain personalities and situations. Sid Luft, that "son-of-a-bitch," and Mel Torme, that "little prick," were two of her least favorite people in the world—in addition to Begelman and Freddie Fields. Please understand that Judy was not a foul-mouthed person. She had a great command of the language, but if a certain word had to be used to express her innermost feelings, she used it.

After another drink, we began to run through a couple of tunes. What great fun it was to accompany these two fabulous singers who were relaxed and giving perfect interpretations of the lyrics they were singing. No audience—just alone with their own personal thoughts and feelings.

The show was taped several days later and, in addition to a medley with Perry, Judy sang two solo numbers. "What Now My Love" and "Just in Time" which started with just Judy and me, seated at a piano. You can imagine how happy I was to be seen on television, accompanying this marvelous lady. At the actual taping, Perry approached Judy after we had performed "Just in Time," and ignoring the script, he said, "I understand you and Nick have worked together before." Judy then went on to say many complimentary things about me. One would think my mother had written the script.

Bill Cosby was supposed to make an entrance about this time, but he screwed up. Unfortunately, they had to stop the tape and re-shoot the entire sequence. You guessed it—all those kind words Perry and Judy adlibbed about me (on the first take) hit the cutting room floor. Ah, dear Mr. Cosby.

Like millions of other people, *The Wizard of Oz* made a big impression on me, as it did upon my entire family. Our daughter, Jennie, at a very early age, memorized every song and each word of dialogue in the movie. Seeing Judy up on the screen was an inspiration to all of us. No matter whether she was singing or acting, she represented the truth. Perhaps one day, I will be able to find the exact words to describe my admiration, gratitude, and love for this fabulous entertainer who made the whole world smile.

CHAPTER 15

COMO ALBUMS—

"LIGHTLY LATIN" and "IN ITALY"

The Bossa Nova became very popular and RCA decided Perry should do an album in this vein. Ray Charles chose some lovely songs and this was my first assignment as the arranger for a Como recording.

Arrangers were typed in those days as being an expert in only one of the following: Broadway, Television and Radio, pop tunes, jazz, or ballads. Several of us crossed over those dumb preconceived ideas.

Lightly Latin was the name of the album. I was happy to finally have an opportunity to write for a string section that included twelve violins, four violas, and two celli. This is small by today's standards. However, cellists George Ricci and Alan Schulman made up for their lack in numbers. David Nadien was the concertmaster. The rhythm section—consisting of Tony Mottola and Bucky Pizzarelli on guitars, Bob Haggart on bass, and Bob Rosengarden on drums—really captured the authentic, sensuous feel of the Bossa Nova. Ray Charles and I wrote the song "Stay with Me," especially for that album. Perry's velvet voice and his relaxed interpretation of the songs made it a musical delight. That album was the first of many that I arranged for Perry down through the years.

Our next project was an Italian album. I jokingly said to Andy Wiswell, the RCA record producer, "So many popular male singers have already recorded Italian albums. Why don't we do something different like actually recording Perry's album in Italy?" Andy thought it was a great idea and off to Rome we went. In retrospect, that was one moment when opening my big mouth really paid off. Again, my friend, Ralph Ferraro came to the rescue. He assembled an excellent orchestra and a vocal choir that could sight-read just like the professional back-up singers do here. Ray Charles was in heaven. We spent the next two weeks making beautiful music and enjoying the delicious food that Italy is famous for. The album is entitled *Perry Como in Italy*.

Perry's birthday came about while we were there recording the album. We all stayed at the fashionable Excelsior Hotel and a dinner party was scheduled at a nearby restaurant called Giovanni's. Judy and I were at a total loss as to what to buy Perry for a birthday present. While walking by an out door vegetable stand, I saw a huge artichoke with a long stem and I got the idea of buying it as a silly gift for Perry. I knew he would get a kick out of it because we both loved to eat the delicious little ones that they served in all the restaurants. The owner of the vegetable stand heard me speak Italian and he became very friendly. I told him I wanted to buy the big artichoke and he answered, "No, no—that's not for you. We sell those to American tourists. Otherwise we feed those big, tough carciofi to our horses." When I told him I was buying it as a gift, he really thought I was nuts. He quickly took my money and turned away. We then went into a fancy lingerie shop on the Via Veneto and the sales ladies were also pleased when they heard me speak Italian. But after they learned that I wanted the artichoke gift wrapped, they too thought I was crazy. At any rate, when Perry unwrapped his gift, he was delighted with the whole idea. He held the artichoke high over his head like an Olympic torch and he proudly led us down the Via Veneto to his birthday celebration at Giovanni's restaurant.

COMO'S FIRST SUMMER TOUR

On our return to New York City, Perry agreed to do an eight-week tour in several Midwestern cities. It may sound strange but he was a bit apprehensive about it. He had not performed for a live *audience,* outside of a television studio, since the old days on the road with the Ted Weems orchestra. It was a difficult job for me because we carried no other musicians with us. I had to rehearse a different orchestra in every city and many of them were not very good. Perry never let it bother him. He would always say to me, "Don't worry, push the piano out a little further and just you and me—we'll do the show." The audience didn't know or care about my orchestral problems. They only came to see and hear Perry, and they loved everything he did.

BEA ARTHUR

The Don Costa swimming pool was the most popular spot in our neighborhood in New City, New York. His wife, Helen, taught all the little kids how to swim, while the adults gathered around a bar that was off to one side of the pool. In the summertime, several of our mutual musician friends, plus local neighbors, gathered almost every weekend to share stories and talk shop. A local lady friend of Helen's, named Bea, was often the center of attention. I thought she was just a neighbor whose son went to school with the Costa's son, Tano. Bea had a marvelous sense of adult humor that kept us all in stitches. I was busy keeping the kids away, because she told many naughty stories and often used the "F" word. Wow, how times have changed.

A year or two later, Ray Charles and I, along with our wives, went to see the Broadway show *Mame*, starring Angela Lansbury. Shortly after the curtain rose, a dramatic entrance was made by a lady seated on what looked like a half moon and it was hanging several feet above the floor. The song she sang and her funny facial expressions provoked great laughs from the audience. I couldn't believe my eyes and ears! Suddenly I remembered that she was the same lady who told those funny jokes at the Costa swimming pool.

Involuntarily, I jumped up and yelled, "My God, that's Bea!" Judy yanked me back down into my seat and I quietly apologized to those nearby. To this day, I can't figure out how everyone else knew about Bea Arthur's great reputation as an actress, and not me. This gifted entertainer, singer, and comedienne is now famous all over the world for her roles on television as the star of *Maude* and also *The Golden Girls*. She is now doing a one-woman show, accompanied by my talented friend, Billy Goldenberg, and they are getting rave reviews. I couldn't be happier for two of my favorite people.

EARLY GRAMMY SHOWS

In the late sixties, George Simon was the head of NARAS (National Academy of Recording Arts and Sciences), and I was one of the governors along with John Hammond, Ray Charles, Phil Ramone, and many other notable music people in New York City at that time. Like now, the award ceremonies were held once a year but not aired on either radio or television. Somewhere around 1966, Phil Ramone and I were selected to produce the show. Woody Herman's band was hired to play the affair and it was held in the main ballroom of the Commodore Hotel. Phil handled all of the technical things like sound and lights and I handled the music. Claus Ogerman, Torrie Zito, and I wrote appropriate eight-bar orchestra play-ons for the various winners and categories. When a winner was announced, Woody was supposed to tell the band which play-on to play, since they were all on one page for each separate category—just like it was done at the Oscar Awards. I thought it strange that Woody didn't seem more concerned about this at the rehearsal.

Tony Randall was the emcee for the evening. When the first winner was announced, Woody just stood there and applauded. From the back of the hall, I kept yelling, "Where's the play-on?" The band members heard me and also tried to get Woody's attention. When he finally realized what he was supposed to do, he became flustered and told the band to play "Perdido." I was dismayed because all of our arranging and copying efforts went down the tubes. For the rest of the evening, every winner or category was played on or off by either "Perdido" or "C Jam Blues"—both tunes the band could easily fake.

GILBERT BECAUD

Gilbert was a big star in Europe and he was known as the "Frank Sinatra" of France. My French friends in Paris gave him my name and he asked me to arrange and conduct a record date for him. He was a good musician and he played the piano quite well. I was impressed with his energy and enthusiasm when he performed. We recorded four sides at Capitol Studios, New York City, and I had a great band that really excited Gilbert. About a month later, I happily learned that one of the songs we recorded became a big hit in France. The song said something about "my home quarters—or where I want to be." I never figured out the translation. He excitedly called me from Canada to tell me the good news. I regret that our paths never crossed again, because I felt certain that he and I could have made lots of exciting music together.

Harry Warren and me—Christmas 1980

HARRY WARREN (1967)

The monthly Como television specials continued for the next two years, and in between, I spent my time doing lots of commercial jingles with Ray Charles and Bill Fredericks. Don Costa persuaded me to fly out to California to case the town, because Hollywood was taking a lot of the recording and television work away from New York City. He introduced me to Harry Garfield at Universal

Studios, and shortly after that, I was hired to score a movie called *Don't Just Stand There*, starring Mary Tyler Moore, Robert Wagner, Harvey Korman, and Glynis Johns. I was very excited because my childhood dream was coming true.

My friend, Carl Fortina, the No. 1 accordionist in Los Angeles and present day orchestra contractor came to my rescue by introducing me to the Knudson click track book, which is essential in determining what tempo and how much music has to be written for each section of a film. Joseph Gershenson was the musical director at Universal Studios and also the conductor of most of their movie scores. He was very complimentary and supportive of my creative efforts because he looked over every cue before it was given to the copyists. This was definitely a "B" movie, but it was still a great challenge for me since it was my first movie assignment.

Gene De Paul, my composer friend, called me and insisted I take a break—drop the pencil and come out to dinner. Ray Charles was in town from New York City and Gene insisted that he join us. When we met in front of our hotel, Gene jumped out of his car and told us that he brought along a couple of his friends, Johnny Mercer and Harry Warren. Ray and I were elated! There we were with two of the greatest talents Hollywood has ever known. We went to dinner at a restaurant where Joe Marino, a great studio pianist, was playing. Ray was thrilled talking with Mercer and I was so happy to be sitting next to Harry Warren, the fabulous Hollywood songwriter. Some of his most popular songs are "Lullaby of Broadway," "You'll Never Know," "On the Atchison, Topeka and the Santa Fe," "That's Amore," "Chattanooga Choo Choo," "This Love of Mine"—and the list goes on and on. That evening marked the beginning of a warm relationship with Harry that would last until the day he died, several years later.

His real name was Salvatore Guaragna. He was definitely Italian and very proud of his heritage. He was born in Brooklyn, New York on Christmas Eve, 1893. In order to become more *American*, his family changed their last name to Warren and Salvatore became Harry. He was born with natural musical talent. Classical and religious music particularly appealed to him. He was a pianist, a drummer, and an accordionist in his teens before coming out to California in the very early days of Hollywood. He ended up writing more hit songs for movies than anyone else. He was known for his outspoken, cantankerous disposition, but underneath, he was a real pussycat. We bonded immediately because I sight-read some classical piano pieces he composed when he first came to California. I became his surrogate son when he realized we both spoke Italian using the same dialect. Gene De Paul was also one of his "adopted" sons.

In his early years, Harry studied classical music, and as a result, had great respect for the correct bass notes in any composition (my kind of guy). His two favorite composers were Giacomo Puccini and Jerome Kern, that dirty bastard. When I asked him why Kern had to be always referred to in that manner, he said that in the early days of Hollywood, his friends gathered frequently for dinner and after that, they sat around and played the parlor games of the day. Kern, apparently, read up and mastered the games before his guests arrived. Then, after dinner he always won whatever game they decided to play—that dirty bastard.

I think a certain amount of artistic rivalry exists in all creative groups. Harry didn't like any other contemporary song composers. He constantly said that during World War II, they bombed the wrong Berlin, referring to Irving, of course.

I moved my family to Los Angeles three years later, and Harry really became a close member of our group. Unfortunately, his own personal family life was filled with turmoil and tragedy. His one and only son died in his late teens and that really broke Harry's heart. His wife and daughters did not give him much comfort in later years, because of various other personal family problems.

He still managed to have a great sense of humor and always loved to hear about all the latest gossip in town. Harry insisted I stop by his house whenever I was in or near Beverly Hills. He was a bawdy old devil and he loved to talk about ladies with large bosoms. One afternoon, Gene De Paul and I both fell asleep during one of the showings of an adult film that he wanted us to see.

When Harry heard Gene snoring, he became very angry and told us two "young punks" to wake up and get the hell out of there.

I enjoyed playing his songs for him, and occasionally, I'd intentionally use a wrong chord or a bass note just to see if he was paying attention. He always smiled as though nothing was wrong. Then, he'd walk up behind me and give me a gentle smack on the side of my head—typical Italian style. He reminded me so much of my own father.

Michael Feinstein was working with Ira Gershwin at that time and he often came over to discuss some interesting projects that Harry had done with Ira. Hearing Michael sing and play some of the songs they had written was a delight. Harry and I were impressed with the singing and playing ability of this young man who had not yet achieved the fame and stardom he enjoys today. Michael was instrumental in getting Harry to compose several new songs (both music and lyrics) for a movie project he was working on at that time. Unfortunately, it never came to fruition.

Harry told me that in his early songwriting days in New York City, he was working on a project with Ira Gershwin and they were in a back room of the large apartment that Ira shared with his brother, George. Out in the front room, a voluptuous young lady was seated at the piano next to George. He was playing many of his wonderful songs in an effort to impress her and, hopefully, get her into the bedroom. After each song, however, she asked him to play *her* favorite song that was popular at that time. She then sang a few bars of it, hoping George would join in. Meanwhile, Harry and Ira could not help but hear all that was going on in the front room. George hated the simple little ditty that she continued to sing and after this routine continued a couple of more times, he slammed the lid down on the piano and shouted, "That tune is a piece of shit!" The lovely lady got up and angrily stormed out of the apartment. Harry was laughing hysterically when Ira asked, "What's so funny?" Harry answered, "George is right. That tune is a piece of shit—but I wrote it."

He often complained to me that nobody was performing his songs anymore. He even accused Perry Como of not singing any of his tunes anymore. I tried to reassure him that his songs were being played and sung by artists all over the world. I mentioned this to Perry when he came out to Los Angeles to do a television special and he said, "Let's surprise Harry and pay him a visit." We did just that. We walked over to his home from the Beverly Hills Hotel. I entered Harry's studio and told him I had a new boy singer with me that I wanted him to meet. He almost came unglued when he saw Perry walk through the door. They knew each other from years back, when Perry was in Hollywood doing movies. It was very touching to see the two of them hugging each other and trying to hold back their tears. After a lot of reminiscing, Harry asked Perry if he would like to see an adult film. Before Como could answer, the video was on and there were several naked beauties on the screen.

Harry's studio was a separate small building out behind the lovely big house he had on Sunset Boulevard. By looking out of the windows, one could see whoever might be coming up the walkway to the studio. What none of us realized was that Harry's wife recognized Perry when we came up the driveway and she immediately called several of her neighborhood lady friends to come right over to meet Como. Meanwhile, the movie was on and at that point it was very explicit. None of us bothered to look out of the window. However, I accidentally caught a glimpse of the ladies just as they were about to make an entrance into the studio. I hurriedly ran to the door and stalled them just for a second or two, which gave Harry a chance to reach for the video remote control. When the ladies came into the room to meet Perry, the video screen was showing *Howdy Doody*.

Old age and poor health finally took their toll on Harry. He often said he was a young man trapped in an old man's body. I agreed with him. Whenever he returned home after a hospital stay, he spoke to me in Italian. His wife took great umbrage at that, but he couldn't have cared less. Unfortunately, their marriage was not a truly happy one, even though it lasted for many, many years.

After several stays in the hospital, Harry passed away. I was asked to deliver his eulogy, but I knew I would not be able to do it without breaking down. Tony Thomas, a very good friend and fan of his, wrote and delivered a marvelous tribute at the funeral. Tony was a highly regarded announcer and author who wrote a very informative book called *Harry Warren and the Hollywood Musical*. I recommend it highly. At the post burial gathering, Michael Feinstein soulfully played many of Harry's songs. It was a sad day for all of us, but I am forever grateful that this gifted man graced my life with such warmth, humor, and love.

We owe Michael a big debt of gratitude for helping to keep Harry's music alive, and also the compositions of other famous composers of that era. Whether the songs be from Tin Pan Alley, Broadway or Hollywood, Michael is doing a magnificent job of helping to keep the history of American music alive. His magical performances introduce beautiful old melodies and lyrics to a brand new generation of music lovers.

JANE JARVIS and MUZAK (1969-70)

Thanks to Andy Wiswell, a record producer, the Muzak Company hired me to arrange and conduct a recording session for them, using a twenty-two-piece orchestra. The lure for me was that I could include two of my original songs in every recording session. I was expected to get twelve songs recorded in three hours. Dick Hyman, Tony Mottola, Al Caiola, and many other top studio players were accepting these dates, both as leader-arrangers and/or sidemen. It was a ball for all of us, because it was a challenge to record that much music in so little time. Wiswell was in charge for many years but later on, a lady named Jane Jarvis took over. In addition to being an executive at Muzak, she was also the organist for the Mets baseball games at Shea Stadium. One day, before the recording session started, she said to me, "I like your two original songs." I said, "How do you know? We haven't played them yet?" She smiled and then started to hum one of them. I was amazed. Later, I learned that Jane had perfect pitch and could easily sight-read all kinds of music. That really got the attention of the studio and jazz players in town. We all love her.

Whenever any of us composers took our kids out to Shea Stadium to see the Mets play baseball, Jane always played one of our songs on the organ over the loud speakers. The fans didn't know and didn't care, but it was a big thrill for us and our families. Thanks to Jane, I did twelve sessions for Muzak over the next ten years. She is highly regarded as a pianist in jazz circles and she has performed all over the world. A real talent.

THE HOLLYWOOD PALACE

In late August of 1969, I flew to Los Angeles to attend the funeral of Mitchell Ayres, who was killed in a tragic auto accident in Las Vegas. Mitch was very supportive of my early efforts on the *Perry Como Show*, and I wanted to pay my respects to this nice man. He was about to start the seventh season of the *Hollywood Palace*, a weekly television variety show. Nick Vanoff, the producer and also an old Como alumnus, asked me to stay on and take over the job as conductor.

The musicians in the orchestra were very cooperative, and we all immediately became friends. I mentioned to them that many of the top players in New York City were always listening to the West Coast guys and admiring their laid-back style. They responded with something like, "While you were diggin' us, we were all diggin' you cats back east." Players like Johnny Audino, Manny Klein, Harry "Sweets" Edison, Frank Rosalino, Charley Loper, Bob Alberti, and Eddie Rosa were just a few of the great players in the band.

Joe Lipman was the arranger for the band, and when he was swamped, the great pianist, arranger Bob Alberti, joined in to help him. Joe got better musical effects by simply writing unison passages than anybody I ever knew. What a talented writer—and a nice guy.

The *Palace* was a weekly variety show and we ended up playing for all of the top stars at that time. I got along famously with all of them except Diana Ross. She acted like a real diva.

Burt Bachrach was very popular at that time and he starred on one of the shows. I knew him from my early days in New York

City when he, Peter Matz, and I were considered the three new, hot, young piano playing conductors in town. On the show, Burt conducted the orchestra playing a medley of his hit songs. However, at the band rehearsal, I was surprised to hear him say to Harry "Sweets" Edison, one of the greatest jazz trumpeters in the world, "Can you play that with a little more of a jazz feel?" All of the musicians had difficulty holding back their laughter. We couldn't understand that Burt didn't know—or care—who he was talking to. I caught Harry's eye and I motioned for him to keep cool, which thankfully, he did. At the band break, he came over to me and said, "Brother, Nicholas, if it wasn't for you, I would have told that—to go—himself." That day, Burt's ego was difficult for the entire band to handle.

"WHITE CHRISTMAS"

At this same time, Nick Vanoff was also producing a television Christmas special for Bing Crosby. Joe Lipman and I were hired as arrangers for the John Scott Trotter orchestra. At our first music meeting, John and Bing told us what songs we each had to arrange, and just as we were all about to leave, Bing said, "Wait a minute— I'd like to have a new arrangement made on 'White Christmas.'" I knew Joe heard him, but he kept walking right out the door. As a result, I was trapped. I tried to explain to Bing that his record and existing arrangement of that song was an international treasure and it should not be touched. He shook his head and said it was now too high for his voice. The fact that it could be easily transposed down to whatever key he desired made no difference to him. He went on to say that he was tired of that *old* arrangement. I could see I was losing, especially when he asked, "You write all that jingle bells stuff for Como, don't you?" I nodded and he added, "I know you'll write something really pretty for me." He patted me on the back and left the room.

I was very concerned about how to go about fixing something that I felt was *not broken*. Sensing my frustration, Nick Vanoff walked me down to a corner bar and bought me a drink. It was a great therapy. I was so relieved when I learned, a week later, that Bing and his entire staff loved the new arrangement I wrote for "White Christmas."

At the final *Hollywood Palace* television show Bing was the emcee. It was appropriate because he had been the emcee of the very first *Palace* show seven years earlier. This final show used only film clips of the many stars that had appeared on previous programs, and Bing sang a few songs in between. Shortly before we started taping, I was asked to go backstage to Bing's dressing room for a little conference. I expected the usual comments that singers generally make like slow down the tempo of the ballad—or hold back the volume of the brass. Shortly after I got there, Bing walked into the room and we began to chat. He said he was very happy with me and all that I was doing with the orchestra. After a short pause, he took a deep breath, and with a very serious look on his face, he said, "How much are you willing to pay me to keep quiet about the accordion?" Well, that really made me laugh. He definitely enjoyed my reaction. Milt Gabler, the head of Decca Records and an old friend of mine, obviously told Bing about a solo accordion album I had made years before on Coral Records, a subsidiary of Decca. I then realized that Bing also remembered our first meeting on the *Ed Sullivan Show,* when he sang "True Love." At any rate, we had a marvelous time doing that last *Palace* show, and it was the beginning of a relationship that continued for seven more years.

Thanks to my good friend, Greg Van Beek, a devout and dedicated archivist regarding the life and times of Bing Crosby, I recently learned that Bing, in his early years, also played the accordion! Now I understand why he enjoyed asking me about the above mentioned "pay off." He, too, in his early days obviously suffered the unfortunate discrimination, in certain musical circles, for playing the instrument.

THE ACCORDION

This is a much-maligned instrument and has been for many years. It is highly respected and appreciated in all corners of the world, but too often here in the United States, it is the butt of many jokes. Players like Lawrence Welk and Dick Contino did nothing to show its many potentialities. The instrument itself has an enormous range and also the flexibility of sound to blend with many different sections of the orchestra.

Jazz artists like Art Van Damme, Frank Marocco, Eddie Montierro, Tommy Gamina, Joe Mooney, Joe Basile, Angelo Di Pippo, and studio-concert artists like Carl Fortina, Dominic Cortese, Nick Ariondo have all shown the incredible possibilities of this wonderful "magic box." Say nothing of the old giants like Charles Magnante, Frossini, and Pietro Diero.

Many famous conductors and artists also originally played the accordion. George Shearing, Marty Paitch, Gordon Jenkins, Jerry Gray (famous old Glen-Miller arranger), Harry Warren, Bing Crosby, and many, many more have had to fight the onus of being a "chordeen player," at one point in their lives.

CHAPTER 16

THE SEVENTIES

W hen the *Hollywood Palace* came to an end early in 1970, I realized that I was going to have to move my family to Los Angeles. More artistic opportunities were opening up for me on the West Coast, but I found myself flying back to New York City at least once or twice a month because I still had many business connections back there. Bi-coastal living became a reality for me. Arranging and conducting for many different recording artists took up most of my time. In NYC, I did an album for a friend of mine named Vinnie Bell, a great studio guitarist. He invented a unique guitar sound and our combined efforts gave him a hit record on the theme from the movie, *Airport*.

COMO IN VEGAS

In the summer of 1970, Perry was booked to perform at the International Hotel (which later became the Hilton Hotel) in Las Vegas. Although he was an established recording and television star, a studio audience is a lot different from a live night club audience. Las Vegas was slowly becoming the *live* show business capital of the world and everyone was excited about what the town had to offer. Perry was apprehensive about this new venture, but Ray Charles and I insisted that he do it. We put together a program of songs that he liked, and we were off to Vegas. Opening night was rather traumatic for him, but after his first song, he realized that he was starting out on a new live-performance career.

People of all ages packed the showroom night after night and he was a smash.

After a record setting three-week engagement, it was customary for a star entertainer to do an extra late-night show for all of the performers, who were appearing at other hotels on the strip. Perry agreed to do the extra show, but on one condition—he insisted that all the chefs, waiters, waitresses, and members of our hotel staff would be seated first. Then, if there was still space available, the workers from other hotels could be admitted. Needless to say, it was an occasion (and a gesture) that all the old-timers really appreciated. He became a hero to the entire staff of our hotel. As a result, none of us ever suffered for want of anything. For the next four years, Perry appeared in Vegas at least twice a year, each time for three-week engagements. Vegas audiences were known to be rather boisterous, but that didn't bother him at all. If on a given night he felt there was too much noise in the room, instead of singing louder, he would do just the opposite and sing softer. At first, I thought this was a bad idea, but I soon learned that his theory worked perfectly. At every performance, he, together with the talented Ray Charles Singers, would stand at the very front of the stage and sing a lovely ballad without microphones. Naturally, the orchestra had to play very softly behind them. The effect was fantastic. As the old saying has it, "you could literally hear a pin drop." The legendary jazz singer, Joe Williams came to many performances with his lovely wife and after each show he came back to Perry's dressing room and remarked about the wonderful effect the *soft song* had on the audience.

Almost every year, Elvis Presley was booked into the showroom right after Perry. He, too, always came backstage after seeing a Como performance to say hello and pay his respects. What a charming, humble, and courteous young man he was. Perry was very impressed with Elvis as a person, and we often sat in the dressing room for an hour or so just shooting the breeze.

Harrah's in Lake Tahoe also became a regular booking during those years. It was always fun for me because the bands in both of these places were very good, and that made my job easy.

DON KNOTTS TV SHOW
COMO IN LONDON
THE "BIG 3" CHRISTMAS TV SPECIALS

Nick Vanoff hired me as the musical director for a new television series starring the comedian, Don Knotts, and it lasted for almost an entire year. I really enjoyed writing arrangements and socializing with the many comedic talents that made guest appearances.

The show ended in early April of 1971, and I was delighted to learn that Como was going to London to do some concerts for Yvonne Littlewood and the BBC. The British people loved everything about Perry, and the feeling was mutual. It was the first of many trips to the United Kingdom that I would be fortunate enough to make with him.

The fall of that year was a memorable one for me, because by some sort of miracle in timing and scheduling, I was able to arrange and conduct the television Christmas specials for each of the "Big 3"—Andy Williams, Bing Crosby, and Perry Como—all giant entertainers identified with the holiday season. My friends jokingly began to refer to me as "St. Nicholas."

It was also about this time that I began working for a television producer named Bob Finkel. I was impressed with his work formula, which was—find the best writer, director, musical director, sound and lighting engineers, etc., that you can, and then stay the hell out of the way and let them do what you hired them to do.

Louis Jourdan and me on a break while filming a television special in Toronto, Canada

LOUIS JOURDAN (1972)

In September, I was Perry's arranger-pianist for a television show we did in Toronto, Canada, that featured the music of Cole Porter. Louis Jourdan, the handsome French movie star was also on the show along with Connie Stevens and Diahann Carroll. Unfortunately, the hotel had misplaced my laundry and one night, on my way to dinner, I stopped by the front desk to make some inquiries about my lost belongings. For some unknown reason, the clerk was being very rude to me and before I could plead my case, Louis Jourdan, who I didn't know was standing behind me, gently pushed me aside and took over. He verbally blistered the woman for her disrespect toward me. When she recognized who *he* was, she blushed and became very apologetic. Suddenly, as if by magic, my laundry appeared—all in great condition. This time, I was very grateful that *he* just happened to be there.

During the taping of the show, if Louis felt uncomfortable or didn't like what he was doing, he would suddenly stand up, wave his arms about and shout, "NO—NO—NO!" Naturally, that got everyone's attention. He explained to me that too many times in the past, when he did something on camera that he was not comfortable with, the producers and/or directors often told him that they would fix things in the editing room—and then when the film came out, they still used the wrong takes. So by shouting out loud, he was certain they would have to use what he knew was his best performance. That made a lot of sense to me.

Perry and I enjoyed watching the ladies' reactions when they recognized this handsome Frenchman. I regret our paths never crossed again, but we had some great dinner conversations.

SHIRLEY BASSEY (1973)

The record producer, George Foster, who produced many of Ferrante and Teicher's later record albums, booked me to arrange a recording session for Shirley Bassey, who had gained fame singing the song "Goldfinger" from the James Bond movie. She came to Los Angeles and we did a pre-record session using just a rhythm section. Dave Grusin was kind enough to come down and play piano for me. He was brilliant, as usual. Then she and George took those tracks back to London and sweetened them with the arrangements that I had written for a forty-piece orchestra. I was sorry not to have been able to go to London for the sweetening session, but they did a great job. She had a lot of the same energy that Dorothy Dandridge had, and she is a very exciting performer.

ANTHONY NEWLEY (1975)

The year opened for me with a job as musical director for the first *Comedy Awards Television Special,* and it gave me an opportunity to work with Anthony Newley. I wrote the arrangement for a new composition he had written especially for that show and it is called "The Entertainer." Tony was a great composer, as well as a gifted performer. I had heard that sometimes he could be difficult to deal with, but again, don't believe all that you hear because two minutes after I began to accompany him at our first rehearsal, we became good friends. He had a certain charisma and a warm, friendly personality that attracted everyone. His way of delivering a lyric was truly magical—a real showman and a dear man.

COMO CONCERTS IN ENGLAND

Later in that year, I was off to London with Perry for a three-week tour of the United Kingdom. We were accompanied by a talented group of English musicians and back-up singers. Just before our opening concert in Bournemouth, England, we learned that the British airlines were on strike. The promoter convinced us that we would be just as comfortable traveling from city to city by chauffeur-driven Daimler limousines. Being able to sit back and enjoy the beautiful English countryside, all the way from southern England up to Glasgow and Edinburgh and then back to London, was a sheer delight. Perry was adored by all the English and Scottish audiences. His good looks, great voice, and mild-mannered approach to music met with their entire approval.

After every concert, no matter what city we were in, the hotel kitchen staff stayed up much later than they were supposed to, just so they could cater to Mr. Como and his friends—Tommy Loftus, Mickey Glass, Ray Charles, myself, and a few others. I am happy to say that the chefs and waiters spoiled us rotten. Every night, we had *fresh* Dover sole along with whatever each chef wanted to surprise us with. Who could ask for anything more? I was privileged to watch and be a part of the love that was exchanged between Como and his adoring United Kingdom fans.

One night in Glasgow, a happy male fan jumped up on the stage at the end of the show and insisted he and Perry share a drink from a bottle of scotch that he was flaunting. He kept shouting, "Ay, mate, ya' gotta 'ave a drink with me." After a lot of hugs and humorous exchanges, much to the audience's delight, Perry managed to finally get him off the stage. What warm, happy occasions these were for one and all.

FESTIVAL HALL

One night at Festival Hall in London, the show was almost over, before Perry realized that a portion of the audience was seated above and behind the orchestra, as is the case in many classical concert halls. On his final bow, he turned to that portion of the audience and asked, "Who are you, the jury?" To everyone's surprise, one gentleman stood up and loudly proclaimed, "Yes, we are, and as foreman of the jury, I pronounce you *not guilty!*" Everyone loved his comment. We couldn't have planned or staged that any better. Perry was deeply moved. Not knowing how to respond to the man, he looked over at me and said, "Always." We had never done that song before, but I played an arpeggio, and just with piano accompaniment and the lights turned down low, he sang, "I'll be loving you, always. With a love that's true, always . . ." etc. It was a very moving moment for the entire audience and all of us on stage. Many of the ladies in the orchestra and the audience were in tears. It was a memorable night for all. On another trip to the United Kingdom, the Variety Club of England, a large charity organization, invited Perry to London to appear in a star-studded command performance for Queen Mary, the present Queen Elizabeth's mother. It took place at the Palladium Theatre. Top performers from all over Europe were there, and after the show, we were privileged to shake hands with the Queen "Mum" herself. She was truly elegant and most cordial.

While waiting in line, along with Perry and Ray Charles, I had the good fortune to stand next to Josephine Baker, the legendary African-American artist who bolted from the United States early in her career and became a major star in Europe, especially Paris, France. I had a very interesting conversation with her. Josephine was well into her sixties by then and her dance performance, earlier in the evening, brought the house down. She was a strikingly beautiful lady, a fabulous entertainer, and a world-renowned leader in the African-American movement for equal rights. Again, I feel so lucky that *I just happened to be there.*

Perry Como, Ray Charles, me and Josephine Baker meeting the Queen "Mum" and Sir Bernard Delfont backstage at the Palladium Theatre in London, England

MOSCOW, RUSSIA

Before returning home from London, Ray Charles was able to obtain tickets for an eight-day tour of Moscow. His wife, Bernice, his son, Michael, and my wife, Judy, and I were delighted to accompany him. We were just ordinary tourists and it turned out to be an amazing trip. At that time, the political tension was still high between our two countries, but we were treated very cordially by all the Russians we encountered. One night after enjoying an incredible Bolshoi Ballet performance, we went into a nearby hotel (the Metropole), looking for a place to have some coffee and ice cream. The ballroom was filled with many people celebrating a wedding. Luckily, the headwaiter spoke English. Although we were not invited guests, he managed to seat us at a corner table near an elevated bandstand. The seven or eight ruffle-shirted musicians were playing American and Latin rhythms and they were very good. When they took a break and passed our table, we tried to compliment them, but they fluffed me off. In the meantime, our gracious headwaiter was serving us vodka, saying that the coffee and ice cream was on its way. Ray explained to this nice man that I played the piano, and he, Ray, was a singer. After a couple of more vodkas, the band started to pack up and, at this point, the head waiter and Ray persuaded me to play a song or two. I climbed up a few stairs to the bandstand and when the leader sensed that I was about to play the piano, he glared at me and slammed the piano lid down. He and the headwaiter got into an argument and I quietly turned to leave. However, they quickly agreed that I should play only one song. The party-goers were all a bit tipsy and were noisily saying goodbye to each other. I must admit I, too, was a little high, but I started right in anyway. For some unknown reason, I started to play "All the Things You Are." I slowly became aware of the fact that the room was very quiet. When I finished playing, it exploded with applause and all of the band members were now shouting for me to keep playing. Ray was trying to interpret what songs they wanted me to play. They knew that Jerome Kern wrote the song I had just played, and now, they wanted "Smoke Gets in Your Eyes." After that, they insisted I play some ragtime pieces. I tried to explain that I was not a good ragtime player, but Ray laughingly looked up at me and said, "You are now." I faked my way through two choruses of "12th Street Rag" and then carefully walked down the stairs to our table and had some coffee and ice cream. The musicians kept telling us to please come back "tomorrow—tomorrow." They didn't know how to tell us that they had the next day off. I felt we had all become good friends. Another wonderful evening I will never ever forget, because I just happened to be there.

On the walk back to our hotel, we all agreed that if the artists, musicians, and scientists of the world could take power away from the politicians and the militarists, we truly could have world peace.

COMO IN MEXICO

The year 1975 ended with a Como Christmas television special that was prerecorded and filmed totally in Mexico. Billy May recommended a wonderful musician named Jose Zavala, who hired all of the musicians for our prerecord sessions in Mexico City. He was one of twelve brothers and sisters known as the "Zavala Family," and they were well-known performers in all of Latin America. Each of them could play the piano and the guitar, and they were all great singers. An amazing group of talented people. They appeared in several sequences on the Como television special. I was a bit apprehensive about doing an entire television score with an orchestra I knew nothing about, but Jose reassured me that everything was going to be OK—and it was.

My wife and kids had taught me several Spanish words and phrases that they felt would help me communicate with the local people. The orchestra was set up in the studio so that all of the musicians faced me—with their backs to the control room. Our morning recording session went very well and during the lunch break, Perry and the producer, Bob Banner, complimented me about how well I was communicating with the members of the orchestra.

After lunch, we were about two minutes into our second recording session when suddenly, all of the musicians stopped playing and began to pack up their instruments and walk out of the studio. I was dumbfounded not knowing why they were leaving. I pleaded to many of the players to explain to me what was going on, but they just waved their hands as if to say, "Get lost!" I felt the whole show was now going to be ruined because of something stupid I unknowingly did or said. At the peak of my misery, I looked up through the large control room window, and everyone in there was convulsed with laughter! Are you ready for this?— Como had set up the entire charade and all the orchestra members happily participated.

An hour or so later, the band took a break and Jose asked me, "Would you like to play a joke on Perry and the producer?" It sounded like a fun idea—but how? He explained that when the band returned and we started to record again, they could all *pretend to play*, but actually, no one would make a sound. I loved the idea! It reminded me of my old friends, the Tasty Yeast Jesters, who had done the same thing to an audio engineer years before. At my suggestion, Jose told our musicians to *play* only the first four bars of the next arrangement, and then suddenly stop making any sound—but continue to *pretend* playing. When they returned from their break, I could tell by the smiles on their faces that they all knew exactly what to do. It was getting late in the afternoon and Perry and the television execs in the control room were obviously getting a little bored and drowsy. I suggested that we start to record immediately, because "time is money and we better keep moving." The money guys all sleepily nodded their approval.

The new arrangement began with a loud brassy intro, but just as we got about ten seconds into the piece, the *silent magic* occurred. I continued to wave my arms around, really hamming it up and the orchestra perfectly mimed playing their individual parts. I noticed the control room quickly "woke up," and I enjoyed watching the audio engineer and the production crew frantically try to figure out what in the hell was wrong. Our band members fought to hold back their laughter; all the while they were pretending to play. Since their backs were to the control room, no one was able to figure out our ruse. The producer kept yelling out over the loud speaker, "Nick! Nick! Please stop—something has gone wrong!" I continued conducting, pretending not to hear what he was saying. Several more seconds went by before I made eye contact with the audio engineer, who was frantically waving his arms at me. Then I cut off the orchestra and silently mouthed the words, "What's the matter?" The producer nervously answered, "We seem to have lost the sound." I paused for a moment, smiled, and then loudly yelled out, "No, shit."

Everyone in the control room poured out into the studio, and along with the musicians, we all had a lot of laughs. Perry came over to me, shaking his finger and said, "You, son-of-a-gun, how in the hell did you do that?" Then he gave me a big hug because he loved the entire caper.

P.S.—I don't think that audio engineer will ever invite me back to his studio.

CHAPTER 17

MORE SEVENTIES

DON HO (HAWAII)

A Como television special, filmed in Hawaii, gave me a chance to get acquainted with Don Ho. Here was a true individualist. He spoke softly and moved very slowly in a real *laid-back* manner. He made Perry look like a bundle of energy. Don had a wonderful family—attractive wife and adult children. But somehow, he enjoyed two different lifestyles. He did whatever he wanted to do when he wanted to do it. After we finished taping the television show, Don invited me to be a guest at his beautiful two-story penthouse that overlooked the beach at Oahu. What a fabulous view! His front room had a giant net set up that would allow one to practice hitting golf balls—with a *driver!* Don was a good sport and we enjoyed playing several rounds of golf together. He was kind and generous to one and all. At night, I attended his shows at the hotel and it was a real hoot for me to see the kind of attention and adoration he got from ladies of all ages. They actually lined up so that they could get up on the stage and give him a smooch. He also had a lovely young lady living up in his penthouse, who catered to his every wish.

Don Costa told me that while recording an album with him, Ho always wore a raincoat when he was in the studio. Standing beside him in the vocal recording booth was a young lady friend who kept *her* hand in *his* raincoat pocket. Whenever he sang a love song, he got some very special encouragement from the warm, caressing hand of his beautiful companion. This inspired Ho to give the lyrics a very sexy interpretation—sounds like a good idea to me.

COMO IN AUSTRALIA

In 1976, a great promoter named Pat Condon booked Perry on a tour in Australia. We played all of the major cities with a local choir and orchestra. The concerts were enthusiastically received everywhere. Again, the ladies all swooned over Perry. We enjoyed the delicious seafood and great wines from Adelaide. Performing a concert in the famed opera house in Sidney Harbor was very interesting. The structure is impressive but the acoustics inside were not what we had hoped for. Perry still managed to please all of his adoring fans.

After a lovely farewell party in Sydney, we boarded a flight for our return home. We were all in first class, and as usual, Mickey and Perry sat together. Linda Wheeler (our vocal group director) and I sat behind them. Our other group member, Frank Marino from RCA records, sat up front next to a loud-voiced, tipsy stranger. Frank, who had a wonderful sense of humor, kept looking back at us and saying things like, "Why me? Just lucky, I guess." He was referring to his drunken seat partner. It was very humorous for everyone in the cabin, and the atmosphere became very festive with lots of champagne and delicious food snacks.

A short while later, we were stunned when Frank suddenly leaped out of his seat yelling profanities at the man next to him. It seems this loud-voiced, inebriated nut had deliberately spilled a large glass of hot liquid all over Frank's crotch. Mickey and I immediately got up and restrained Frank from hitting the guy. We took him upstairs to the upper cabin, followed by many fellow passengers. Everyone sat down and collectively complained about this awful drunk's behavior. Perry and Linda soon joined us.

After ten minutes or so, everyone was surprised to see this drunken idiot come up the stairs with a large glass of brandy in his hand. He walked directly toward Perry, but at the last second, he turned and threw the entire glass of brandy into Frank's face, burning his eyelids. Before I could do anything, Mickey and Perry had this madman on the floor and Perry was about to punch him out! I used every ounce of energy I had to control Como, who had his arm around the man's neck and was yelling, "Are you going to behave yourself, you son-of-a-bitch!" I had never seen Perry so angry. Up to this point, he had been jovial and doing his best to make light of the situation. But in typical Italian style, he exploded when somebody harmed *his family*. The flight crew now took charge and the drunk was ushered back downstairs. The captain came out and apologized profusely to everyone. He then informed us that the plane was going to make an emergency stop in Fiji to deplane the troublemaker.

The flight attendants took care of Frank's eyes, and Linda and I were able to get Perry and Mickey to calm down and relax. The rest of the passengers were also very supportive, and after some more conversation and champagne, things settled down.

VIENNA and SALZBURG

This was really a trip to the *old world* for me. In early November of 1976, the Como Christmas special was totally recorded and filmed in Austria. In Vienna, a large studio orchestra was assembled and the choir came from the opera house. What could be better? Senta Berger and Sid Caesar were the guest performers along with the Vienna Boys Choir.

I had arranged a medley of Viennese waltzes for the show, and when it came time to record it, I told the orchestra I was just going to throw a downbeat and then let them go on their own. I was not about to tell *them* the correct tempo of a Strauss waltz. I figured, "When in Vienna, do as the Viennese do." They all laughed and were somewhat flattered. They played it beautifully and I learned a lot—an everybody-wins situation.

The orchestral pre-record took all day, and after a dinner break, we overdubbed the choir. The singers all came from the Vienna Opera and they could sight-sing like angels. The recording studio was only a block away from the opera house. We actually recorded the choir during a break in that evening's performance of a long Wagnerian opera that they were a part of. It was such a kick to see all of them enter the studio, fully clothed in their flowing robes, tiaras, etc. and sing whatever music we put before them. We finished in about an hour and they hurried back to the opera house in time for the grand finale. What delightful, talented people they were.

A portion of the show was filmed in Salzburg, and I was able to visit Mozart's apartment. What an emotional experience that was for me to know that I was in the same room where this genius once lived. His piano-harpsichord was roped off, but when the guard wasn't looking, I must confess that I reached over and gently touched one of the keys—hoping maybe something wonderful would rub off on me. I figured, nothing ventured, nothing gained.

EVEL KNIEVIL TV SPECIAL (1977)

The show originated in Chicago, and it was called *Death Defiers*. Marty Pasetta was the director-producer, and it became obvious right from the very beginning that he and Evel were not compatible. Actually, nobody was compatible with Evel. It was to be a two-hour *live* telecast with remote pickups from all over the country photographing people who would be performing life-threatening feats. A man in Minnesota was going to blow himself up in a barrel. The Flying Wolenda's were going to walk on a high wire suspended between the Eden Roc and Americana Hotels in Miami, Florida. Evel was going to *fly* his motorcycle over a man-eating, shark-infested pond inside a giant covered arena in Chicago. The live orchestra that I conducted was set up on various tiers in the arena. The brass was upstairs to my right, the strings and reeds were upstairs to my left, and the rhythm section was scattered all over the floor in front of me. They expected us to be able to play together and hear each other with the use of headsets.

My podium was located at the side of this giant pool with what seemed like a hundred big sharks swimming around in it. One false backward step from me, and my ass would have been in that pool. Got the picture? Definitely, not a lot of laughs. Juilliard never warned me about that kind of situation.

The afternoon before the actual taping of the show, a production meeting was held in a lush, carpeted conference room at our hotel. We were supposed to finish around 6 PM so that the room could accommodate the sponsor's many friends and associates for a posh dinner celebration starting about 7 PM. During our meeting, the waiters were quietly bringing in ice sculptures and all of the necessary provisions for dinner. The guests, however, were not allowed to enter until after our meeting was over. Television production meetings can be long and tedious, and this one was exactly that. I sat in the back of the room with my script on my lap and making notes. Evel was seated in a large padded easy chair directly in front me. He kept ordering Jack Daniels whiskey on the rocks from an accommodating waiter who was roaming amongst us. I was amazed to notice that Evel never finished a drink. He would take a couple of sips and then pour the remains of the glass onto the carpet behind his chair. I couldn't believe what I was seeing! When the meeting finally ended around 10 PM, and the guests were finally allowed to enter the room, the hors d'oeuvres counter was a mess. The ice sculptures had melted and they were now just unrecognizable blocks of ice.

When we videotaped the show the next night, the outside temperature was below freezing and the arena was very uncomfortable—mainly because there was a big opening at one end which allowed Evel to make his grand entrance after starting his motorcycle ride outside. With a long-enough runway, he could generate enough speed to fly over the shark-infested pool as soon as he entered the arena where the audience was seated.

The show was scripted (all written out), because Telly Savales and Jill St. John were the cohosts and neither of them were noted for their ability to ad lib. The orchestra had to play lots of play-ons and play-offs, and it was a challenge for all concerned. At the last production meeting before the show, Marty and Evel really locked horns and Evel stormed out of the control room. The rest of us just crossed our fingers and hoped for the best.

Fifteen minutes before show time (remember this was live television), the musicians and crew members assembled and prepared for the broadcast. Suddenly, we heard the roar of a motorcycle. What no one expected was that Evel was about to make a test run. He roared into the arena and took off into the air. He barely reached the other side of the pond before he lost control and crashed into a scaffold upholding TV cameras. Two cameramen were seriously hurt and Evel emerged with only minor wounds—but he was still rushed to a nearby hospital. What chaos resulted! The script went up in smoke when we appeared live on the air a few minutes later. It was madness. Poor Telly and Jill didn't know what in the hell to say, but they hung in there and improvised as best as they could. Marty and the tech crew were going crazy in the control room and the orchestra kept staring at me, wondering what was going on. Sheer madness! However, the show-must-go-on theory prevailed, and the next two hours were pure agony for all of us.

Six months later, I learned from my nephew, Bob Perito, in Washington, DC, that the show was voted as the "worst television program of the year." I wonder why.

BING CROSBY 50th SHOWBIZ ANNIVERSARY

I have already told several stories about this incredible man. He was a professional in a class all by himself. A natural-born performer who could do just about anything that was necessary to entertain people. Act, dance, sing, tell jokes,—you name it—Bing could do it all. He kept a tight schedule and he was never late for a rehearsal or performance. On one particular Christmas special, Buz Kohan and Bill De Angelis created a brand-new ten-minute musical segment especially for him—all original music and lyrics. We rehearsed it a couple of times and that was it. We didn't have personal audio cassettes then. I wrote the orchestral arrangements and three days later, we videotaped the show and Bing performed it perfectly—no cue cards—nothing! He obviously had a photographic memory.

Many times during a long production meeting, he would get bored, leave the table, come over to the piano and say quietly to me, "Play some jazz." Whatever I quietly chose to play was fine with him. He would take the pencils he had in his pocket and start to beat rhythmic patterns on top of the piano. And then, he'd quietly hum or whistle some jazz licks.

The producer would many times yell over, "Will you guys please hold it down?" No big deal—we'd just go looking for another piano. The pre-record sessions with the band were always very relaxed. After listening to an arrangement of mine, he often times said to me things like, "you really wrote your ass off on that one," or "that's beautiful, my friend." We generally made only one vocal take on any song, and he'd insist that we move on.

Bing's 50th Anniversary in Show Business Television Special started out to be very exciting because so many famous stars showed up to honor and pay him respect. But at the end of the show, a tragic mishap occurred. While making his final exit he forgot that he was supposed to walk out *into the audience*. Instead, after saying good night to them, he instinctively turned his back and started to walk offstage. He forgot that the middle of the stage had been lowered one floor because of the previous act's performance. The audience gasped as they watched him fall into the large gaping hole. While conducting the closing theme with my back to the audience, I suddenly realized the orchestra was in a state of shock. They all saw Bing fall. The lady violinists were in tears. I remember seeing Tommy Tedesco pack up his guitar and leave the stage. Poor Kathryn Crosby and her children were all there, and it was a traumatic time for everyone. Fortunately, dear Bing was not seriously hurt. We were so relieved to see him wave and smile as he was carried out on a stretcher.

I choose to remember Bing as the giant entertainer that we all loved. He was the man who blazed the trail for many of the talented crooners who followed in his footsteps. In later years, Perry Como insisted on doing a fifteen-minute medley honoring Bing at the end of every one of his live concert shows. He said that if it wasn't for Bing, he would still be back in Cannonsburg, Pennsylvania, cutting hair and Frank (Sinatra) would own a pizzeria in Hoboken, New Jersey.

Perry renamed me "Little Daddy" and he wrote, "remember the 'guitar (slipped out of my hand).'" I was pretending to play the concertina and we were on board a sailing vessel in the San Diego harbor filming a Como Spring television special along with Kenny Rogers and the U.S. Navy men's choir. This photo was taken after more than half of its members were taken back to shore because of "sea sickness."

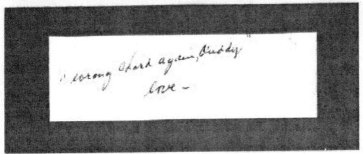

Same cast as above but Perry's written caption saying,
"wrong chords again, daddy"
(This will be explained in a later chapter.)

COMO SPRING SHOW IN SAN DIEGO (1978)

Bob Banner, the legendary television producer, decided to film the *Como Spring Television Special* in San Diego, because it was going to be shot totally outdoors. After much research, it was discovered that the San Diego area was the least likely to have bad weather at that time of year. Kenny Rogers, Debbie Boone, and the U.S. Navy men's choir were the guest artists. Guess what—it *poured* rain every day that we were there filming the show. The costume designer was despondent because the only thing the television audience saw throughout the entire show was the performers wearing yellow rain slickers.

One segment was to be filmed out in the San Diego Bay area, aboard a big sailboat. Kenny Rogers, the Navy men's choir, and Perry were to do a medley of sea chanteys. I had to put on fake sideburns and pretend to be playing the concertina while accompanying the singers. We all assembled at a dock early in the morning before being shuttled out to a large vessel where we would shoot the scene. Caterers served sweet, sugary doughnuts and coffee and cocoa to all those who were interested. Perry and I, both being fishermen, realized that that was not a good idea before going out into the open ocean that sometimes could be a little rough. However, everyone else, including our technical crew and all of the Navy singers, happily consumed many of the sweet goodies. We boarded the tenders and the sea was a little rough. By the time we got to the big fishing boat just outside the harbor—you guessed it right—more than half of our tech crew *and* the Navy singers were throwing up all over the place. They were shuttled right back to shore. So there we were—Perry, Kenny, myself, and about twelve of the original thirty-five-member Navy choir members—wondering what in the hell we were going to do. Luckily, two cameramen, one audio engineer, and a couple of other technicians survived sea sickness, and we were eventually able to film what we had originally intended. Fortunately, the music and the singing had all been pre-recorded and we all pretended we were having a great time. I often wonder how some of the Navy guys explained to their families and friends back home as to why they weren't seen on the big fishing boat out in the ocean on the *Perry Como Springtime Television Special.*

DENG XIAO PING— KENNEDY CENTER (1979)

Nick Vanoff hired me to conduct a concert at the Kennedy Center in Washington, DC that celebrated the meeting of President Carter and Deng Xiaoping, the Chinese leader. The orchestra was stationed in the pit and many talented entertainers performed that evening. At the suggestion of George Stevens, Jr. (Nick's co-producer), I wrote a big orchestral arrangement on the song "Getting to Know You." We used it as a theme to usher President Carter and his Chinese counterpart on and off the stage.

Before the concert began, I was in a dressing room putting on my tuxedo. There was a sudden knock on the door and two well-dressed gentlemen came in to have a chat with me. They asked if I knew every member of the orchestra, which I didn't. I explained that I was a visiting conductor and they understood. They asked if they had my permission to sit in the orchestra pit along with the musicians. It was then I realized that they were U.S. undercover security agents. They also said that if I saw anyone in the pit that didn't look like he or she belonged there, all I had to do was give them a nod with my head and then look over at the stranger. They would quietly do the rest. Thank goodness, nothing like that transpired. The show went off perfectly, and I still remember how exciting it was for me to conduct the orchestra playing "Getting to Know You" and looking up at two of the most powerful political figures in the world at that time.

COMO CONCERTS IN JAPAN

On my first trip to Japan, I didn't know what to expect in the way of musicians, particularly since Perry never took any other musicians along but me. Don Costa had just returned from a tour with Frank Sinatra and he tried to reassure me that the Japanese musicians were very good. Since I wrote all of Perry's arrangements, I knew that I had to have versatile musicians who could play many different styles of music.

At the first rehearsal, I immediately got the *bends* when I saw a trombone player pull out an instrument that looked like a reject from some Midwestern college marching band. Also, one trumpeter had an instrument that was all dented and the bell pointed off to one side. Listening to the band warm up told me I had my work cut out for me. After we ran through four or five arrangements, I was told it was time for a break. I started to walk off the stand, but

I noticed no one in the orchestra moved. Terry Terajima, the producer, and I went for a cup of tea. When we returned, I heard a lot of noodling from the band. Perry then walked into the rehearsal room and asked me how I liked the musicians. I hesitatingly answered, "Uh—they're OK." He didn't like the look on my face and he asked to hear one of the pieces we had rehearsed earlier. Well—the orchestra played it perfectly! Perry looked at me and said, "What do you mean, OK? That was great!" I agreed with him and I happily realized then that these musicians would not tolerate goofs and errors. They practiced on their own until it was perfect. How's that for a good work ethic.

We developed a mutual respect for each other and the following concerts were a joy for everyone. These musicians especially enjoyed the moments when Perry and I did a song alone and I played something different each night while accompanying him. They all loved any kind of improvisation, even if they could not do it themselves.

This was the beginning of many Como tours to Japan, all of which were booked by Terry and Yoshiko Terajima. Each time we were accompanied by the great Sharps and Flats orchestra from Tokyo.

MATSUO KAZUKO and KAYAMA YUSO

Perry was greatly admired by many famous Japanese singers, and as a result, I was later hired to arrange and conduct albums for them. The first artist I recorded was Matsuo Kazuko. She was the "Dinah Shore" of Japan, a delightfully charming lady with a beautiful voice. I flew to Tokyo for a five-day rehearsal, and one month later, Kazuko came to Hollywood to record her album. She loved being surrounded and accompanied by so many famous American musicians that she had long admired.

Several years later, Kayama Yuso, a handsome movie actor-singer, invited me to Japan. We rehearsed on his yacht for a couple of days, and then I returned to Los Angeles to write the arrangements. After three weeks, I flew back to Tokyo and recorded a beautiful album with all Japanese musicians. Yuso was also a good musician and it was a joy to work with an artist who understood exactly what was happening in the orchestra behind him. At one of the sessions, he realized that he felt more comfortable singing a particular song one-half tone higher—and I had already written a rather ambitious arrangement on it featuring the string section. I jokingly told him that *he* would have to inform the orchestra to play it up in another key, because I didn't want them to be angry at me. There was a little bit of grumbling from the players when they heard his request, but after a few minutes of noodling and practicing—lo and behold—we made the recording, and they played it perfectly. Yuso knew what they had just accomplished and he was most complimentary to everyone concerned. The entire project was a very satisfying and happy one for me.

CHAPTER 18

THE BIG SHOW (1980)

This very ambitious project was conceived and produced by Nick Vanoff. It was a weekly one hour-and-a-half musical variety extravaganza, the likes of an old Busby Berkeley movie. Every show included an underwater ballet, an ice skating production number, various popular singing stars (both classical and pop) and comedy sketches, starring many famous American and English comedians. We finalized the selection of weekly music on a Monday afternoon and then pre-recorded the orchestra on Wednesday afternoon or early evening. Very demanding schedules also held true for the script writers, set designer, costume designer, lighting engineer, and the entire crew involved in the show.

I called upon Bob Alberti, Jon Charles, Joe Lipman, Angela Morley, and Peter Myers to help me with the arranging. The copyists, headed by Terry Woodson, literally worked around the clock. This schedule went on for ten weeks. Vanoff did a magnificent job as producer because he was hoping to bring back the old Hollywood musical format to television. Each individual show was a masterpiece, but unfortunately, the television audiences did not respond like he hoped they would.

JAY LENO

What was to become an annual Perry Como summer concert tour, started in Detroit, Michigan, in 1980. A new young comedian named Jay Leno opened every show and he was an immediate smash. Everyone loved him. Perry was particularly fond of Jay because he never used any vulgar language or blue humor. Ray Charles assembled a young vocal group and we toured all over the East Coast and Midwest for over six weeks. This same troupe performed together every summer for the next four years. Jay and I often shared the same dressing room, and that was always a million laughs for me. He constantly kept me and our entire group amused with his practical jokes and crazy backstage humor. Perry loved his spontaneity and unique way of turning a tense moment into a silly laugh-in. None of us realized, at that time, that "our Jay" would become the giant television personality that he is today. We are all delighted with his success. Hopefully, many more wonderful old Leno memories will be recalled in another book one day.

THE RAY CHARLES SINGERS

This group included several beautiful, talented young ladies who brought great energy and spirit to every show with their marvelous singing and dancing. The standouts were Tina Halverson, Karen Harper, Cheryl Crandall, Hollis Payseur, Cassie Miller, Sally Spencer, Robin Funk, Donna Garcia and Cassie Monsieur. They were an integral part of every Como live performance. When they weren't dancing or singing with Perry, they sat up on high stools in front of the orchestra. Often times, while Perry was singing a solo, I couldn't help but notice their shoulders moving while they were trying to suppress laughter. Como sometimes forgot the correct lyrics of a song and he would then make up a new set of words as he went along. As you can imagine, we all had lots of fun, both on and off stage during those wonderful years on the road with Perry.

THE EMMY AWARDS

In late July of 1980, I received an unexpected phone call from a friend at the television academy, and she told me that I had been nominated for an Emmy Award for my work as musical director for one of the *Big Shows*. I was thrilled! My friend had actually violated a strict law, which stated that the nominations were not to be made public for at least another three or four weeks. I was sworn to secrecy. It was so frustrating not to be able to share this great news with my friends. I only knew that the Emmy Awards ceremony was going to take place on live television, Sunday, September 7.

Jay and all of the Como gang generally spent afternoons by the side of a hotel pool. One week, Jay's lovely girlfriend, Mavis (who is now Mrs. Jay Leno), joined our group and she entertained us by card-reading our fortunes. I was very impressed with her psychic power because she told me things about my early childhood and my family that were right on target. As I was getting ready to leave, she said that she saw something exciting coming up for me in the future. September 7 was going to be an exciting day for me. It was a well-established fact that the untelevised television craft awards, which included musical direction (my category), were always presented one day before the usual televised Emmy Awards, and this year they were going to be on September 6. I sat back down and asked her if she could possibly be mistaken by one day or two. She thought for a moment, staring at the cards, and then said, "Absolutely not. September 7 is the day." My heart sank— but I still couldn't share my frustration with anyone.

We all returned home after the successful tour. One week before the Emmy telecast, the actors and writers called a totally unexpected strike against the television industry. This really took the whole town by surprise. Everyone expected the TV Emmy Awards Show to be cancelled. You can imagine my surprise the following day when I read in the newspaper that, since the actors were on strike, the TV Emmy craft Awards would be presented *on television*, September 7—Mavis was right!

When we arrived at the Pasadena auditorium for the awards ceremony, it was very exciting with all of the news cameras and reporters surrounding us. My fellow arrangers Bob Alberti, Joe Lipman, Peter Myers, and Jon Charles and their wives sat with Judy and me. My acceptance speech was etched in my mind, and I only hoped I wouldn't stumble walking up to the stage to accept the Emmy. I was certain that the academy would understand the very tight schedule that we worked under to do the *Big Show* and I would naturally be selected as the winner. I felt as though I was about to explode with excitement. When the winner was announced, and it wasn't me, I couldn't describe my disappointment. My wife and friends were very comforting, but I was still in a big funk. During the ensuing years, I was nominated eleven more times—but I never won an Emmy. On many occasions, I knew that although I had been nominated, I was not going to win because other musical directors had done bigger or more complex shows. However, one particular year, I again felt positive that I was going to walk away with the trophy. My daughter, Jennifer, a talented actress had guest-starred in several television drama shows and she joined Judy and me at the awards ceremony. My friends and fellow musical director nominees were all seated nearby with their wives. Again, I had my speech memorized. Angie Dickinson opened the envelope to announce the winner and we all held our breaths. When she said, "And now, the winner is—Elliot Lawrence," my daughter Jennie, loudly blurted out, "Ah, shit!" Some of the nearby guests cracked up at her remark, as did Judy and I. A good laugh definitely helped my morale at that point.

Years later, I told Elliot Lawrence that story and he howled. He added that his daughter would have probably said the same thing if I had won.

One day, while rehearsing with Perry Como for another television special, I noticed a large package by the side of the piano. I asked Perry and Mickey Glass, his manager, what it was. They looked puzzled and said they didn't know because it was addressed to me. I immediately ripped open the package and you can imagine my surprise when I saw a beautiful Emmy statue before me. Perry then laughingly said, "If those schmucks don't have enough brains to give you an Emmy, then I will give you one." He went on to say he chose one that he had been awarded years before, but since it had not been specifically inscribed to him, I could write "whatever the heck I wanted to on it." Mr. Nice Guy—what an appropriate name for that man.

COMO IN ISRAEL

In early October of 1980, we went to Jerusalem to videotape the Como Christmas show, again with the Bob Banner television crew. I was very apprehensive because Israel was unfortunately in turmoil. We stayed in a lovely hotel in Hertzlia on the Mediterranean coast. Soon after we arrived, Perry, Mickey, and I went for a stroll on the beach. It was beautiful and tranquil. We soon noticed two men about one hundred yards away who seemed to be trailing us. We were never able to make eye contact. Upon returning to our hotel, we spotted them at the cigarette counter. Perry approached them and asked why they were following us. They reluctantly admitted that they were undercover agents whose job was to look after our group at all times. Both were well-built, handsome young men and very friendly. I said to them, "How can you protect us if you have no weapons?" One of them answered, "My partner has a weapon but I can kill anyone with just my hands!" I playfully punched him on the arm and said, "Show me." Perry smilingly nodded his approval. With that, the young man grabbed me, and in a matter of seconds, he picked me up, held me high over his head and began twirling me around, much to the delight of all the Como group members who suddenly showed up. As you can imagine, these two young men became our buddies for the entire trip. Videotaping that show in Israel was a learning experience in many ways for all of us.

Conducting the Kennedy Center Honors orchestra playing the
National Anthem *in Washington D.C.*

THE KENNEDY CENTER HONORS

In 1979, I became the musical director and arranger-conductor of the annual *Kennedy Center Honors* television program. Jimmy Carter was president at that time. While conducting the "Star-Spangled Banner" at the very opening of the program, I accidentally lost control of my baton. It went sailing over the orchestra and landed up in the brass section. The orchestra members all chuckled, but kept on playing. You can imagine my embarrassment. When I turned to acknowledge the audience, I saw President Carter had a big grin on his face. I was certain that he, too, was amused by my *baton act.*

I continued as the musical director for this prestigious annual honors program for the next fourteen years, earning several Emmy nominations in the process. In the beginning, it was co-produced by George Stevens, Jr., and Nick Vanoff. Each year the program became more and more challenging. But because of budget restraints—sound familiar?—I was not allowed to bring along any copyists or people who could help me when extra or different musical numbers were added at the very last minute. Some members of the production staff didn't seem to understand or care that orchestral arrangements took time and had to be written and copied by hand. When I knew in advance what arrangements were necessary, I managed to write them all. But when time was running short, I called on my friends Bob Alberti, Torrie Zito, or Jon Charles to come to my rescue. Sometimes, I was able to fax my scores of the unexpected musical changes to Terry Woodson in Los Angeles, and then pray that Federal Express would deliver the copied orchestra parts back to Washington, DC, in time for either the Friday or Sunday-morning rehearsals.

In 1987, Sammy Davis, Jr., was one of the honorees and several of his old tap dancing pals were invited to perform. Ray and Jon Charles made contact with a couple of them, and two weeks before the show, Jon wrote the orchestral arrangements they needed for their performances. Unfortunately, none of them were able to get to Washington, DC, in time for our first orchestra rehearsal on the Friday morning before the Sunday evening telecast. But they all managed to show up for a makeshift rehearsal on Saturday evening at 7 PM. After we assembled and the actual rehearsal began, they began joking around and improvising various new dance steps. As a result, they all decided to do *different routines,* instead of the ones which we had already written arrangements for. Nobody seemed to care about the fact that we were going *on the air* at 7 PM the following evening, and *time* was of the essence. Now, new arrangements had to be written and copied for their altered routines. Realizing that my pleas were falling on deaf ears, I turned on my little portable tape recorder and proceeded to play on the piano whatever they wanted. At about 10 PM, I went down to my office and started arranging for the orchestra what we had just rehearsed. With the help of a young lady volunteer named Jan Ivy, I managed to arrange and copy four new orchestral jazz arrangements for our 9 AM orchestra rehearsal the next morning. Jan kept going over to the printing machine, duplicating parts for various members of the orchestra and serving me coffee to keep me awake. She was a mad fan of Gene Kelly and a devoted backstage helper. Naturally, I didn't get any sleep that night.

Nick Vanoff knew what had transpired in that short period of time, and after the show was over, he gave me a hug and apologized for having put me through the wringer.

Perry Como was also one the five honorees in the 1987 *Kennedy Center Honors* television special. Vic Damone, Diahann Carroll, and a one-hundred-voice male choir called "The Harmonizers" performed in honor of Perry. This choir consists of men from all walks of life and they sing beautiful four-part harmony, a la barbershop quartet, arranged by John Hohl and conducted by Scott Werner. They sang a long medley of Como's hit songs that Ray Charles and I had put together. Their performance began with only four men singing on stage, but as the medley progressed, various curtains and screens were lifted or pulled back until at the end of the number, all one hundred of the Harmonizers were in view singing their hearts out. The audience went wild with applause! Their performance was very touching because each and every one of them was a devout Como fan. They all wanted to shake hands with Perry after the show, but that was impossible to do backstage.

Later on, when Perry opened the stage door to leave, he was flabbergasted by what he saw. Waiting patiently there to see him was every single member of the Harmonizers. Knowing that they all wouldn't be able to shake his hand, they immediately started to sing Perry's signature song "Sing to Me, Mr. C, Sing to Me." Then they quickly segued into the beautiful classic Christmas song "Toyland." It was gorgeous. I still get chills up and down my spine when I remember the sound of their beautiful voices echoing in the cavernous halls of the Kennedy Center. It was another one of the big musical moments in my life that I can gratefully say, "I just happened to be there." Months later, this same male choir, The Harmonizers, made a beautiful recording of a song that Ray Charles and I wrote called, "A Gift of Music." I hope you have an opportunity to hear it one day.

The *Kennedy Center Honors* TV shows were performed before very dignified audiences, headed by the president of the United States at that time, his wife and many of his cabinet members and their wives, along with notables from every other walk of life. Technically, we regarded the programs as live performances, and rarely did we ever have to do any retakes after the audience left the theatre. Here were a few of my favorite moments when truly exciting things occurred while we were "on the air."

LEONARD BERNSTEIN

The overture to *Candide* was to be played as a part of Bernstein's tribute, and Michael Tilson Thomas was chosen to conduct it. He was to arrive on Sunday, the day of the show, and rehearse the orchestra in the morning. But the director wanted to be able to move in with his camera crew for close-ups of various musicians, and that would be impossible with a live audience present. So I was asked to conduct the *Candide* overture on the pre-record session two days earlier. I memorized the score and also listened extensively to both Bernstein's and Zubin Mehta's recorded versions, which were only three seconds apart in time. The orchestra was dressed in tuxedos for the videotaped recording, as was I. That was only in case my arm accidentally got in a camera shot. On the Sunday evening program, Thomas would naturally be videotaped conducting the orchestra, but when it was time for an orchestra close-up, later in the editing room, they could cut to the already videotaped version—wise artistic planning. When we finished taping my version on the Friday morning before, I was surprised to hear someone applauding in the vacant theatre. I turned to discover that it was Zubin Mehta, and he gave me a big thumbs-up sign. He was there waiting to rehearse with the orchestra his portion of the tribute to Bernstein. Michael Tilson Thomas arrived on Sunday. He conducted the piece *his way*—and that he did very well.

Betty Comden and Adolph Green combined to sing (along with a large choir) the song, "New York, New York," which they had co-written with Bernstein. I wrote the arrangement and it was the last number performed on the show. Soon after we started, Adolph apparently got confused and started to rush the tempo like crazy. My arms suddenly became *six feet long,* and the orchestra followed me beautifully. I wasn't aware that Zubin Mehta was standing in the wings, viewing the entire thing. As soon as we were off the air and I complimented the orchestra, I started to step down from the podium when I felt someone pulling on the back of my tuxedo. There was Mehta telling me, "Good job, junior!" I blabbered something in response, and he interrupted with, "I'm glad it wasn't me. You and the orchestra did a great job." I appreciated his kind words, and we all applauded him as he walked away.

Bernstein was one of my musical idols. Jeanne Behrend, my piano teacher at Juilliard referred to him as a *triple threat* musician, meaning he was a master composer, pianist, and conductor. His television seminars back in the fifties are gems for people of all ages who want to learn and appreciate the basics of music. On the 1988 *KC Honors* television special, I had written an arrangement for Fredrica Von Stade, a marvelous soprano, who sang one of Bernstein's songs called "Take Care of This House." At the end of the show, Bernstein came backstage unannounced. Just as I was taking off my headset, he walked up behind me on the podium and put his arms around me. My headset and eyeglasses fell off, and the orchestra enjoyed seeing him in such a happy mood. I am so grateful that I had the good fortune to know him—and learn from him. What a phenomenal musician he was.

THE RUSSIANS

When the Berlin Wall came down in 1989, the entire world rejoiced. It was certainly a time to celebrate. Nick Vanoff and George Stevens, Jr., saw it as a great opportunity to establish artistic ties with an exciting group of Russian entertainers (dancers, singers, and musicians), who were on a tour in the USA. It so happened that they had just played at the Kennedy Center a couple of months before our *KC Honors* show was going to be televised. Fortunately, a videotape of their performance was made available to us, and it was fabulous! There was lots of fantastic dancing and singing, and they ended their show with a tribute to the people of our country by singing "God Bless America." Nick and George decided that those Russian entertainers should be featured in the finale of our next *KC Honors* television special. There was only one problem—they were booked solid, and it was difficult to coordinate a date and a time for rehearsal. However, they did have a concert scheduled in Detroit on the first Sunday afternoon in December (the same day we were to videotape our show in Washington, DC). Weather permitting, they could fly out of Detroit immediately after their afternoon concert and arrive at the airport in Washington, DC, at just about the time we actually began videotaping our program at the Kennedy

Center. When we broke for our show intermission, we could all meet backstage and have a brief "talk over" rehearsal.

Does this all sound crazy? You bet it was. However, Vanoff was determined to make it work. It would be a monumental task for Ray Klausen, the set designer; Bill Klages, the lighting designer; Ed Greene, the audio engineer; Dwight Hemion, the director; and the entire technical crew. Without having an actual rehearsal, we were going to videotape a performance involving several hundred people—in front of the president of the United States and his many honored guests. Call it madness? Yes—but we all accepted the challenge.

Our entire technical crew practically memorized the video of the show the Russians had done at the Kennedy Center months earlier. Their background music was all prerecorded. But when it came time for the "God Bless America" closing portion of their act, our producers decided to add the large choirs of the U.S. armed forces. At this point, the existing Russian orchestral music track was to be stopped, and I would start to conduct our live orchestra, which was set up at the back of the stage behind a large grandstand that would hold all of the Russian dancers and chorus members. Then by adding the various choirs of our armed forces, the stage would be filled with hundreds of singers. Since this was going to be a live performance, Dwight Hemion, the director, assured me that a special camera would be focused only on the Russian conductor, so that I could always see him on my video monitor and thus be able to transmit his tempos to our orchestra. From a front-row seat in the balcony, Ray Charles would also be able to see the conductor, and that would enable him to direct the American singers down stage in front of the Russians.

Copies of the Russian orchestral parts were faxed to us from Detroit, and they looked like chicken scratches—very difficult to read. Our musicians miraculously were able to decipher the music, and after our Friday morning rehearsal, we all understood when and where to make our live musical entrance when the Russian sound track faded out.

Just as we began videotaping our show around 7 P.M. on Sunday evening, the Russians landed safely at the Washington, D.C. airport and were quickly transported to the Kennedy Center. At intermission, we were delighted and relieved to see them waiting backstage. Their musical conductor, a very short man, approached me and, through a translator, asked when the rehearsal was going to take place. When I informed him that we were already *on the air* and would not have the luxury of a rehearsal, he grunted and angrily replied, "In Russia, even the circus acts rehearse." After I told him that I would be watching his every move on my TV monitor, he angrily strutted off in a very militaristic manner.

At a commercial break just before the Russians were to make their entrance on stage, a large curtain was lowered over the back of our orchestra showing the American and Russian flags side by side. It was very impressive, except it covered up the top row of my musicians and I could not see the three French horn players or the percussionist. Ray Klausen, the set designer, walked by at that moment and he saw my problem. We both knew it was too late to make any changes. I still remember the sad look on his face when he said, "Can you live with it?" I had no choice.

The Russians were greeted with thunderous applause when they made their entrance and they proceeded to wow the audience. Our orchestra, on platforms, was pushed to the back of the stage, and I was happy to be able to look up and see the shoulders of many of their singers, as their large grandstand rolled in behind me and they began to sing. My video monitor clearly showed the little Russian conductor out in front of them waving his arms, and we made our Kennedy Center live orchestra entrance perfectly. All was going well, until the U.S. armed forces choirs began coming up on the stage.

The tall singers, who traditionally stand up in the back of a choir, now totally *blocked out* the small Russian conductor. I couldn't see him at all. I was flying blind! Dwight was aware of my dilemma, but he had his own problems directing cameramen all over the hall. It was every man for himself. This was a perfect example of live television chaos. At the end of "God Bless America," the audience went wild. All of the musicians and singers, including the Russians, knew about our agreed-upon reprise of the last half of the song. When I got my cue to start up again, I conducted a short intro, and the singers were supposed to enter, singing, "From the mountains, to the prairies,"—but *nobody came in*! I pleaded with the control room asking them whether I should continue playing or stop, but the roar from the audience in my earphones was deafening, so I just kept on conducting the orchestral background. Fortunately, the singers all realized musically what was happening, and as if by magic, they all made a perfect entrance at the last eight bars of the song where the lyric says, "God Bless America, my home sweet home . . . etc." What a triumphant moment that was for every one of us backstage. The audience reaction was truly inspiring. The cheers and applause lasted for several minutes. It was like a giant love in.

Every one of the musicians and technicians connected with that show deserved a standing ovation. And Nick Vanoff was the first to acknowledge us all. His dream had come true.

When I finally took off my headset at the end of the program, I was delighted to see Benny Carter, one of America's greatest jazz musicians, coming over from the side of the stage to the podium to congratulate me and the orchestra members. He was in the audience during the entire show and he understood exactly what was going on, musically, onstage and backstage.

Just as Benny left, I was approached by the little Russian conductor. Through his interpreter, he angrily told me that I didn't follow him correctly during the last four bars of the finale. Using hand signals and some old charade tricks, I politely tried to explain that I could not see him on my TV monitor because the tall singers had blocked him out. He still kept ranting. I finally asked the members of my orchestra, "Do any of you speak Russian?" When they asked me why, I answered, "Because I want to be able to tell this little man to go screw himself!"

To Nick Perito
   With best wishes,
Nancy Reagan   12/7/86   Ronald Reagan

My visit to the White House in 1986 and meeting President and Mrs. Reagan

THE "GREEN ROOM" and
WHITE HOUSE PARTY

The "Green Room" backstage was the place where all of the notables hung out before their respective appearances came up on the actual program. It also served as a waiting area for performers before the show started. When my friend, Harry Belafonte, was honored, many of his famous associates showed up to pay him tribute. Before the program started, it was exciting for me to be able to sit and chat with people like Sidney Poitier, Desmond Tutu, and other guests of that caliber.

Every year, before we videotaped the Honors program, a party was held in the East Room of the White House where the five honorees were toasted and feted by the then president of our country. It was a very elegant affair attended by many celebrities and important government officials accompanied by their wives or husbands. George Stevens, Jr., graciously invited me to attend this function in 1987, the year that Perry Como and Ray Charles were two of the honorees. Before returning to the Kennedy Center to do our show, several of us were invited to shake hands with President and Mrs. Ronald Reagan. They were most cordial, and it was a very special moment for me.

While waiting in line, along with many dignified guests, Miles Davis and his lovely wife, Cicely Tyson, were standing in line in front of me. She was very friendly, but Miles seemed annoyed by the whole affair and kept mumbling about when they were going to "get the hell out of there." Here was a perfect case of different strokes for different folks.

CHAPTER 19

1980's AWARD SHOWS

AMERICAN FILM INSTITUTE

The American Film Institute (AFI) award was annually presented to an outstanding person in the film industry. Nelson Riddle had been the musical director for several years but apparently got into a squabble with the producers of the show and he chose to quit. I received a call to replace him, but before I accepted the offer, I called Nelson (not knowing he had already resigned) and told him I didn't want him to think that I had solicited his former job. He thanked me for that consideration and then said, "Don't be a damn fool, Nick. Take the job, because if you don't, they will only get somebody who isn't nearly as qualified as you are. Oh, and by the way, lots of good luck dealing with those assholes who are running the show!"

I arranged and conducted the show for five years. The honorees were all people I had high regard for—John Huston, Gene Kelly, Barbara Stanwyck, Billy Wilder, and Gregory Peck. Their acceptance speeches were very stimulating and they should be read and reread by all young filmmakers. I remember John Huston pleaded that "the industry should be taken out of the hands of the accountants and the lawyers and given back to the artists."

I will never forget the evening that Barbara Stanwyck was honored. She was getting along in years and a special dressing room was set up for her backstage so that she would not have to make the long walk through the audience and up to the podium to receive her award. The orchestra and I were in very cramped quarters behind the curtain. Barbara, with cane in hand, was slowly helped over to where I was standing in front of the orchestra. She seemed very weak and fragile, but she still had that lovely face that the entire world admired. I whispered into her ear how lovely she looked and she responded with a feeble "thank you." I got my cue to play her entrance music and after I gave the band a downbeat, I offered to help her out to the microphone. Well, as soon as that curtain opened and the spotlight hit her, she lost sixty years—me—*and the cane!* She proudly strutted out on the stage, to the delighted cheers and applause from the audience. Talk about a miraculous recovery!

THE WHITE HOUSE
WASHINGTON

December 19, 1985

Dear Mr. Perito:

I understand that you put forth a special effort for the Variety Clubs Tribute and I thank you for your participation in what will long be a cherished memory for me and Nancy.

It was apparent that a lot of hard work was devoted to the occasion. I know this is in large measure due to the friendship and capable skills of individuals like you.

Again, my heartfelt appreciation for all you did. Nancy and I send our hopes for all the best in the future.

Sincerely,

Ronald Reagan

Mr. Nick Perito
5798 Penland Road
Hidden Hills, California 91302

The letter I received from President Reagan regarding my efforts on a
Variety Club television special that honored him.

THE VARIETY CLUB

The Variety Club also had an annual television special that honored famous personalities. Paul Keyes was the writer-producer, and again, I got the job as musical director when Nelson Riddle became ill and he recommended me as his sub. The format of the program was more like a loving "roast." One of the honorees was President Ronald Reagan, who was affectionately referred to as "Dutch" Reagan by his friends back in his Hollywood days. Other honorees, in subsequent years included stars like Joan Collins and Clint Eastwood. Clint's tribute stands out in my mind because what many of you may already know, he is a lover of jazz music. He composed a simple melody and Sammy Cahn wrote a lyric for it. The producer, Paul Keyes, informed me that Clint had already selected a lovely young lady to sing it at his tribute. Merv Griffin would accompany her on the piano, along with my orchestra. I wrote the arrangement and when we got on the air, Merv, who acted as emcee for this portion of the show, now also had the extra responsibility of playing the piano, which he can do very well. Something must have technically gone wrong because the piano accompaniment was not recorded as it should have been. When the show ended, Merv and all of the principals involved left immediately. There was no way we could re-shoot the scene. Since the program was to be aired in a few days, Paul was in a predicament. He asked me if I would overdub the piano part. He had never actually heard me play, but he had no other choice. I agreed to show up early the next morning at the studio editing room to help solve the problem. The finished film had to be delivered to the network later that same day. As soon as I got home that night, I practiced the piano part and got it down pat.

The editing engineer turned out to be a real pro and an old acquaintance of mine. He was well aware of my piano-playing ability. Since Paul was late in arriving at the studio the next morning, I told the engineer, "Don't ask any questions, but I might pull a silly stunt on Paul." His enthusiastic nod told me that he loved the idea. We both knew that Paul had a great sense of humor.

I sat at a piano in a tiny adjoining studio and I was able to make visual contact with the engineer and Paul, who now was seated next to him at the recording console. Time was of the essence and Paul insisted that we do a run-through immediately. I mumbled something like I hadn't had a chance to practice the piano much lately because I was so busy writing, but "let's have a go at it." The tape started to roll and I proceeded to play the piano part—very badly—hitting lots of wrong notes and showing off with lots of fancy arpeggios. I couldn't help but notice that Paul was miserable. He put his face in his hands and just sat back in his seat. He was ready to flip out! Before he could make any comment, I said to the engineer, "Why don't we go for a take? I don't know if it's going to get any better, but what the hell, let's give it a shot." He agreed and the tape began to roll. Now, I played it perfectly. There was silence when I finished and walked into the control room proper. Paul, still with his face in his hands, said something like, "You miserable son-of-a bitch! How could you do that to me?" Before I could even attempt to explain, he stood up, gave me a big bear hug and with an understanding smile on his face, he muttered, "Thanks a million. Now, get your ass out of here."

Along with his great ability as a writer or producer, he was really a fun, off-the-wall kind of guy. For example, as a result of car trouble, I was fifteen minutes late for a production meeting at the beginning of the second year. As I entered the room, Paul said to the entire staff, "You all know Nick and what a great conductor he is. Next year *would have been* his third year with our show."

ADULT FILM FESTIVAL

This was an event that honored XX-rated pornographic films and the people who created and starred in them. My buddy, Joe Soldo, was hired to get an orchestra and a conductor for the award ceremony. I declined his offer to conduct the show because I felt it would be harmful to my career since I was so closely affiliated with Perry Como and the *Kennedy Center Honors* program. Our mutual friend and pianist-conductor, John Berkman, accepted the job. I must add that Joe had no trouble assembling the greatest Hollywood studio orchestra ever.

Adult films were still in the "hush-hush" category at that time and it was something everybody knew but no one wanted to talk about. Berkman did a great job conducting a jazzy type overture and then all of the play-ons and play-offs—just like a regular television awards show. These annual programs took place at the Palladium Ballroom in Hollywood. They were not televised. Don Costa and I attended every year, along with some other musician friends. We'd sit at bar tables in the back of the ballroom, sip wine, and have lots of laughs listening to the acceptance speeches of the winners. Very handsome young men and lovely young ladies would get up after winning an award for some obscene film and thank their *moms* and *dads* for being so supportive of *their acting careers.* It was a bizarre yet hysterically funny situation, depending on what role one played in the whole operation.

One year, John canceled out at the last minute and Soldo insisted I take over as piano-conductor. We agreed that my name would not appear anywhere and I would keep a low profile. That year, the awards ceremony was held at the Ambassador Hotel. Soon after I arrived, I learned that the show was going to be videotaped for the Playboy Channel. Just my luck. The orchestra members, led by my friends Rick Baptist, Chauncey Welsh, and Pete Fanelli chided me about my anxiety and they decided to give me a new name. They chose, "Mario Dante."

A beautiful white grand piano with a mirrored keyboard, was placed conspicuously in front of the orchestra. After a short rehearsal, a young video director approached me and we discussed the play-ons and play-offs for the show. The whole thing was getting pretty silly at this point when I learned that one of the nominated songs was "Keep Your Nose Out of My Pantyhose."

Every major porn star was there and the cameras were rolling. I was still concerned about being seen in this environment. The show went off without a hitch and afterward, the young director came running over and paid me many compliments about my conducting. Just as he was leaving, I heard him yell back, "And boy, did I get some great shots of you!" The band musicians loved hearing that, and after lots of joking around, they told me to relax and not to worry. I took their advice and we all did the show for the next two years. It was interesting to observe the different reactions of people who were intimately involved with the show. To some, it was just a hoot, but to many others it was very serious business.

PONTIAC INDUSTRIAL SHOWS

These lavish productions, using lots of singers and dancers, were created by my friends Eric and Peggy Lieber. They gave the Pontiac Automobile people an opportunity to show off their new car models each year. The shows played in six or seven different cities throughout the country and they were always very well received. In 1984, I became involved as the arranger-conductor for these productions.

One particular performance stuck in my mind. Just before our initial show of the season, Eric, Peggy, and I had a meeting with the then CEO of the company. He wanted to make a big welcome speech to all of the dealers and special guests in the audience, and at the end of his speech, he would pause for just a second and then say to me, "Hit it, Nickie." That was to be my cue for the tympani roll and the show would begin.

After a short lunch break, everyone took their positions. I had my earphones on, the band was all set, the lights dimmed and the CEO walked out on stage. His rousing welcome speech was well-received and, when he paused to give me my cue, I sensed that he couldn't remember my name. Suddenly he blurted out, "Hit it . . . ah . . . ah . . . *nooky.*" I cued the tympani, but I couldn't continue with the rest of the orchestra, because the brass and reed players were laughing so hard that they couldn't play. Through my earphones, I told the director to kill the click track until I got the band under control. After one of the longest tympani rolls in showbiz history, the band calmed down enough so that we were able to start the show.

CHAPTER 20

FRANK SINATRA

Frank became a part of my life from the first moment I heard him sing. Starting with Tommy Dorsey and then the Axel Stordahl years—all the way up to the present time. I always hoped that one day I would get an opportunity to work with him. When Don Costa got the call to do the *Sinatra and Strings* album with Frank, I was there with him, vicariously. Don was so worried that his arrangements wouldn't please Frank, but I kept urging him on by saying things like, "Don't worry, just put down on the score paper what you feel in your heart." That, he certainly did, and Frank loved it.

"CYCLES"

My second actual meeting with Frank occurred in New York City on July 24, 1968, when I was hired to play keyboard on the "Cycles" recording. Frank became unhappy with the person who was conducting at the beginning of the session, so he took the baton and demonstrated to the orchestra what he wanted, and he was very effective. When he went back into the singer's booth, I was chosen to be his substitute conductor. We got along great, right from my first downbeat. Don Costa, along with Frank's daughter, Nancy, kept making a lot of changes as the date wore on. They eventually ended up with a hit record for Frank. Since Don was my closest buddy, I shared all of his ups and downs as an arranger and sometimes conductor for Frank in the years that followed. I want to thank Charles Pignone for keeping such an accurate account of what really transpired in the musical life of Frank Sinatra.

"SHE SHOT ME DOWN" ALBUM

In the summer of 1981, Costa reminded me that he was going to produce an album for Frank called *She Shot Me Down*. I had written a song with lyrics by Artie Malvin called "You're Free," and Don flipped over it saying it would be perfect for this upcoming album. Since Gordon Jenkins was doing the arranging, Don suggested I submit the song to him. Gordon's reaction was even more positive than Don's and I was delighted. He called Frank and said it was the best ballad he had heard in fifteen years. Frank gave the go-ahead sign and a demo tape and lead sheet were immediately sent to him in New York City.

Gordon flew back to the big city to conduct the three sessions for the album. Joe Malin was the contractor of the orchestra and he promised that he would telephone me as soon as my song was recorded, so that I could crack open a bottle of champagne and celebrate.

After the first night's session was over, I got no phone call. The same was true for the second night. Now, I was really on pins and needles. Two of my good friends, Don and Gordon, were in charge of the recording dates and I was figuring, "how I could I miss?" Well, the third night came and still no phone call. I was heartbroken. When I was finally able to get in touch with Joe, he said, "Your tune was the last song to be recorded on the date. Frank was all set to sing and Gordon was just about to throw a downbeat when Lee Iacocca (former Chrysler CEO) walked into the control room. Frank dashed in to say hello, thinking it would only take a second. Gordon and the orchestra were waiting to go on with the recording. Inside the control room, Iacocca told Frank that he needed a big favor. Lee wanted him to overdub some comments on a recorded commercial advertising of a new product he was sponsoring. Don Costa kept reminding Frank that he still had one more song to record, but Iacocca would not be dissuaded. Costa even suggested that they do the Iacocca overdub after the music session was over. Apparently it did no good because Frank, knowing time was running out, insisted that the band be excused and they would use something they already had in the can (storage vault) to finish out the album.

Don, Gordon, and all of my friends in the orchestra were disappointed, but not nearly as much as I was. You can bet I will never ever buy a product associated in any remote way with Lee J. Iacocca.

March 25, 1982. Sinatra and Como at the White House performing for President Pertini of Italy, the Reagans and honored guests. The musicians are (left to right) Tony Mottola, guitar; Gene Cherico, bass; me, piano; Bucky Pizzarelli, guitar; Irv Cottler, drums; and Vinnie Falcone (who was not in camera range)

THE WHITE HOUSE

Perry and Frank enjoyed a mutual love and respect for each other, even though their paths hardly ever crossed. In April 1982, President Reagan asked Frank and Perry to do a joint concert honoring President Pertini of Italy, who was coming to Washington on a state visit. Frank was to be accompanied by his own rhythm section, which was headed by Vinnie Falcone on piano. I played for Perry, using the same rhythm players. Our first rehearsal was a ball. Vinnie and I made notes as Frank and Perry suggested various tunes for their closing medley. After their opening duet on "I'm Sittin' on Top of the World," each would do a solo or two, followed by an Italian version of "Santa Lucia." Then Tony Mottola and Bucky Pizzarelli would play an exciting guitar duet. The closing duet of popular old classics would bring the concert to an end. What a joy it was to see these two vocal giants joke and kid around with each other.

The entire White House staff was invited to attend the dress rehearsal the following afternoon in the East Room. Frank had just begun to sing "The Lady Is a Tramp," when suddenly Nancy Reagan entered at the back of the room and began walking down the main aisle on her way up to the stage to give Frank and Perry a welcome hug. Frank was at the point in the song when he was supposed to say, "and that's why the lady is a tramp"—but just as Nancy reached him, he adlibbed, "and that's why the lady is a *champ!*" Yo, Frank.

Before the show that evening, we musicians had dinner downstairs in the White House staff dining area. Perry and Frank naturally had dinner upstairs with the president, Mrs. Reagan, and all of the honored guests. Since this was a very important Italian-American event, several famous Italian sports figures were present, namely Tommy Lasorda and Joe Montana.

After dinner, everyone assembled in the East Room and the show began. Needless to say, it was a smash. Perry and Frank genuinely had a ball kibitzing with each other and when they sang, everybody was in heaven.

At the end of the show, President Reagan said that since the two stars and all of us accompanying musicians were of Italian descent, with the exception of Irv Cottler, President Pertini was taking us all back to Italy. Reagan teased us by saying that he hoped we would come back one day and pay a visit to our families and our old American friends. The audience loved it. I was disappointed that KCET or some other major television network had not chosen to televise this fantastic Italian-American musical event. But you can imagine how happy I was to learn, one week later, that at the very last minute, Frank had managed to get someone to make an audio-video copy of the concert.

All the party guests at the White House left early. I enjoyed sitting at a bar area, just outside the East Room, with Joe Montana, Tommy Lasorda, Frank, Perry, and our musicians. After a while, we decided to leave and return to our hotel. As we were walking down the steps of the White House, I remember Frank saying, "I'd kill for a good plate of pasta." That really made me laugh and I told him he sounded like Dom De Louise in the movie *Fatso*. Frank added that it was also one of his favorite movies. The word *pasta* suddenly got the attention of everyone in our group and Frank decided that, although the hour was late, he would make a couple of calls. He did exactly that, and as if by magic, shortly after we returned to our hotel and the management was persuaded to open up a small bar-dining area, several large platters of pasta arrived. Frank was the perfect host, making sure that all of the musicians' wives were served cocktails and everyone was comfortable. What a party that turned out to be! I couldn't believe that we all had eaten dinner just a couple of hours before. But again, thanks to Frank, we all realized that pasta takes precedence over everything when the "Paisanos" get together.

As the party began to wind down, Perry went off to sleep. I was still very energized by the entire evening and I found myself at the bar having a wonderful discussion with Frank. We shared our mutual respect for the great talents of Axel Stordahl and so many other musicians and arrangers that we both knew and admired. Frank is the only entertainer I have ever known who always acknowledged the orchestral arranger of whatever song he sang. What a great professional thing to do. Being the naturally gifted musician that he was, he knew the important contribution an arrangement can make to the success of any performer or performance.

PARTY FOR THE QUEEN

Almost a year later, Queen Elizabeth came to Los Angeles, and a big party was planned for her on a giant sound stage at the 20th Century Fox lot. Sinatra and Como were invited to do their "White House act" one more time. I was surprised to get a call from Dorothy Uhlemann, Frank's secretary, who said, "Mr. S wants to know if you would kindly play for him also." I told her that I had only been waiting thirty years for the opportunity. She told me later that Frank got a kick out of my response to her request.

The show was star-studded. Ed McMahon was the emcee. George Burns and other celebrities performed. I was so sorry that I didn't have a tape recorder backstage to tape Frank's comments regarding certain performers who he felt were "less than capable." He had me on the floor laughing. Anyway, he and Perry did their thing again and the queen was delighted—as was the entire audience.

KENNEDY CENTER HONOREE

In December 1983, Sinatra was chosen as one of the five honorees on the Kennedy *Center Honors* television special. Como appeared, along with other stars, to pay homage to him. Together with a children's choir, Perry gave a very touching performance of "Young at Heart."

In December 1987, Como was chosen as one of the five honorees, and this time, Sinatra volunteered to make a "surprise" appearance to pay homage to Como. The *KC Honors* show was videotaped on a Sunday night, and although Frank was appearing at a venue in Long Island, New York, that afternoon, it was agreed that he would fly down to Washington, DC, after his show and arrive at the Kennedy Center in time to sing his tribute to Perry. Frank was scheduled to sing "But Beautiful" with special lyrics by Sammy Cahn. The producers were a bit anxious, because there would be no time for a rehearsal. Knowing that I was the musical director of the show, Frank reassured them by saying, "Nick can accompany me on the piano—no orchestra. I sing it in E flat and he knows what to do."

I was excited about the challenge and everything was all set. However, when Frank finished his afternoon performance in New York, a terrible thunderstorm hit the area and prevented all aircraft from taking off. As a result, he was never able to get to Washington, DC, in time for the taping. What a major disappointment that was for all concerned.

MICKEY RUDIN

I was surprised to get a call to attend a meeting with Mickey Rudin, Frank's lawyer-agent at that time. He was very cordial and got right to the point. He asked if I would consider being Frank's conductor, pianist, and musical director. I was thrilled with the offer, but I told him that Como had the first call on my services because we had been together for so many years. Mr. Rudin said he and Frank both understood that, but and as long as I would provide an adequate substitute, we could work it all out. How wonderful! I went on to tell Mr. Rudin that I would have to have total musical control, because I knew that there was a big power struggle going on backstage with Irv Cottler, the drummer who aspired to be the leader since the first day he played for Sinatra. Rudin assured me that would not be a problem because he, too, was aware of the tension that existed with the musicians backstage.

When the topic of money came up, I gave him a figure equal to what I was making with Perry and without blinking an eye, he said that he would be in touch with me in a day or two. Well, I waited for two weeks and still no call. I phoned his office and told his secretary that if Mr. Rudin did try to contact me, I never received his call. She politely said she would get back to me. He never got back to me.

DEAN MARTIN

I had worked with Dean a couple of times before when he appeared as a guest on a Como television special and also on the

Big Show for Nick Vanoff. He was always fun to be with and musically no problem at all.

Mort Viner, his agent-manager, called me one day and said that Dean's long-time piano-conductor, Ken Lane, had had an accident and would not be able to work with Dean for at least five or six months. I called Ken to express my concern and he gave me his blessing to be his substitute. Sinatra, Sammy Davis, and Dean were just about to start the "Rat Pack Together Again" tour. Mort immediately agreed to the fee that I wanted and everyone seemed happy. The next evening, I unexpectedly met Dean in an Italian restaurant in Beverly Hills. We exchanged greetings and I asked him when we could meet and rehearse. He answered, "Eh, Nickie, I know you can play and conduct. We don't have to rehearse, but—uh—how well do you read lines?" He laughed when I told him I was a big ham. A large dish of Italian escarole arrived at his table and we both inhaled the lovely garlic aroma. He mentioned that his folks were from Abruzzia, Italy and they knew good Italian cooking. I agreed. He then took a big sip on whatever he was drinking, gave me a hearty handshake and said he would see me at the first rehearsal with Frank and Sammy. He was definitely my kinda' guy.

Mort provided me with a couple of videos of Dean's act and my buddy, Terry Woodson, gave me his conductor book. I did my homework and I was all set. Two days later, the entire orchestra contracted by Joe Malin, came from New York City to Los Angeles and everybody assembled on a huge sound stage in Hollywood for the first rehearsal. It was great to see so many of my old New York musician buddies again.

Dean came by to say hello and mentioned that his stomach was very upset because of some terrible food he had eaten the previous night at a fancy dinner party. I saw Frank sitting several feet away at a table, studying his lyrics for the big medley he did with Sammy and Dean at the end of the show. I went over to greet him and he barely looked up at me as he shook my hand. When I asked how he was feeling he said, "Lousy," and just kept rubbing his stomach. Then I foolishly said, "I guess you were at that same awful dinner party that Dean was just telling me about. What you need is some good Italian food." He didn't respond and I added, "I hope you feel better,"—then I walked away. I hadn't taken more than a dozen steps when I realized what a terribly rude thing I just said. I had totally forgotten that in that morning's paper there was an article about a lavish dinner party Barbara Sinatra had hosted the night before to celebrate the reunion of the "Rat Pack." I continued what I felt was a death march as I walked over to see Joe Malin and my New York buddies. When I told them of the major goof I had just committed, they roared with laughter. Joe said something like "Don't worry—Como still likes you."

The rehearsal went very smoothly and two days later, we opened in San Francisco. My long-time arranger friend, Morty Stevens, conducted for both Sinatra and Sammy Davis. It soon became apparent that Frank, for some unknown reason, was unhappy with the way things were going on stage. On one particular night he shoved Dean's microphone right up into his face while they were doing the closing medley. The audience always loved whatever these three giant entertainers did on the stage. I had a chat with Dean in his dressing room before each show and he was upset by Frank's behavior toward him on stage. One night, after he showed me how to hit an eight-iron golf shot, he said, "Can you imagine?— This guy thinks I'm drunk and I don't know how to handle a microphone. Nickie—I've been doing this for forty fucking years and I ain't going to change now!"

It was a very cold night and we were performing in Chicago. Mort Viner told me before the show that he wanted to talk to me later. Just before the final medley, Dean and Sammy got into an adlib comedy thing that had the audience and the entire orchestra in stitches! At the peak of the hilarity, Frank suddenly turned to Morty Stevens and angrily demanded that he start the closing medley *immediately*! The musicians were all taken by surprise, as were Sammy and Dean. None of us could figure out what possessed Frank to do what he did. Anyway, when they finished singing the closing medley, the audience was on its feet cheering wildly. It was so exciting to watch and hear their thunderous applause.

After the show, Dean, Mort Viner, and I were all bundled up because of the frigid weather. We were about to walk out the stage door when Frank suddenly appeared. Dean had just put a cigarette up to his lips when, as if by magic, Frank produced a lighter. He proceeded to ignite not the cigarette, but instead he lit the red scarf Dean was wearing around his neck. I couldn't believe what was happening as we doused the flames with our gloved hands. Fortunately, no one was burned or harmed in any way. Frank made a big joke out of it and I honestly believe that his intention was not to hurt anyone. However, what was done, was done. Short goodbyes were exchanged and we all parted.

As soon as I reached my hotel room, Mort Viner called and said, "Don't ask questions. Take the morning flight back to Los Angeles—we'll talk later." What I didn't know was that, at that very moment, Dean was on his way back to California by private jet, and upon arrival in Los Angeles, he was going directly to a hospital. He would be diagnosed as suffering from intense fatigue. That was it. My job was over and that made me sad. Playing and conducting for Dean was one of the easiest and most entertaining jobs I've ever had. He was a delight to be with. The entire experience was something I will never forget. Liza Minnelli was called to fill in for Dean, and the rest of the tour went off as planned.

CHAPTER 21

BOB and DOLORES HOPE

Bob and Dolores Hope at a Christmas party in 1993

How does one begin to describe the likes of a Bob Hope? He has been a part of every American's life and we are all grateful for the humor and fabulous entertainment he has brought to all of our lives. I conducted for him several times when he appeared as a guest on a Como or Crosby television special and he was always a gentleman and a real entertainer. When the spotlight went on, you name it, he could do it. He will forever be a true American Legend.

For many years Bob Alberti, a great pianist and arranger, was the musical director of the Hope television specials. He wrote the new arrangements for the Les Brown band and did all of the necessary pre and post musical chores. A couple of times he called me in to play the accordion and also to write an arrangement or two for one of the guest artists. When I was growing up in Denver and the big bands came to town, Les Brown's was always my favorite. The arrangements they played were exciting and tasteful and the comedy of Butch Stone brought joy to one and all. So needless to say, I was always happy to be a part of the Bob Hope shows.

Bob's wife, Dolores, is as extraordinary in her way as he was. Their sixty-nine year marriage is amazing, especially in Hollywood. Dolores Reade was a singer when they met back in the thirties. George Murphy, Bob's co-star in "Roberta" took him to a smart club in New York to hear her sing. She had a rich sultry voice and according to Bob, "it was love at first song." Bob was hooked. They shared a terrific sense of humor (she was more than a match for his quick wit), a love of golf and dogs. Dolores put her career on hold while she raised her family and tended to her many charitable causes, but she always loved to sing. She accompanied Bob and performed on many of his famous overseas trips to entertain the troops and from time-to-time, Bob would insist on her singing on his television specials. Dolores is a talented musician and had a great sense of what she wanted. She also had a reputation for being a perfectionist and later on I would come to admire that quality in her.

Bob Alberti informed me that Dolores, after much coaxing from her family and friends, decided to record an album of her own and she was looking for an arranger. Several of my friends, who could have done the job for her didn't work out, so Bobby asked me if I would like to give it a try. Since my schedule was not too hectic, I agreed to meet with Dolores. We had tea the next afternoon and she was delightful . . . very gracious, polite and lots of laughs. I gave her some recordings of my favorite arrangements and singers so that she could get an idea of exactly what it was I did. I felt we already had a lot in common because she said she loved Art Tatum and many of the same artists I had great musical respect for.

We met again a couple of days later. After we exchanged the usual pleasantries and had tea accompanied by an absolutely sinful dessert, I asked her how she liked a particular Como album I had given her . . . it was one of my favorites. She quickly responded, "I hated it." Not expecting that kind of an answer, I asked if we could listen to some of it together, so she could point out to me the places she hated. She agreed and after several bars had gone by she said, "See, there! What's all that clunking going on in the piano part?" As the recording continued, she admitted that the strings were lovely and after a while she confessed she didn't really hate the album after all. I was relieved . . . but only for a short time. I was asked to play something on the piano and I thought that was a good idea since I sensed we would be working together soon. I only played about four bars when she said to me, "Why do you have to play all those runs?" I answered that God only gave me four bars that I could play like Art Tatum and that was it; reminding her that she had already told me he was one of her favorites. Her laugh greatly helped to lighten the growing tension in me.

I suggested we run through a song or two so that we could get more musically acquainted. She started to sing, "There'll Never Be Another You." After a bar or two, I sensed she wanted it in rhythm and I fell right in and started to have a good time. She was singing beautifully, but before we got to the middle of the song, she stopped and said, "What's all that thumping going on in you left hand?" I tried to explain that since we had no bass player present I was indicating his part. I would play differently, of course, when we had the full band. She wasn't convinced with my explanation and at that point my Italian temper was beginning to rise. We chatted some more and she thanked me for allowing her to express her opinions. She added that most Italian musicians, at that point, would have told her the equivalent of "Go to Hell", which she actually said in Italian. Her accent was perfect because she came from an Italian father and an Irish mother. Her maiden name was Dolores De Fina. Now I realized the source of her energy and forthrightness. Geoff Clarkson, Bob's personal accompanist and a long-time member of Les Brown's Band had accompanied her on many occasions, so I suggested that she rehearse with him and decide on the songs for her album. After all, I thought, Geoff knew what Dolores liked in an accompanist. I added that she should get some great players who could adlib and all go into a studio and record. Then she could tell each one of them exactly what she wanted to hear. We agreed that this was the way to go.

As soon as I got home, I called her daughter, Linda, and said the equivalent of "there's no way in hell your mother and I will ever work together." Linda politely said she understood and asked me to send a bill. I assured here there would be no bill and wished her and her mom lots of luck. Unknown to me at the time, Dolores had also called Linda and said, "That Nick Perito is a wonderful musician, but I don't think there is any way that we'll be able to work together."

A week later Linda called me back and said her mother insisted that I (that nice man) attend the recording sessions. My contractor, Joe Soldo, also thought it would be a good idea. I went to the first session and stood in the back of the control room sipping coffee and trying to keep a low profile. I soon realized people weren't communicating and tempers were beginning to rise. I offered a few suggestions to the engineer and the musicians to hopefully satisfy what Dolores was asking for. Lo and behold, it started to come together and when the session ended, they had two very good sides. The musicians, namely Gary Foster, Warren Luening and Geoff Clarkson improvised perfectly and everybody was happy. The same thing happened on the next recording date two days later. When that session ended, Dolores had Michael, the Hope's butler, come by with a tray of Italian antipasto hors d'oeuvre and a large jug of Manhattans. The control room became a real party scene and Dolores was in Heaven, complimenting everyone in sight, including me. Saying that I was a magician. Well, after a couple of drinks she asked my honest opinion of what was going on. I opened my big mouth and out came, "I'm delighted that you are so pleased with the musicians and everything but honestly, Dolores, sometimes you can be a real pain in the ass." The smile disappeared from her face and a hush fell over the room. The next thought came directly from my heart and I quickly added, "Do you want to know why?" While she continued to glare at me, I said, "Because it takes one to know one." With that, all those in the control room burst out laughing, including Dolores. She gave me a big hug and to this very day, she often refers to me as "PITA."

That album called "Dolores Hope: Now and Then" was finished with additional arrangements by Bob Alberti and John Oddo, Rosemary Clooney's musical director. It was enthusiastically received. After all, how many eighty-seven year old singers had a sound like Dolores? How many singers, period, had a voice like hers? Over the next few years we did four more albums which I arranged and conducted. Our mutual trust and respect grew with each new project. I was thrilled that Bob Hope agreed to sing on two of those albums, "Somewhere in Time" (music of the World War II era) and also the Christmas album called "Hopes for the Holidays." I am so honored that both Bob and Dolores recorded several of my original songs and their performances were perfect.

Bob's 90th Birthday TV Special in 1993, "Bob Hope: The First 90 Years" was planned as a three hour retrospective with major guest stars, clip packages and big production numbers. It was a challenge for the production team. So many years! So many memories! So many choices! By this time, Bob Alberti had moved to Hilton Head, North Carolina and I inherited his position as Musical Director. The tech crew and I burned the candle at both ends along with Linda Hope, the Executive Producer, and Don Mischer. Our collective efforts made for a great television special and it won an Emmy that year as "Outstanding Special." But again, I lost out on an Emmy for the music because I had already nominated myself for the Kennedy Center Honors. I continued as Musical Director for subsequent Hope Christmas Shows and it was always a ball working with Linda and her crew.

I spent many afternoons rehearsing with the Hopes at their

beautiful home in Toluca Lake. We'd often have lunch and I was delighted to learn that Bob was also a great audience. He spoiled me by listening intently to many of my old Italian stories. One day, he really broke up when I told him I wanted to write a book entitled, "I Made Bob Hope Laugh." I regret not having had a tape recorder to preserve all the great stories he told me about his early days in show business with all of his famous friends and sidekicks . . . the people he loved and admired so much. I suggested to Bob that the title of that book should be, "These are the Guys Who Made Me Laugh"

Shortly after Bob's 90th Birthday TV Special, he and Dolores were invited by Skitch Henderson to appear with the New York City Pops Orchestra at Carnegie Hall. It was a very special occasion because it gave us all a chance to make beautiful music together and share many great memories with old friends. Skitch insisted I conduct for the Hopes and it was a joy for me to see so many of my old buddies like Sid Jekowsky in the orchestra.

As a result of the acclaim, Dolores was getting from her new albums; she began to entertain the thought that she might perform in a nightclub again. I warned her that nightclub audiences were not as quiet and attentive as she remembered them to be. To demonstrate my point, we went to dinner at "Tavern on the Green" in Central Park. My friend, Torrie Zito and his wife, Helen Merrrill, a great singer, were appearing there. Shortly after their show started, Dolores became very annoyed because the waiters were still serving food and drinks and the audience was noisy and inattentive. I asked her if she would be willing to perform under those circumstances. After a moment, she turned to me with a mischievous glint in her eye and an amused smile and said, "No thank you. I'm too old and too rich to have to do that again." We enjoyed a good laugh.

As a kind of post-script to this story, in 1997 Rosemary Clooney who had always been one of Dolores' staunchest supporters, invited Dolores to appear with her at "Rainbow and Stars" a famous cabaret venue in New York. Dolores agreed and she did two shows a night for two weeks. The show was sold out and a huge success.

So much for too old and too rich. Dolores is a singer who could not turn down a great gig.

50th ANNIVERSARY OF D-DAY

In January 1994, Bob and Dolores were approached with an offer to do a week of shows aboard the luxury liner QE II in honor of the 50th Anniversary of D-Day. The idea was that we would build a show around "Somewhere in Time," our World War II album. The ship was already sold out to various veterans groups returning to honor their fallen comrades at Normandy Beach.

Linda came up with a great concept weaving together the period's music with wonderful film clip packages featuring Bob and Dolores. Bob as usual was going to do an opening monologue and handle the MC chores. He was also going to do a couple of his songs from his regular personal appearance act. In hindsight, it was a pretty intricate show but Bob and Dolores were ready to give it a shot. After several rehearsals, we began to realize that at ninety-one Bob was having some difficulty handling some of the complicated cues. We all thought that maybe the whole thing was too much. Maybe we should cancel. Dolores, Linda and I had tea with him one afternoon and Linda, who was producing the show, tried with the utmost delicacy to broach the subject of the possibility of canceling the date. Bob, who was used to running things, quickly shot back, "Are you trying to tell me I don't know what I am doing?" Linda tried to explain further and getting nowhere, she rose from the table and quietly left the room. A few minutes later, the exact same thing happened when Dolores diplomatically tried to get across the same message to him. Another uncomfortable silence . . . and then she got up and left the room. There I was, sitting across the table from this incredible performer and I was at a loss for words. Needless to say, he was a bit angry . . . so I started talking about golf, thinking that topic would lighten up the atmosphere. When I tried to segue back into what the real purpose of our meeting was, he roared back at me, "You too? Are you trying to tell me the same damn thing?" Not knowing exactly what to say, I also left the room. When I walked into the kitchen, both Linda and Dolores were there sipping tea, and almost in unison they said, "We were wondering how long it was going to take before you'd be joining us." We all hugged and laughed and slowly returned to where Bob was seated in the living room. He realized then that we were really concerned about his well-being and we only wanted the best for him. A calm conversation ensued and we all decided not to cancel out. We reworked the act and everyone was excited. We were going to England and take our chances. We did and it was a fabulous experience—one I will never forget.

ABOARD THE QUEEN ELIZABETH

An English Glenn Miller type band was hired to play the show. Rehearsals went well and the film clips were all set to roll on cue. After the overture, a screen would light up over the orchestra and a film clip would be shown of all the zany entrances Bob made on his TV shows down through the years. Then the band would play Bob on stage with his theme song "Thanks for the Memory." After a few opening comments and jokes, he would introduce the next film segment featuring his many movie dance partners. Then more comments followed by film segments of his movie songs . . . his various leading ladies, etc. and at the very end, Dolores would appear and sing a couple of solos. After that, Bob would join her for a closing song or two, at least that was the plan.

Opening night came and the front row was filled with many English dignitaries and our own, Walter Cronkite. The rest of the room was filled with World War II Veterans and their families. Many of these men had seen Bob when he did shows throughout England, North Africa and the South Pacific during the Second World War. After the orchestral overture and the opening film clip, we played "Thanks for the Memory" and Bob walked out on the stage. The place went wild!

His opening comments were perfect and, as usual, he had the audience in the palm of his hand. All of a sudden, he started to introduce Dolores and I was taken by surprise. She wasn't scheduled to make her first appearance until at least forty minutes after the show began and I knew she was not ready to walk out on stage. I was conducting the band behind him and as he crossed near me, I tried to get his attention but he ignored me. Finally, he became annoyed with my persistent, "Psst . . . Pssting" . . . and he came over to me and stuck the microphone right in my face. The expression on his face told me he was very annoyed. I don't know where the inspiration came from but I adlibbed something like, "Ladies and Gentlemen, we have a great surprise for Bob tonight. He doesn't know this but we have put together a film clip showing the many famous dancers he has performed with in the movies down through the years. So, sit back and enjoy this marvelous composite of Bob's terpsichorean talents with some of the world's greatest dancers." I was so relieved to see the house lights dim; the screen lit up overhead and the film clip began to roll. Fortunately, Bob's microphone was shut-off because he said to me something like "What the hell are you doing?" I quietly reminded him that we still had many film clips to show before Dolores was to make her grand entrance. He paused for a moment and then, with a little grin on his face, he said, "Thanks for reminding me." The rest of the show went very smoothly and the audience's reaction was thunderous. We did the same program at Albert Hall in London and also in Glasgow, Scotland. The UK audiences were thrilled to see their native son return.

Dolores and me in a recording studio

MORE ALBUMS

Dolores received such great accolades in Britain that she decided to make another album, which is exactly what we did as soon as we returned to Los Angeles. People are amazed that a woman of her age can still sing so beautifully and give each song such a special interpretation. If you didn't already know Dolores' age you would never guess from her voice. It is strong and true and rich. What people don't know is that she can also play the piano and is a good musician. She doesn't like to practice, but who does. Improvisation comes easy to her when she sings and that's what makes her such a special performer. It is a commonly agreed fact that had she chosen, in her early years, to pursue a singing career, she would have been a big star in her own right. The guys in the band loved working with her and we had lots of laughs.

We are currently involved with album number six, which has temporarily been titled, "Just for Fun."

In the recording studio, Dolores can still be very demanding and that I certainly respect. The great musicians that Joe Soldo always hires are only too happy to grant her every wish. On one particular session, we had several players of Italian descent and Joe reminded Dolores that the band was very "Wop-sided." She loved his comment. We always have a good time and, yes, she still makes sure that the Manhattans and hors d'oeuvres are served after every recording session. "To walk among kings yet keep the common touch" is only one of many complimentary phrases that accurately describe this incredible lady. She is, and will always be, a very special person in the lives of every member of my family. We love her!

Dolores and my sister, Marian, bonded as soon as they met. It was as though they had known each other forever. Dolores enjoyed calling her by her Italian name, "Marianna." They had so much in common and it was party time for one and all whenever they were together.

ORSON WELLES
and
JERRY ABBOTT

I first met Jerry Abbott in March of 1966. He was a very successful jingle writer-producer in Chicago, and he often flew to New York City to record some of the jingles he was doing for Wrigley's gum or any number of other products. He always presented me with a challenge, because he would arrive in Manhattan very early in the morning, meet me at my office about 9 AM and hum to me the melody of his new jingle. After figuring out how many bars we needed to fill up a minute or so, I would write the orchestrations for a couple of different versions, using whatever size of the orchestra that we had discussed on the telephone prior to his coming to New York City. Bob Rosengarden, my contractor, would have booked already the studio and hired the musicians. Bill Kratt, then copied the orchestral parts and we'd all meet at a studio around 2 or 2:30 PM. The recording session generally lasted an hour or so. Jerry would then rush to the airport and be on a 6:30 PM flight back to Chicago.

On one occasion, he brought a lady account executive to one of our recording sessions. The ad agency was promoting a European product and the music called for some ethnic flavoring so I played accordion on the recording. Everything went well with the singers and the orchestra, but the lady executive quietly complained to Jerry that my accordion playing was *too Jewish!* OK?

The jingle business allowed Jerry the opportunity to make friends with many well-known stars in the entertainment world. The most famous was Orson Welles. Jerry composed both the music and lyrics to a lovely song called "I Know What It Is to Be Young (but do you know what it is to be old?)" I wrote the orchestral and choir arrangements and Orson Welles agreed to narrate the lyric. We did the actual recording on December 19, 1983.

Orson came to the studio to overdub his part after the choir and orchestra had gone. He made a dramatic entrance as he swept into the room wearing a long black cape and a big bowler hat.

When he laughed, the whole room shook. After hearing the music that he was to narrate over, he told me he loved my arrangement and then jokingly added that he would try not to "get in the way." When we started to overdub his voice, he insisted I sit across from him and a hanging microphone would be suspended between us. After a couple of rundowns, Orson was still having trouble staying in sync with the singers and the orchestra. He asked me to direct him with a series of hand signals that would tell him when to read a little slower or faster. That made me laugh because I told him my showbiz friends would never believe that *I directed* Orson Welles! He, too, thought that was funny and again, his laughter shook the room. What a memorable afternoon that was for me, sitting across from this amazing actor/director making small talk and exchanging funny stories.

CHARO

In April of 1982, Charo was one of the guest stars on a Como television special from Guadalajara, Mexico. She insisted on playing a guitar solo in the middle section of one of her solo vocal numbers. At the orchestral pre-record session in Los Angeles, I had to keep reminding Tommy Tedesco, one of Hollywood's greatest guitarists, to stop "noodling" around so much on a particular arrangement because Charo was going to be playing a guitar solo at that point. I preferred that he would just play the rhythmic chords that I had written for him. Tommy had great improvisational talent and he always got bored by simply playing the rhythm parts. However, he agreed to do as I asked.

Charo was late getting to the studio and as a result, we had to overdub her part. No problem. It was common procedure for many artists. When she did start to record, it became obvious to all concerned that her guitar playing was not what we expected. It was *her* idea in the first place, so you can imagine our mutual frustration. Ordinarily, Charo can play the guitar very well—but on this particular day she was having difficulty. She apologized to the producer and the director and the control room became uncomfortably quiet. In order to relieve the growing tension, the engineer began testing and opening up various orchestral audio tracks. Suddenly, as if by magic, the room was filled with exciting improvisational guitar playing. Charo was overcome with joy. She gave me a big hug and kept repeating that I was a magician. I tried telling her that it was Tommy Tedesco who was the magician—not me—but she didn't want to be confused with the facts.

All she had to do now was "fake playing" what she had just heard. The director and producer were very relieved and everyone was happy. When I got home, I called Tommy and thanked him for *disobeying* my instructions. Unknowingly, he had saved the day for Charo—and me. Later on, he enjoyed reminding me of that story whenever we were amongst a group of fellow musicians. Tommy was a real pro in our industry.

DINAH SHORE

Here was a person that I can honestly say was a real doll. Everything about her was beautiful. Her looks, her voice, and the way she related to every person she met. Years back, I accompanied both Steve and Eydie at various times when they made guest appearances on her television shows. She had such a relaxed, casual manner that it was always fun to be around her. In addition to Dinah's great talent as a singer and actress, she also loved to cook and, as a result, became a real connoisseur of good food. She compiled a cookbook that became very popular with all of her television fans.

Whenever her long-time conductor friend and piano accompanist, John Rodby, had a booking conflict, I was privileged to take his place. This occurred several times down through the years and one incident, in particular stands out in my mind. It took place in Sun City, Arizona. Dinah, myself, and a couple of her assistants were greeted by several local dignitaries upon our arrival there. After our group climbed into a big limo, we were surprised to hear Dinah tell the driver to forget about going directly to the hotel. Instead, she suggested that he drive us to the best restaurant in town. It was about 6 PM and we all agreed that was a good idea.

The restaurant was jammed with diners and we had no reservation. But as soon as they recognized Dinah, the headwaiter magically opened up a table for our party. Dinah ordered for all of us and the food was delicious. I was amazed to see the outpouring of love and respect the fellow diners showed her. She graciously signed every autograph, and after her great performance the following evening, I thought that she could have easily run for governor of Arizona. What a classy, intelligent, regularly down-to-earth, warm and wonderful lady she was.

With Placido Domingo after the concert in Fukuoka, Japan,
January 28, 1999

THE TENORS and THE DIVA
(DOMINGO, CARRERAS, and DIANA ROSS)

My good friends in San Francisco, Terry and Yoshiko Terajima, were the promoters who booked Perry Como for all of his concerts in Japan beginning in 1976.

In early 1997, Terry asked me to make an arrangement of what he called "The Movie Medley" for an upcoming concert in Osaka, Japan, starring José Carreras, Placido Domingo, and Diana Ross. Initially, I thought that was a rather strange combination of talents, but I learned later that it was absolutely dynamite for true music lovers. A full ninety-piece symphony orchestra was imported from Hungary and a one-hundred voice choir came from Osaka. They accompanied the three major stars. The soloists each performed their individual spots and at the end of the program, they all sang "The Movie Medley" together. It proved to be a fantastic finale. Terry had chosen five great songs and we worked out the various sections that each star sang. I also arranged and orchestrated a medley of three Italian songs that featured the choir and the symphony—excluding the stars. This was performed in the middle of the concert and it gave both Placido and José a chance to rest between their respective solos.

Here is what occurred before the actual concert took place. Eugene Kohn, Placido's conductor, was the leader of the orchestra and choir for the entire concert. Diana Ross insisted upon having her own personal drummer, guitar, bass and piano player added to the ensemble. That worked out fine, particularly when it came to the sections in the closing medley that needed a contemporary rhythmic feeling. The Terajimas flew me to Osaka to attend both the rehearsal and concert to make sure that the European orchestra would play the American music with the proper feeling. I arrived late at the initial orchestra rehearsal, because of bad weather on the flight to Osaka. Kohn was in the middle of the Movie Medley rehearsal, and as I walked into the back of the hall, I heard him say there were some wrong notes in the French horn parts. I had already heard what *he* thought was wrong. As I continued to walk toward the podium, I said loudly, "Don't change a thing. Those notes are correct." My forthrightness immediately garnered me the respect of Diana's musicians who were not very fond of the conductor. Placido and José were very pleased with my arranging and orchestration and we got along beautifully.

Two great gentlemen and real pros. On the other hand, Diana, the pop diva, was aloof and "above it all." What a giant ego!

At the dress rehearsal on the day of the performance, Kohn, who I knew was still a bit miffed by my comments at the initial music reading, asked me to come up to the podium and conduct the choir and orchestra for the Italian medley I had written. He wanted to hear what it all sounded like at the rear of the arena. All of the choir singers and musicians were not sure what my role was for this affair, but as soon as I threw the first downbeat, they responded enthusiastically. When we finished, the entire orchestra stood up and applauded. The choir members, up on the elevated platforms, were all waving their music in the air. What a happy musical and emotional experience that was for me.

Forty thousand people attended the concert, which took place in an indoor baseball stadium on March 4, 1997. The theatrical chemistry of the two classical tenors and a pop star, was really electrifying.

This same concert was repeated on May 24, 1997 in Taiwan. Here it took place outdoors in front of the Chiang Kai Shek Memorial. Over sixty-five thousand people attended. This time, the orchestra was imported from Czechoslovakia and David Gimemez, José Carreras's nephew, was the very capable conductor. I sat in the sound booth area (which was situated out in the audience) about one hundred twenty yards from the stage and I cued the very capable Japanese audio engineers. They were very appreciative of my suggestions since we only had one rehearsal before the actual performance.

Months later, Terry Terajima called me again to orchestrate a medley of three popular Japanese songs for the two tenors and Diana. This time, in order to attend the rehearsals with a different European symphony orchestra, Terry and I flew from Los Angeles to London, to Paris, to Prague, Czechoslovakia, and then to a small city nearby called, Ostrava. After a two-day rehearsal there, conducted by David Gimenez, the three of us flew back to Paris and then over Russia to Japan—as did the entire orchestra. The three stars and a Japanese choir met us in Fukuoka, Japan and the rehearsals went smoothly. The concert took place one day later on July 28, 1999 and the soloists all gave thrilling performances. I returned to Los Angeles the following day.

What an exciting experience it was for me to travel *around the world* for just one concert—and the entire project only encompassed ten days.

It was really gratifying for me to see the enthusiasm, appreciation, and love that the Japanese audience showered upon these three great artists—José Carreras, Placido Domingo, and Diana Ross. I am grateful to Terry and Yoshiko Terajima for making it all possible.

REGIS PHILBIN

One of Perry Como's biggest fans was Regis Philbin. He never missed a chance to be with Perry and have an opportunity to just sit and talk. I am happy to say that Perry felt the same way about Regis, who is also a very good singer. These two men really had a lot in common.

One afternoon, Perry was late for a rehearsal at the Westbury Theatre in Long Island, New York and *Regis* just happened to be there. All the while I was rehearsing the orchestra, he stood up on the stage and sang Perry's songs. When Perry did finally show up, the two of them happily took turns singing various sections of the remaining songs. I am sorry that we didn't do a television special showing those two great guys singing together, kidding around, and sharing stories.

Perry appeared on the *Regis & Kathy Lee* television show several times and I was always there to accompany him. On one specific occasion, Perry said (before the show) that he did not want to sing—he just wanted to sit and chat. Privately, Regis and I agreed that the presence of a piano *on stage* might convince him otherwise. After a commercial break, a piano was quietly wheeled in so that when Perry was introduced, he would have to notice the instrument as he walked into camera range. His smile told both Regis and I that we had done the right thing.

After some warm conversation, Regis and Kathy cajoled Perry into singing a song. When he saw me sneak in and sit down at the piano, he happily acknowledged that he had been *set up*. I started to play quietly as they continued talking and Perry knew I was suggesting that he sing "It Could Happen to You." That song has never received a better rendition than Perry gave it that day. Another magical moment for me, and I thank you, Regis.

JULIA MIGENES

I first met this magnificent soprano while working on a Como Christmas television special in 1987 that was filmed in San Antonio, Texas. Julia was very easy to get along with and a musical delight.

We learned that she began her career as a dancer-singer on Broadway in *West Side Story*. At an early age, she studied classical singing and really came up through the ranks of show business.

She grew up in New York City near the midtown tunnel on the east side of Manhattan. Her father was Greek, and her mother was Puerto Rican. Therefore, she considers herself to be a "Greeko-Rican." That makes sense to me.

To gain attention early on in her career, I was told that she sang a very ambitious classical program before a large, dignified audience. When she finished her final aria, she received a standing ovation and the applause went on forever. After taking her bow, she politely raised her gown just high enough to allow her to roller-skate off the stage! The audience went crazy when they realized that she had sung the entire concert with *roller skates on*. As you can see, she had a wonderful sense of humor, but it did not interfere with her dedication to her craft.

Placido Domingo made a movie of the opera *Carmen* and Julia sang the lead role. She won a Grammy for her performance. When you see the movie, you will agree that Placido made a very wise choice. I have had the pleasure to conduct for Julia on several occasions and each time, the audience went wild.

It was suggested that she repeat her roller-skating act when we filmed the Como Christmas television show in San Antonio, but she refused saying, modestly, that she now considered herself a "diva"—and I agreed with her 100 percent. What a magnificent artist and performer she is.

JERRY LEWIS

In August of 2000, I was hired to conduct the Jerry Lewis Muscular Dystrophy Telethon. Before I accepted, I called Lou Brown, who had been Jerry's conductor for the previous forty-something years. In his usual humorous but brusque manner, he said, "Who in the hell do you think recommended you?" Knowing I had Lou's blessing, I accepted the job.

Jerry was a comic legend, and I was looking forward to working with him. I had heard many stories from various people in the industry about his ego, but I had no idea how big it was until I actually met him. At first I thought he was acting or putting me on, but I soon discovered he was serious.

Lou Brown was still connected with the program as a conductor, for whenever Jerry sang his solo pieces, but everything else the orchestra did was my responsibility. The initial rehearsals went as planned, until Jerry wanted to rehearse an old arrangement of "Fascinating Rhythm." After a few bars, he insisted that the band was not playing the correct arrangement. Lou reminded him that it was the same one they had been doing for the past thirty years. Jerry would hear none of it and angrily stalked off. During a break, I walked into the production room and made the mistake of saying I was sorry that he didn't have the arrangement he wanted. He sat me down and proceeded to sing a bunch of musical phrases around the melody of "Fascinating Rhythm." Then, he insisted that I take down what he was improvising, then write the band arrangement and have it ready for rehearsal the next afternoon! He was furious when I told him I couldn't write it and have it copied for the orchestra in such a short time. He angrily roared back that his secretary could get on the telephone and hire four different arrangers to show up within the hour and have it all scored and copied by the next morning. I excused myself and went back to the band rehearsal. I couldn't believe what I had just heard.

Peter Myers, who had written an arrangement for the show, just happened to be at the rehearsal and I asked him to go in and try to appease Jerry. Peter wisely recorded what Jerry sang to him on a small portable Walkman and then promised he would write the arrangement overnight. But he managed to convince Jerry that the music copyists needed an extra day to do their necessary work. Two days later my son, Danny brought the music to the rehearsal and Lou Brown conducted the orchestra playing the new arrangement. Jerry seemed pleased with what Peter had miraculously done—but when he saw Peter's name on the conductor part as the arranger, he flipped out! He insisted that Peter's name be erased *immediately* and replaced with his name because he boasted, "I wrote that arrangement!" A common joke among the musicians was that Jerry wouldn't know if the music was upside down or not if the title wasn't printed on the page.

I tried to keep a low profile during all of this madness. Believe me, it was difficult to keep my mouth shut. After watching me conduct the rest of the rehearsal, Jerry, surprisingly became very complimentary regarding my ability to communicate with the orchestra. The next day we were going on the air, and I couldn't believe that now, I was a big hit.

When I arrived at the studio early the next morning, I was flabbergasted to learn from the orchestra contractor, Jack Eglash, that on Jerry's orders, Lou Brown was fired! I couldn't believe that on the night before the telethon was actually going on the air, Jerry fired a man who had been his conductor for over forty years— *and* he didn't have the guts to do it himself. Jack had to call Lou on the phone and tell him that he was not to show up the next day. I was devastated, as were all the members of the orchestra.

Since I had not conducted Jerry's solo numbers, we had an early rehearsal so that I could learn exactly what he wanted at various times during his performances. After several songs, he said in front of the entire orchestra that he had never been followed so well. Again, I was a big hit.

Wait, it's not over. Greg Huckins, our lead saxophonist, had to play a very difficult flute solo on a jazz arrangement that Jerry mimed during one of his comedy skits. Playing it was rough and Greg did a great job. Yet, Jerry was convinced that if Greg would watch him mime it, Greg would actually play it better. The whole band couldn't believe the reasoning behind Jerry's request—it didn't make any sense.

The telethon began on a Saturday in the early evening, and all went well for the first portion. The orchestra was dismissed around midnight and we were told to be back early the next day, Sunday. As soon as we got started the next morning, I sensed something had changed. Jerry found fault with everything and everybody. He was extremely rude and disrespectful, and he chastised certain stagehands and the television director right "on camera" for no apparent reason. A short time later, I too, found myself in the line of fire. He kept saying that I was not stopping the orchestra at the right time after a play-on or play-off. At one point, he actually came over to the podium and tried to show me how to conduct a fanfare. I politely gave him my baton and he proceeded to conduct, but the orchestra fell apart because he didn't know what in the hell he was doing. It wasn't meant to be a comedy skit and it only proved to be an embarrassment for all involved.

All of my professional life I have had the good fortune to work with performers from every facet of show business, but I have never ever had to deal with an egotist, the likes of a Jerry Lewis.

CHAPTER 22

MY SPORTS HEROES

I participated in many charity and celebrity golf tournaments as a result of being musical director for Perry Como. Each event ended up with a closing night dinner, followed by a quickly put-together variety show, featuring many of the famous sports and show business stars who were present. The annual Como-Duke University Charity Golf Classic in Durham, North Carolina, was one of my favorites. It attracted guest stars like Bob Hope, Dinah Shore, Andy Williams, Sinatra, and many others. The emcee was always my dear friend, Woody Woodbury. He was a former WWII marine fighter pilot who, after the war, became a well-known comedian in film and radio.

He has a very special down-home sense of humor and can improvise silliness at the drop of a hat. There was never a dull moment when Woody was around. He also is a good golfer and plays the piano with a unique style all his own. We have played many zany piano duets together, much to the enjoyment of our many old friends.

DICK GROAT

Dick Groat, the all-star baseball shortstop from the Pittsburgh Pirates and a graduate of Duke University, became a real pal of mine. To this day, whenever I start to talk to him about baseball, he always manages to switch the conversation to piano playing. In addition to being a big Como fan, he loves all kinds of music, especially jazz. When he was playing with the Pirates, he often took a four-hour train ride from New York City to Boston on a day off just to hear the great jazz pianist, Dave McKenna. Dick was happy to learn that Dave was a mad baseball fan *and* he had a small portable radio under his piano bench so that during intermissions, he could check up on all of the baseball scores of the day and, when possible, listen to a live Boston Red Sox game.

I never figured out why so many of my musician friends are and have always been devoted sports fans. What I was delighted to learn later was that so many of my sports heroes were also music fans.

What fun it was to walk eighteen holes with Como on different occasions when he played with golfers like Arnold Palmer, Sam Snead, and Jack Nicklaus. I was the envy of every duffer within a one-hundred mile radius of those events. Willie Mosconi, the famous pool player and I played several rounds of golf together. One day, I asked him what went through his mind when he had a difficult shot to make on the pool table. He immediately answered, "I never *leave* myself a difficult shot!" I guess that's what *planning ahead* is all about. Along with Willie, I was lucky to be a part of a foursome that won the Como-Duke golf tournament one year.

THE SUPER BOWL

The Warner-Lambert Pharmaceutical Company held an annual golf tournament on Super Bowl weekend that was also one of my favorites. Thanks to men like Ron Demczak, Joe Dilger and the former CEO, Joe Williams, they managed to attract many famous sports stars for several days at a time. In the early years, the emcee was the famous television announcer-host, Dennis James, whose real name was Dimitri Sposa. He, too, grew up in an Italian family. On the evening before the big game, Dennis, Woody Woodbury and I would put together a variety show featuring the musical stars who were present. It was all adlib and I accompanied anyone who wanted to sing—great fun for all.

Can you imagine sitting next to Otto Graham, Hall of Fame quarterback from the Cleveland Browns, watching a Super Bowl game and discussing what John Elway of the Denver Broncos would be thinking or planning on each new play? Like Dick Groat, he preferred talking about music because what very few people know was that Otto studied piano when he was a young boy. His favorite piece was "Claire de Lune," and I played it for him whenever I had the chance.

Off the football field, some of the supposedly *meanest* players were just regular guys—polite, gentle, and kind. I'll never forget walking up to the football great "Night Train" Laine, a massive athlete, giving him a light punch in the stomach (which was at my eye level) and telling him, "If anybody ever gives you trouble, just tell 'em to see me." Then I had to brace myself for a loving hug that I felt was going to crush every bone in my body.

I really enjoyed the opportunity to hang out with my baseball heroes—like Don Newcomb, Alvin Dark, Bobby Thompson, Yogi Berra—and talk about what they were experiencing in a crucial game while the whole world watched. It was always fun to talk about sports with Bryant Gumbel, who was also a lover of good piano music. One night in a cocktail lounge in Palm Springs, California, he introduced me to the one and only Joe DiMaggio. I was so happy to have the opportunity to tell him what an inspiration and role model he was for all of us young kids growing up in Italian families all over the country. He was very surprised when I reminded him that on his first day at bat with the New York Yankees, he hit three for six—a triple and two singles. He bowed his head and there was a moment of silence before he reached up and shook my hand. I will never forget the wonderful look on his face at that moment. Joe deserved all of the accolades he received. What a hero he was for me!

ROGER MARIS

While attending a Chet Atkins golf tournament in Nashville, Tennessee, Como and I, along with some mutual friends, were enjoying an afternoon glass of wine in his suite when someone mentioned that Roger Maris was in the lobby and he wanted to meet Perry. He was immediately invited up to join us. We were all impressed with his quiet demeanor. Perry couldn't resist asking him why the New York City press was giving him such a hard time since he broke Babe Ruth's homerun record. Roger proceeded to explain that Red Smith, a popular sports writer at that time, was a great admirer and old friend of Babe Ruth and he was unhappy about the fact that *anybody* broke Ruth's record. As a result, Red was instrumental in creating the asterisk after Roger's name in the record books. What angered Maris and all of his Yankee teammates most of all was the fact that although Roger played in two more season games than Babe did—Roger still went to bat *less times.* The press, in general, never addressed that fact and that caused him a great deal of frustration. I wonder how Red Smith, that old bastard, would handle the homerun hitters of today. I guess showbiz and sports have a lot in common.

After Perry and I finished the show that night at the Atkins tournament, we returned to the hotel, and just before getting on the elevator, I saw Roger in the lobby bar surrounded by several lovely "southern belles." He ran over and pulled me out of the elevator and insisted that I join him at the bar for a drink. I didn't resist. After meeting all the ladies, I tried to excuse myself, but Roger would have none of it. Instead, he bid the *ladies* goodbye and then began telling me how much he enjoyed the show. We sat there and talked and drank for at least another hour or two and I was thrilled to hear what life was like in the dugout with the likes of Billy Martin, Mickey Mantle, Yogi Berra, Whitey Ford and all the rest of my Yankee heroes at that time.

TONEY PENNA

This legendary golfer was a good friend of Perry's, and he was a guest pro at many of the benefit golf tournaments. Although he was small in stature, he could still hit a golf ball a mile. Toney loved telling funny stories and he also had an eye for the ladies. One day out on the practice tee, I asked him to take a look at my golf swing and give me some pointers. He was very helpful, but I sensed he much preferred talking to me about music.

When I returned home after one particular tournament, I was surprised to discover a brand-new set of golf clubs waiting for me. They were a gift from Toney and Perry. I eagerly tore open the attached card and this is what Toney had written:

"Dear Nick—it was great hearing you play the piano last week. You asked me for my advice regarding your golf swing. I remember watching you take several practice shots, and now I have a suggestion to make: Don't play any golf for several days—just relax and take it easy—then after a week or so—give up the game completely. P.S. When do I get my piano lesson?"

RMIGB TOURNAMENT

Thanks to the initial efforts of Ray Valente, Al Carmosino, and a few of my other Italian hometown buddies in Denver, Colorado, the "Rocky Mountain Italian Golf and Boccie" tournament became a reality in the late seventies and it has since become an annual event. All of the proceeds go to the Colorado University Cancer Research Program. In 1981, I persuaded Perry Como to make a guest appearance. We all had such great fun that he returned for many years after that and generously gave of his time and talent. In the following years, I was also able to bring stars like Dolores Hope, Scott Record, Donnie Conn, and Kevin King to entertain.

When I began having booking conflicts, the gifted comedian and musician, Pete Barbutti, became the emcee of the after-dinner party shows. He still holds court along with Buddy Greco, Danny and the Juniors and many other talented performers—all of them accompanied by the versatile Dick Buckley Trio.

CHAPTER 23

MUSICIANS OF "NOTE"

Celebrating with Don Costa on his birthday in 1981

DON COSTA

I can't find the words to describe my love and admiration for him, both as my friend-brother and as the brilliant musician that he was. I have already mentioned Don many times in this book because he has been present throughout my entire life.

He had the ability to tell a funny story that would make any comedian jealous. Here are some of his experiences that he enjoyed telling me about. They will give you an idea about who he really was and what a wild sense of humor he had.

He was born and raised in a strong Sicilian family in Boston. His father was the *boss*, as was the case in many Italian families. One day, Don came home from elementary school crying. He told his father that a certain male teacher had slapped his face. Papa Costa became furious and the two of them hurried back to the school. When they found the teacher, Papa yelled at him, "Eh, you—you no toucha my boy!" He then grabbed the teacher, dragged him across the classroom floor and hung him up on a peg protruding from the wall in the clothes closet. Justice, Sicilian style. Don was never bothered again.

In his teen years, Don's older brother Leo, was obsessed with buying a motorcycle, but his father said absolutely no! And that was it. No more discussion. However, Leo did not give up his dream and diligently saved his money. Months went by, and one Saturday afternoon Don, along with his dad and other family members, had just finished digging a large hole in front of their garage. They were waiting for a cement truck to come and pour in the concrete for their new driveway. To everyone's surprise, Leo appeared with his big, shiny new Harley Davidson motorcycle—at the same time the cement truck arrived. Don and his other brothers were very excited about the beautiful new motorbike, but Papa was not a happy camper. He pointed his finger at Leo, and while angrily shouting several Sicilian curse words, he took the brand-new motorcycle away from Leo, pushed it into the large hole they had just finished digging-and then motioned to the operator of the cement truck to start pouring the concrete—which he did. OK? Case closed.

Don loved the thought of being a cowboy, but since he lived in New York City in the early fifties, that wasn't about to happen. In order to satisfy his ongoing desire, he bought a horse saddle, put it over the radiator in his tiny room at the Capital Hotel and occasionally, to make his friends laugh, he pretended that he was Buffalo Bill.

Shortly after Don became involved in writing arrangements for Sinatra, he suffered a serious heart attack. Frank flew him to

Texas and Dr. Debakey performed his magic. Don survived the open-heart surgery—but after a while, he went back to drinking and using drugs again. While conducting for Frank in Atlantic City, he had a second heart seizure after their closing night performance. He was rushed to a local hospital and all the necessary life support systems were applied to him. He had tubes coming out of every opening in his body. His condition stabilized after a day or two, but he was still listed as critical. Sinatra went on to New York City to conduct the album that Don had arranged for Sylvia Sims. Still being listed as critical, Don was visited one day by a local priest who said that every good Catholic should be given last rites, just in case his condition suddenly worsened. He had no idea that Don was definitely not a religious person. The priest then made the mistake of saying that he had heard that Don's mother passed away without having been given the last rites of the church and thus, she would not be in heaven. Don's reaction was like an eruption of Mount Etna, the Sicilian volcano. Up to that point, he was only able to answer questions by uttering, "Uh-uh," but now the tubes came flying out of his mouth and nose and he proceeded to verbally blister the priest, yelling things like, "My mother was a saint, and she didn't need anybody's help to get to heaven. Now, get the hell out of here!" The priest made a hasty exit and Don's tubes were re-inserted by the attending medicos.

The next day an attractive young nurse came by his room and she recognized his name at the foot of the bed. The tubes were still in his nose and throat. She excitedly asked if he was the man who arranged the music on all the hit records for Paul Anka. Don was only able to utter "Uh-uh." With every subsequent question she asked, his answer was always "Uh-uh." Not wanting to leave this wonderful musician, she asked if he would like to be bathed and, of course, you know the answer. She gently pulled the sheets back and began to bathe and massage Don's arms and legs. You guessed it. He became aroused and the young nurse smilingly said, "Oh, Mr. Costa, what have we here?" The usual "Uh-uh" crossed Don's lips. She then quietly closed the door to his room and orally began to relieve his "condition." Fortunately, no one interrupted this great therapeutic treatment.

The following day, the priest kindly paid Don another visit and before he could say one word, Don yelled, "Have you forgotten what I told you yesterday? Now, get out of here—and send that pretty nurse back in."

When he told me this story one year later, I roared with laughter and then chastised him by saying, "Didn't you realize you were on a life support system and were being monitored? You could have died right then and there!" He laughed and said, "Can you think of a better way to go?" He made a good point.

I was absolutely devastated when Don passed away on January 19, 1983. He died in New York City, and his body was shipped to Los Angeles at the request of his wife and family. The family decided to have a very religious ceremony at the Church of the Good Shepherd in Beverly Hills. I had a lengthy discussion with the priest who didn't seem to care that we were going to honor a famous musician. He was only concerned about his mass. He didn't give a damn about anything else. However, I got him to promise that after the mass, he would provide a microphone so that we could all share with each other our personal memories of Don. Quincy Jones agreed to deliver the eulogy that I had written.

It was raining like mad the day of the funeral and the church was jammed with Don's family and friends. I had put an audio cassette together with all of the songs that I knew Don loved and especially some compositions by Robert Farnon. Unfortunately, one of Don's nephews accidentally locked the playback machine in his car and he had misplaced his keys. I yelled at him to kick in the window and get the necessary equipment to play the cassette, which he eventually did. The music was quietly playing as mourners entered the church.

Shortly thereafter, we learned that the vehicle that was to transport Don's casket from the mortuary to the church had unexpectedly broken down and it would take another fifteen minutes to correct the situation. I was about to lose my mind, but somehow I managed to stay cool. Quincy got up on the altar and adlibbed, "Wouldn't you know that even at Don's funeral, we would start with a ten-minute break?" That certainly helped to ease the tension that was building up in the church.

When the mass finally ended, Quincy delivered the eulogy with great warmth and dignity. When I introduced Nancy Costa, who wanted to sing an original song in her dad's honor, the priest cut off the microphone. We carried on in spite of that mean old man's behavior and after a few more people spoke, we were all satisfied that we had paid our last respects to our dear friend, Don. Before closing out this chapter on Don, I would like you to read a little of what I wrote in his eulogy. Here it is:

If Don had one enemy in this world, it would have been the clock on the wall. He never seemed to have enough time. Of course, the fact that he was a great procrastinator never quite got through to him. He loved to hang out, to sit and rap about music, the record business, or whatever—never a dull moment. Phones were always ringing and what seemed like total confusion to most of us, was standard operating procedure for him. But somehow, at the very last minute, the arrangements got written and all of the tension and anxieties that many of us experienced disappeared ten seconds after the first downbeat. Whether it was a lush string sound, a stompin' jazz band, or a funky rhythmic feel, all those concerned with the recording date would sit back and bask in the glory of this man's great talent. He always said, "Give me a pencil, some score paper, a band, good singers, a studio, and leave me alone."

I hope that wherever his soul and energy are right now, things are calm and serene and all of his dreams and wishes are coming true.

GORDON JENKINS

In 1958 I got a call to play the piano on a record date for Gordon. He had a fabulous reputation as a composer, conductor, arranger, and songwriter. All of us New York City musicians were very attentive to this well-known person from Hollywood. You got the impression from his appearance that he was a stern taskmaster. But, somehow, underneath we sensed that he was a regular guy.

About fifteen years later, after my family had moved to Los Angeles, I received a phone call one evening from a man who sounded like he was drunk. He asked if I was the guy who had written a Bossa Nova album for Perry Como. When I asked him why he wanted to know, he answered, "That's the way to write for strings." When he told me he was Gordon Jenkins, I almost dropped the phone! What a great compliment coming from a man of his stature. We made a date for lunch the next day and I was surprised to learn that he had a serious speech defect that made him sound like he was a heavy drinker. It was the beginning of his bout with Lou Gehrig's disease. We bonded as friends immediately. He was warm, friendly, and knowledgeable about so many different things—*and* he had a great sense of humor. He loved sports and I soon realized that this man was not only a musical maven, but also a literary giant. We all know that he wrote both the music and lyrics to several standard pop songs like "P.S. I Love You," "Goodbye" (the Benny Goodman theme)) and many more complicated projects like "Manhattan Towers," "The Letter," starring Judy Garland, and "What It Was, Was Love" for Steve and Eydie. On the classical side, he wrote a very passionate anti-war *libretto* to the music of the "Sibelius First Symphony." It was really a significant piece of work called "The Voices of War" and one of which he was most proud.

He also wrote the arrangements on the hit records of "Lover," for Peggy Lee, and "Sleepy Time Down South," for Louis Armstrong. He always spoke so lovingly of Louie. I suspect that deep down, Gordon really wanted to be a jazz player.

He was born in St. Louis and, at an early age, learned to play the ukulele, guitar, accordion, piano, and organ. An early morning radio show gave him an opportunity to be four different, imaginary people. At fifteen-minute intervals, he would play one instrument and have a fake name. I asked what name he assumed when he played his fifteen-minute accordion section and he said, "Abe Snake." I never got that connection, but to this day, it still makes me laugh. He added that if after an hour, the personnel for the next show wouldn't arrive, he would start at the top and play the "whole damn program over again!" That reminded me of my watermelon story when I was a little kid.

He enjoyed telling me how he aspired, as a teenager, to go to New York City, study music and learn to arrange and conduct. (Boy, did that sound familiar) As we all know, he realized his dream.

I've always admired Gordon's versatility. He was perhaps one of the few men in our business who did it all. He was a player, an arranger, a composer, a conductor, a producer, and a lyricist. A real poet. Do yourself a favor and study the lyrics to "This Is All I Ask" or "The Red Balloon" and any number of others.

His association with Frank Sinatra was now legend. Frank once said of Gordon, "The way he writes for strings—if he were Jewish, he'd be unbearable!" Gordon had a very dramatic sense of orchestrating. His harmonic choices were not always what some of the contemporary musicians liked, but that didn't matter in the overall picture. His aim was to capture the true feeling of what the song was all about and what the performer was trying to transmit with his or her vocal rendition. It was no wonder that Sinatra loved him. He was a true dramatist.

When I asked him if he had ever studied classical orchestration, he said, "Hell, whenever I heard something I liked, I bought the score and stole the voicing." That confirmed the old saying that *good composers borrow, but great composers steal!*

Golf was one of his favorite hobbies. He got lucky one day and shot a hole in one on a par-three hole. His wife, Beverly, placed the trophy he received up on the mantelpiece in their front room. It actually embarrassed him because he said, "I topped my drive and the damn ball hit every stone and pebble on the way to the green. Then it just accidentally fell into the hole!"

My buddy, Terry Woodson and I spent many hours out at his beach house in Malibu, just yakking about sports, current events, and whatever was happening in the music business at the time. Gordon surprised Terry one day with a birthday gift package. When the wrapping was removed, we were surprised to see it was a cardboard egg carton. Strange gift, we both thought. However, Terry peeked inside expecting to see a dozen eggs, but instead, there were twelve shiny new golf balls.

On another afternoon, I played him a melody that I had written many years before after having seen the movie *The Diary of Anne Frank*. It brought tears to his eyes and he asked if he could write a lyric for it. I was thrilled. He titled the song "That's Love," and these are his beautiful lyrics:

> Like a flame made of ice, that's love.
> Sometimes mean, sometimes nice, that's love.
> There is no way to know, how a romance will go,
> First the blues, then the shoes and the rice.
>
> Love will aim shooting stars at you,
> And make those words that are old, sound new.
> And on that special day, if your heart flies away,
> Let it go, let it go, that's love.

His physical condition worsened day by day until he could no longer speak because of the paralysis of his tongue. But he still had all of his faculties. He communicated with me by writing on a large yellow paper scratch pad. We "talked" about how some of the best songs ever written were composed in just a short space of time. "This Is All I Ask" was one of my favorite songs of his and he admitted that it took him just an hour or two to write both the words and the music. He then proceeded to tell me (by writing on a scratch pad) how it all came about. He said he was walking by a large construction sight on Fifty-fourth Street in New York City one day when he noticed a crudely scribbled sign over a doorway used by the hard-hat workers. It read, "Pretty girls, walk a little slower."

He said that the rest was easy—however, "Somewhere in the Bronx, there is a pipe fitter I owe a bundle to." Then he added, "Don't get too close to me because I'm drooling a lot today." He never lost his sense of humor no matter what his physical condition was at the time.

The American Society of Music Arrangers and Composers wanted to honor him with a very special award. Since he was not able to physically attend the ceremony, I was chosen to inform him of the great honor that was being bestowed upon him. At this point, he was unable to speak, but his mind and wit were still as sharp as ever. When he printed out on his computer screen: "What in the hell are you trying to tell me?" I said that the members of ASMAC decided that he had made a great contribution to the world of music and we were going to honor him. He gave me a very disbelieving stare, and then I continued saying something like, "Listen, pal, you've written a lot of notes in your lifetime and—well—ah—some of them were even pretty good." He, of course, knew I was kidding. I went on to tell him how much we all loved and admired him. After a short pause, these two words came up on his computer screen, "No shit!"

As we all know, for over forty years Gordon wrote many beautiful, sensitive, dramatic arrangements and songs for perhaps every big singing star in the business. He was an incurable romantic, a perfectionist, a dreamer, a dramatist, a task master, and yet a guy who could be reduced to tears of joy by any singer or musician who really knew how to *turn a phrase*.

After an extended hospital stay, as a result of a bad auto accident, Gordon sent me a picture of the great body of George Atlas with all the rippling muscles showing. But somehow he managed to paste his own face on top of that body and printed at the bottom of the photo: "How's that for a recovery!"

One last story to illustrate his crazy sense of humor. He had just returned home from another hospital stay due to the Lou Gehrig's disease and was having difficulty walking and speaking. Although he was ambulatory, he still had many tubes protruding from his body and the stares of a fellow patient annoyed the hell out of him. Here is what the note read that he had waiting for me when I paid him a visit.

"When I was still in the hospital, my son Bruce was walking me around, and there was this guy staring at me and all my tubes.

Bruce said, 'Why don't you go over and speak to him?' I went over to him and said, 'Fuck you!' He answered, 'I'm fine. How are you feeling?'" Gordon's note ended with, "That's when I knew I had a speech problem."

Gordon had amazing stamina to hang in there for so many years, in spite of all his medical problems. However, he finally gave up and one morning I was saddened to receive a phone call from his son telling me that "Dad took the midnight train last night." I had heard Gordon use that expression before—referring to an old friend of his who had passed away.

We shared many good times together and I am grateful that he brightened my life.

How's That For Recovery!

How's That for a Recovery!

Gordon's face on the torso of George Atlas

HENRY MANCINI

Henry and I first met when he was a guest star on the Perry Como *Music from Hollywood* television special in 1977. I enjoyed sitting in the control room, listening to him record his beautiful music for the show. It was a long and tiring day and the last thing we recorded was an arrangement I had written for Perry on the theme from the movie *Love Story*. When the session ended, Henry came over and gave me his baton. Before I could ask why, he shook my hand and said, "That's for your arrangement of *Love Story*." Talk about making my day—I felt so honored.

At the actual taping two days later, the director told Henry and Perry about how he was going to photograph the scene with the two of them performing *The Days of Wine and Roses*. Henry knew exactly what key he wanted to play his piano solo in, but Perry was not sure of what key he wanted to sing it in (as he was prone to do at times). At this point, Henry said to me, "After I play my solo part of the song and the camera moves away from my hands on the keyboard and pans up to Perry singing, why don't you accompany him [in whatever key he wants] on that piano over there in the wings, and I will pretend to keep on playing." The director, the audio engineer and Perry all agreed. Henry and I had a ball trying to second guess each other. When I played an arpeggio, he would move his arms toward the upper register of the piano keyboard and vice versa, when I played something in the lower register. The video monitor, placed beside my piano, made it possible for me to watch every move Henry made. During the rehearsals, we really had a good time trying to trick each other. Como enjoyed our shenanigans, knowing that when we got on the air, everything would be OK—and it was.

Ginny and Henry hosted many fund-raising parties at their home to benefit the Jack Elliott Symphonic Jazz Orchestra. For a couple of years, I was the piano accompanist for the celebrity singers who appeared. Henry was most cordial and we always had a good time together. I regret that our paths didn't cross more often because we were both raised in strong Italian families and I felt that we were from the same cut of the cloth in so many ways.

Prior to Henry's untimely death, as a result of cancer, he was honored at a giant benefit concert at UCLA. I will never forget the inspiring speech he made, directed to all of the students sitting up in the balcony. I know many of them have gone on to achieve success as a result of Henry's encouraging words. Particularly now, with the establishment of the Henry Mancini Institute in Los Angeles headed by the great composer, arranger, conductor, Patrick Williams. It's a summertime program where carefully selected young music students from all over the country can study and perform with some of the best musicians in the world.

At the recommendation of John Williams, I was called by the Pittsburgh Symphony in 1995 to conduct some of Henry's compositions at a concert celebrating the one hundredth anniversary of the orchestra. Henry was born in the nearby town of Aliquippa and his musical compositions were an integral part of this exciting event.

In April of 1998, I was privileged to return to Pittsburgh to play piano and conduct the symphony orchestra for five concerts featuring the many pop and symphonic compositions of their famous "hometown boy," Henry Mancini. It was indeed an honor and I will cherish those wonderful musical memories for the rest of my life.

JOHN WILLIAMS

I first met John while I was conducting the *Kennedy Center Honors* television show in Washington, DC. Lerner and Loewe were being honored and John was there to pay his musical respect to them. It was a heavy program for me to conduct and I had also written a ton of orchestral arrangements for the occasion. Knowing that John Williams was in the wings, watching and listening to all that was going on, really kept me on my toes. At the end of the program, I gave him back the baton he had left on the conductor's stand during his appearance. He smiled and said, "Thank you,

Nick, but after watching how you handled the orchestra, it's yours—
if you would like it." I loved it.

A year or so later, John was again, a guest conductor on the
Kennedy Center Honors. On that same program, I arranged and
conducted a medley of Jerome Kern songs for the world famous
soprano, Fredrica Von Stade. John liked what he heard and he
asked Fredrica to include that medley in her upcoming concert
with the Boston Pops orchestra. I was invited to be her piano
accompanist. It was very exciting for me to sit at that beautiful
concert grand piano and make music with John, Fredrica and the
wonderful Pops orchestra.

In 1988, Perry Como was hired by Bill Cosell and the Boston
Pops to perform his Bing Crosby tribute. I was delighted when
John asked me to re-orchestrate the entire medley for the Pops
orchestra. Strange as it may seem, Perry was a bit apprehensive
singing in front of such a large ensemble. He didn't think they
could play *softly* enough for him. They certainly could, and they
did, and he was very happy with everything that transpired. As
soon as we got back to the hotel after the concert, I was happy to
see Perry rush to a phone and call John to thank him for the
wonderful musical experience we had all shared.

NELSON RIDDLE

Back in the early fifties, Don Costa, Marion Evans, and I often
sat and listened to the latest recordings from the West Coast. Along
with Billy May, Nelson really got our attention. He had a unique
style that was all his own and I could tell a Riddle arrangement
after hearing just the first few bars.

It wasn't until many years later in Las Vegas, that I finally got to
meet him in person. I was conducting for Steve and Eydie at Caesar's
Palace and I had arranged a long medley of contemporary rock-type
songs. One night after the show, I walked into Steve's dressing room
and there was Nelson Riddle. I was surprised because I had no idea
he was even in town. He was most complimentary of the medley I
had written. I told him how much he had influenced me and many

of my musician friends back in New York City. He was very modest and changed the subject. We sat and drank and chatted for a long time and Steve kept us entertained with lots of funny stories.

Back in Los Angeles, a couple of years later, Terry Woodson set up a lunch date with Nelson. We had a great time and this meeting gave me an opportunity to get to know the real man. He had a troubled personal life, but he still had a great sense of humor and he was fun to be with.

He rejuvenated Linda Ronstadt's career with his arrangement of "What's New" and the albums that followed. He had already done that many times for other artists as well. His association with Linda lasted for several years until he became ill.

He called me one day and asked if I would sub for him and conduct the orchestra for an upcoming Ronstadt concert in Las Vegas. Naturally, I agreed to do whatever he wished. He told me to get the music from Terry Woodson and to send a big bill to Linda. I told him I would be his sub for no fee—I just wanted him to get well and back on his feet. He thanked me for the kind, consoling words but absolutely insisted that I ask for lots of money. Just before we hung up he said, "You gotta remember Nick, you and I are the last of a dying breed." I must admit that Linda's manager was most cordial and generous. And I was off to Las Vegas. The concert was a big success.

In the meantime, Nelson's physical condition grew steadily worse and on October 6, 1985, he passed away. I was called in to finish conducting the album that he and Linda had almost completed. It was an emotional recording session for me and all of the musicians in the orchestra, many of whom were his personal old friends. Nelson will live forever in the hearts and souls of all of us who loved the good music of his era.

For several years, I continued conducting for Linda Ronstadt, but eventually we could not reconcile our personality differences. She had a great voice, but musically, we were poles apart. Although she was a famous recording star, her rudeness toward many of the live audiences was difficult for me to handle. I don't expect our paths will ever cross again.

PERCY FAITH

I have always been aware of Percy Faith and his great talent as an arranger, composer, and conductor. It was not surprising to learn he was one of Robert Farnon's early mentors. My only regret is that in all my years in New York City, our paths never crossed.

Thanks again to Terry Woodson, I was chosen to conduct a series of albums featuring Percy's music for a large Japanese company (JVC). They wanted to have it recorded in a digital format. Over a period of approximately three years, we made four albums. Our contractor, Joe Soldo assembled a fabulous studio orchestra. I studied Percy's scores so that I knew almost every note in them. Terry Woodson produced all of the sessions and he sat in the booth with the recording engineer, Armin Steiner. We did our best to recreate precisely what Percy had originally done. His wife, Dolly and his daughter, Marilyn often told me that they were pleased at how sensitively I interpreted Percy's music.

While reading an article one day about Percy, I was surprised to learn that we were both born on April 7. It all seemed so strange because just at that time, we were recording another of Percy's albums. During one of the orchestra breaks, I showed Marilyn my driver's license, hoping she would notice my birth date. She took one quick look at my photo and said, "That's the ugliest picture I've ever seen." We both laughed, but when she noticed my birth date, she couldn't believe it. We all got teary-eyed when she told her mother that Percy and I were both born on April 7. I remember Dolly saying, "I knew it, I knew it." She felt that that was the reason I understood Percy's music so well.

For years, Japanese audiences have loved Percy's music and his tours of Japan are always sold out. His arrangement of *Summer Place* was and still is very popular over there.

Percy himself, along with a great studio orchestra from Hollywood, toured Japan many times in the sixties and seventies. I was told that on one of their early tours, a very humorous incident took place.

The concert began with a tympani roll—the lights were dimmed, and just as the curtain slowly began to rise, a Japanese announcer was heard saying over the loud speakers, "And now, radies and gentermen, here is the music of Pussy Face." Well, this became another one of the longest tympani rolls in history because all of the musicians in the orchestra were laughing so hard that they could not play. Ever since then, many musicians jokingly refer to Percy by his mispronounced Japanese name.

I have been privileged to conduct the Percy Faith orchestra tours of Japan in 1996, 1999, and 2001. Because of unexpected back surgery, I was unable to make the tour in May of 2003 and Terry Woodson ably took over for me.

On our tour in 1996, I learned from the promoter, Mr. Ito that one of our concerts was going to be videotaped and I would be interviewed afterward. I decided to put on a brand-new white jacket for the occasion. After the opening downbeat, the curtain slowly began to rise and when the lights came up, I was horrified to notice that I had absent-mindedly forgotten to remove a large price tag that was sewn on to the left arm sleeve of my jacket! The store name, size, and price were boldly printed in black. The tag was very visible to the orchestra members and people sitting down front in the audience. You can imagine my embarrassment and frustration during the next two selections as I tried to make my conducting moves coincide with my efforts to rip that damn tag off my sleeve. I finally succeeded and everyone, except me, found it to be very amusing.

Percy's arrangements deliver a very special message because they capture all of the human emotions that are pertinent to the melody and lyrics of the song. Many times, while I'm conducting the orchestra in the middle of a concert, I feel a lump come up in my throat because his orchestration of certain passages is so very personal. Perhaps that is why his music transcends all language barriers. It really deals with one's emotions.

Having a drink with Gene De Paul in my kitchen

GENE DE PAUL

Our paths crossed several times when I was living in New York City. But after I moved to Los Angeles, we became very close friends. Besides the fact that we both came from Italian families, we also had a lot in common regarding the way we felt about music, the melodic and harmonic structures of popular tunes.

Gene wrote most of his songs while he was under contract to various film studios and when the movie was released, his music was automatically heard by audiences all over the world. The composers in Hollywood, who worked under those conditions, had a big advantage over the songwriters from Tin Pan Alley or any other place in the country because they got immediate exposure for their tunes. But no matter where he was, Gene's talent would not be denied. Along with Don Raye as his lyricist, he wrote such beautiful standards as "I'll Remember April," "Star Eyes," "He's My Guy," "You Don't Know What Love Is," and many more. Two of his big Hollywood successes were the movies *Lil Abner* and *Seven Brides for Seven Brothers*. Gene wrote all of the songs and Johnny Mercer was the lyricist.

After his wife Billie passed away and his children grew up, Gene became a member of our family. We all enjoyed his crazy sense of humor and, as a result, we shared many holidays and birthdays together. Golf became a different game when we played by a very silly set of rules that he made up. Great fun.

Gene always pleaded poverty even though we all knew he made a good living as a result of his American Society of Composers, Authors and Publishers (ASCAP) royalties. Every Halloween he locked up his house and came over to our place so that he didn't have to go out and buy candy for all the neighborhood children who would come by trick-or-treating. Gene's own kids and my family often recall his many miserly traits, which have endeared him even more to all of us. Those memories will always provide us with a lot of laughs.

At Gene's funeral, Sammy Cahn told how they were turned down by over thirty different singers and publishers when they tried to promote one of their songs. As a result, they published it themselves and along with Gene, it ended up earning Sammy more money than any other song he had ever written. I will always love "Teach Me Tonight"—and that story.

DICK HYMAN

We actually grew up together in the music business back in New York City in the early fifties. His versatility as a pianist is astounding. Dick can immediately improvise and play whatever style you might choose. His technique and imagination defy description. One afternoon at a lawn party with several musicians and their families, he was persuaded to play a couple of tunes. Bob

Rosengarden requested the Beatles' song "Let it Be," and to make it worse, he added, "and play it in a Chinese style." Dick thought for a minute while we were all laughing about that silly request. He then proceeded to improvise an absolutely magical jazz version of the song, using the traditional Chinese melodic and harmonic sounds. We were all blown away.

He has a remarkable sense of humor, and I find it interesting that Woody Allen has chosen Dick to score practically every one of his films.

Early on in his career, he had a hit record on "Mack the Knife." I was told that it happened quite by accident at the end of a regular recording session. When someone realized that they still had some time left, Dick whistled the tune and accompanied himself on piano along with bass and drums. The record became a smash and the recording company was anxious to re-sign him immediately. Dick agreed, but only on the condition that he be allowed to record a piano concerto that he had just composed. They agreed to pay for a fifty-five-piece symphonic orchestra, which was unheard of in the pop recording field at that time. I was privileged to be the conductor. The composition was challenging for all the musicians because it encompassed both classical and pop thematic material. Many New York Philharmonic musicians were hired along with the top pop jazz studio players in town.

It was recorded in two sessions. The first day, we did the opening movement, and the following day, we did the second and third movements. All was going well but I sensed that some of the classical players were bored with the pop jazz portions of the composition.

As is customary in almost all concertos, the third movement is where the solo cadenza takes place. In the days of Mozart and Beethoven, this was the moment when a performer was expected to improvise on the thematic material previously played. I mentioned in an earlier chapter that improvised cadenzas became a rarity shortly after the beginning of the twentieth century.

After having made a good recording of the last movement, we decided there was still time to make another take. After we finished that, Dick was still not pleased and he insisted that we immediately make another final take. I suggested that in the interest of time, and since he had already improvised two different solo cadenzas, we should skip the cadenza and cut directly to the coda. He would not hear of it, and we started off again. We all, including Dick, had our eyes on a large clock that was in the studio because we knew that overtime would not be allowed. Dick, loving the challenge of all this, played another *entirely different improvised* cadenza which surprised and thrilled everyone. Now *all* of the classical musicians were really enthused. Shortly after I made the final orchestral cut off, the entire orchestra stood up, applauded, and cheered Dick. After the noise subsided, I yelled over to Dick and invited him and his wife Julia, to come to a party at my house. We were going to have a "piano burning"—mine!

When the record was released, I was pleased that Dick took my advice and included the extra two cadenzas at the end of the album. It is called *Concerto Electro,* and it's on Command-ABC Records.

STAN FREEMAN

Shortly after graduating from Juilliard, I met Stan Freeman, a fantastic pianist. In addition to being a top-notch studio musician, he performed in many east side nightclubs. Stan also had a good reputation as a comedy writer and as a singer-performer with a very low, raspy voice. Years later, he did a one-man show impersonating Oscar Levant, the chain-smoking humorist and pianist friend of George Gershwin. Sadly, the show never got to Broadway, but Stan was absolutely brilliant.

In the late eighties, Carol Burnett asked Stan to come to California and work as a comedy writer on her television show. He was reluctant to leave New York because he was born and raised there, and the thought of having to uproot, sell his apartment, move to Los Angeles and change his entire lifestyle was definitely not appealing to him. However, Carol's management team did not give up and they finally persuaded Stan to make the move to Hollywood.

Near the end of his very first season in California, he was crushed to learn that the Burnett show was not going to be renewed for the following year. It was going off the air. *Now*, Stan was *really unhappy* for having left New York City.

At the closing night party, everyone had a chance to sing or say something nice in honor of Carol. Stan chose to sing "You Light Up My Life," a very popular song at that time. What nobody knew was that he had written a new set of lyrics for the chorus of the song. He started out and sentimentally sang the verse, exactly as it was written. Then, after a long piano arpeggio, what everyone expected to hear was, "you . . . light up my life," but what came out of Stan's mouth was "*Yooooooooooooo* fucked up my life—" That's all anybody heard of the rest of that song—they were all on the floor laughing, Carol included.

JERRY BRUNO

Jerry and I first met in NYC in the late forties when he was playing with the Vaughn Monroe band. We soon became close friends and from our very early days in the recording business, he played bass on practically every recording Don Costa or I ever made—particularly those we did at Bell Sound. Since I was the conductor, he, along with all of the other musicians became accustomed, and sometimes annoyed, with me constantly asking them to play *softly*, especially when we were accompanying a singer. It made the recording engineer's job so much easier because we didn't have the luxury of re-mixing the over-all sound once the orchestra departed.

Many years later, I got a call from Jerry asking me to put together an orchestra because he was coming out to L.A. to *conduct* for a new performer. Joe Sold assembled a great band consisting of many of our New York buddies like Chauncey Welsch, Bobby Tricarico and Don Ashworth. We were happy about the fact that Jerry had a new gig as a conductor, in addition to being the great bass player that we all knew him to be. Even Don Costa showed up and played guitar— I played piano. It was a happy reunion for all of us.

After rehearsing a couple of arrangements, I noticed that the next selection was only for piano and voice. The soloist wasn't there so I asked Jerry to give me an idea if it was to be played in tempo or ad lib. He said he wasn't sure, but he wanted to hear me play the song anyway. Shortly after I started, he came up beside me—paused for a moment—and then suddenly, at the top of his voice, he yelled out, "SSSHHHHH!!!! Play it SOFT!" I was so shocked by his outburst that I stopped playing. With a big smile on his face, he said, "I've been waiting twenty fucking years to tell *you* that!" The band broke up laughing because I think that (in their minds) many of them had also been wanting for years to say the same thing to me.

At lunch with Terry Woodson and Joe Soldo

JOE SOLDO and TERRY WOODSON

In the early seventies, two men became an integral part of my professional life—Joe Soldo and Terry Woodson. Joe and I originally met and worked together in New York City. He played with many big name bands and was one of the best 1st alto sax-reed players on both coasts. He eventually became a first call studio player. After we both moved to California, I chose him to be the orchestra contractor for all of my personal recording and television projects. In addition to being an excellent instrumentalist and knowing who and where all the best players are, he has a very special sense of humor. His unique comedic talent enables him to come up with words and phrases, on the spur of the moment, that can change a potentially tense moment into a laugh riot. Yo, Joe!

Initially, Mac McDougald and Newcomb Rath were my California music copyists. But as years went by, Terry Woodson gradually became my No. 1 man. Bass trombone was his original instrument, and he played with several well-known orchestras, namely Henry Mancini and Percy Faith. He is also a composer and an arranger, but as years went by, he became more and more involved as a copyist and music supervisor. Because of his instinctive music and incredible technological skills, he is invaluable to any arranger or orchestrator. Currently, he is also the conductor of the orchestra for Frank Sinatra, Jr.

In addition to being my business associates, both Joe and Terry are two of my closest personal friends. We have shared many good times together, along with our respective families, and I know that we still have lots of music to make and wine to drink in the coming years.

CHAPTER 24

"OFF CAMERA" HEROES

Nick Vanoff and I at the Kennedy Center in Washington D.C.

NICK VANOFF

In the early fifties, Nick started out as a cue card boy on the early fifteen-minute *Perry Como* television show and eventually worked his way up to become an assistant to Lee Cooley, the director and producer. But after a while, he decided to move on to greener pastures. He worked hard behind the scenes of other early television shows and finally in 1960, he returned to the Como show as the producer. He loved Perry and the feeling was mutual. Perry was a father figure to Nick. Around 1960, he moved to Los Angeles and became an important figure in television production.

I can thank Nick for making me the musical director of the *Hollywood Palace*, *The Don Knotts Show*, *The Big Show*, and *The Kennedy Center Honors*.

In 1974, he again produced several television specials for Perry. During the rehearsal period for one of the shows, we had a production meeting in a small cottage out behind the posh Beverly Hills Hotel. I sneaked off into the tiny kitchenette in Perry's suite to make some pepper and egg sandwiches that I knew he loved. While I was slicing the peppers, Nick walked in. When he saw what I was doing, he started to laugh and said, "Move over and let me show you how to do it." I thought he was kidding, until he added, "My father owned a diner in Buffalo when I was a little kid, and I grew up in the kitchen." He really did show me how to slice and fry the peppers. That incident further served to cement our relationship. P.S. . . . As a youngster, he also played the accordion.

Nick produced a one-man show on Broadway for Jackie Mason, the comedian. On one of my trips to New York City after finishing the *Kennedy Center Honors* television special, Nick left two complimentary tickets for me at the box office. My buddy Marion Evans, was busy that night and none of my other friends were available to go with me. I phoned Nick and told him not to waste a good ticket because I was coming alone.

I had a perfect seat in the middle of the theatre and was pleased to see an attractive young lady sit down beside me with her date next to her. Just before curtain time, another pretty escorted young lady sat down on the other side of me. We exchanged pleasantries and the show began. Jackie, of course, was brilliant and he had the audience in stitches.

At the end of the show, I noticed a lot of black electric cables in the aisle going from the stage to the back of the theatre. After meeting Nick in the lobby and thanking him for the great seat, I asked him why all the cables. He said, "Oh, didn't you know? We videotaped the show tonight. Why don't you go outside to the remote truck and say hello to the guys?" When I opened the door of the trailer truck control room, I recognized all my old pals. We yakked for a few minutes and as I started to leave, Dwight Hemion, the director thanked me for being such a great audience. I didn't understand what he meant by that, but I waved goodbye to the guys and left.

Como's wife, Roselle saw the show when it aired on television in Florida and immediately called Mickey Glass, Perry's manager, in New York City. She told him that it was disgusting that I allowed myself to be photographed with what she thought were two obvious "hookers"—one on either side of me.

A week or so later, my son Terry called me from San Diego where he was employed as a stockbroker. He was a bit uncomfortable trying to explain to me that he had also seen the *Jackie Mason* television show and saw me sitting there, very conspicuously, with a beautiful "babe" on either side of me. Before I could explain, he went on to say that I should make sure none of our other family members saw the program. Boy, talk about "getting the name without the game." It was then that I realized why Dwight Hemion thanked me for being such a good audience. Vanoff had told them where I was seated and they had a camera trained on me.

Along with his wife Felice, a gifted choreographer, Nick and I climbed *many mountains* together during the production of several Kennedy Honors television specials. He knew, many times that he was asking for the impossible, but for Nick, the entire production crew rallied to the cause. He died much too early and I will always miss him. He was a true friend and a giant in the television entertainment industry.

I am one of the few still around who started working and performing on television when it was in its infancy, and I have had the opportunity to work with many different producers and directors. Besides Nick Vanoff and Dwight Hemion whom I have mentioned many times before, I must mention some other individuals who are real pros in the field of television.

BOB BANNER and MARTY PASETTA

Banner has been in television since the very beginning. I feel safe in saying that he is one of the very few who "wrote the book" on how to produce a television show. I speak for many of my colleagues when I say that I've never worked with a kinder, more considerate and knowledgeable gentleman. We combined efforts on many television specials for Perry Como, in cities all over the world and his very presence always made things easier for everyone. Why he is not in the television Hall of Fame is a perfect example of the injustices that often occur in the entertainment industry.

Stephen Pouliot, one of Bob's close associates, was a major participant in all of the Banner television productions that were done for Como. He is a marvelous writer and director. Like Bob, he is a kind, gentle, courteous, and talented man, who currently is one of the busiest individuals in television—a position in the industry he justly deserves. And, as an aside, he is also one of the people who encouraged me to write this book and arrive at the title *I Just Happened to Be There*.

Buz Kohan is another dear old friend and talented writer-producer who fits the same description I just gave Steve Pouliot. I have great respect for men like Buz and Steve, who have the magic ability to put words together that really communicate—whatever the moment or the occasion may demand.

Marty Pasetta was one of the most technically knowledgeable of all producers. He sometimes made impossible demands, but if he changed his mind at the last minute, he'd always ask, "How much time do you need to fix it?" Marty totally understood the inner workings of everyone's job. We did many projects together and no matter how involved they were, I always felt he was right there beside me.

I have had the privilege to work with many other creative behind-the-scenes people. George Stevens, Jr., Bill Harbach, Don Mischer, Jeff Margolis, Saul Turtletaub, and Sterling Johnson are just a few of the other directors and writers who have helped me learn and grow in the exciting world of television. The list could go on and on, but I will save that for another book that I hope to write one day.

SAMMY CAHN

To say "he had a way with words" is really being much too simplistic. We met many times down through the years at various functions and he was a big fan of Perry, and he always suggested that we write a song together.

In 1988 I called and made a date with him to play a new song I had just written. He was very cordial and hospitable when I arrived at his home in Beverly Hills. We chatted for a few minutes and then I started to play my song. After only a few bars, I was asked to stop because he had to answer an important phone call. After another few minutes, I started playing again, but his wife suddenly burst into the room saying the pool man was there and they needed Sammy's advice. He apologized when he came back into the room and said, "Sorry, Nick—please play it again." This time I got about as far as the twelfth bar when still another interruption occurred. Again, he excused himself. Then I was ready to leave and come back another day. I mentioned that to him when he returned, but he assured me that nothing else was going to happen. He sat at his typewriter and told me to start once again from the top. I finally played the entire song all the way through. I had a dummy title for the tune thinking it might be of help to him, but he didn't want to hear it. After a moment of silence, he asked me to play just the first eight bars, which I did. He started to type immediately and then asked for the next eight bars. We went through this same routine eight bars at a time until in a very short time, the song was over and he had finished the lyrics. I couldn't believe his speed.

He removed the paper from the typewriter and proceeded to recite his lyrics to me. I fell in love with his beautiful poetry. When he got to the middle of the song, he stopped and asked me, "What was that dummy lyric of yours?" I answered, "Screw you, you are doing just fine!" Then, he read the rest of what he had written. It was absolutely perfect. All told, I was there for only forty-five minutes and he had captured lyrically all of the passionate feelings that I had hoped the melody would inspire. The song is called "Making Love to You." I recorded it with Perry Como, but until you hear him sing it, take a look at Sammy's passionate poetry.

> I'd love to spend my whole life through, making love to you.
> It's just the nicest thing I do, making love to you.
> Each time we're face to face, music fills the air.
> And then, when we embrace, I hear violins, our song begins.
> I never dreamed that you could be making love to me.
> That dream is now reality, you are here with me.
> Each night the miracle of rainbows come in view,
> Because I'm making love to you.

Sammy was one of the greatest popular lyric writers the world has ever known. His fans are legion and I am forever grateful that I had the opportunity to work with this poetic genius. We all know he also had a great sense of humor. He was once asked," When you are working on a new song, which comes first, the words or the music?" He quickly answered, "The check."

BOB WYNN

In 1987 Bob Wynn was hired to be the director and the producer of a Como Christmas television special emanating from San Antonio, Texas. I enjoyed conducting the local symphony orchestra and chorus. Bob performed a difficult task because Perry, at this point in his professional career, was ambivalent about any and all things connected with rehearsing. He was never angry or disrespectful to anyone, but it was clear that he felt we all knew what we were doing and everything would be fine. Along with Dick Williams, our choral director; the wonderful actress-entertainer, Angie Dickinson; Julia Migenes, the incredible operatic soprano and a great crew of technicians with my pal, Terry Woodson advising in the audio booth; the show came off very well.

In the early nineties, Como indicated many times to both Mickey Glass and I that he had lost his desire and enthusiasm to continue going on the road. For the first time in his life, he kept referring to his singing career as "work." Mickey remembers him saying, "In what other profession do you see an eighty-year-old man running around the country doing what he did better thirty years ago?" He still had a great voice and we, along with Bob Wynn, tried to convince him that his fans worldwide still wanted to see and hear him sing. I think our pleas fell on deaf ears, but somehow he was talked into doing one more Christmas television special and again, Bob was the producer and director. That television special was prerecorded in Dublin, Ireland and videotaped on a Friday night, January 21, 1994. The show aired on television in the United States during the Christmas season—*ten months* later!

Bob Wynn and I, along with Dick Williams, our choral director, arrived in Dublin, Ireland in early January 1994, in order to rehearse the various acts and choral groups that were scheduled to perform on the show. As a Christmas present for my two sons, I brought them along to Ireland. They had a ball visiting all the famous historical landmarks and sampling various ales in the local Irish pubs. I wanted go along on their fun trips, but I was too busy rehearsing or writing arrangements.

The Glasnevin choir was a delight, both musically and socially. It was made up of local citizens from all walks of life. Dick Williams did a great job rehearsing them nightly with the help of their director, Niamb Mcdonough. At the end of each session, I came in to inform the choir of what I wanted musically so that it would all coordinate with what I knew the orchestra was going to play, especially since I had written all of the orchestrations. Their enthusiasm and desire to please was overwhelming. Since it was Christmas music we were singing, I kept telling them I wanted to hear *angelic* voices. I rehearsed some portions of the music over and over and I told them, "When it's right, we will all know it." A few nights later and again after a lot of rehearsing, that *magic moment* occurred. When I cut them off, there was a dramatic moment of silence—and then all hell broke loose because they realized what I was trying to achieve. At around 9 PM, it was time to call it quits, but they all refused to go home. We continued rehearsing and making music for another hour and a half. I felt like I died and had gone to heaven.

One day, after a long rehearsal, I jokingly asked a lovely young lass behind the hotel counter if I had any messages from anyone asking for my body. She was a bit embarrassed, but after a moment, she very politely informed me that "there are none, suh." The next day after another very long rehearsal, I was really exhausted as I approached the counter and again, I asked the question about anyone wanting my body. This time the lovely lass very politely asked me to "wait a moment, suh," and, in a matter of seconds, she and all of her friends in the back room brought out three big boxes, filled with small scrap pieces of paper. The ladies, in unison and with big smiles on their faces, told me, "Here are all your messages, suh."

A production meeting was scheduled in Perry Como's suite for 1:30 PM on January 17. I was busy in my room writing an arrangement and I knew I was going to be late for the meeting. Suddenly, the phone rang and Bob Wynn said, "Turn your television set on immediately to station CNN." Well, when I saw what had happened and was still happening in Los Angeles, I was horrified! A giant earthquake had just hit the city and all I could see were fires burning all over the area. When the announcer mentioned names of streets right near my home, I almost panicked. I tried telephoning my wife and my daughter, but I could not get through to them. I raced up to Como's suite, and he, Mickey, and Bob were all watching CNN. Perry sensed my panic and he came over and put his arms around me and wouldn't let me go. He just kept saying in my ear, "Don't worry, Nicolo, everything is going to be OK." After several more agonizing minutes, we received a phone call from Bob's secretary Annette, in Los Angeles saying that Bob's wife, Cecile and their house were OK but shaken up pretty badly. She then said that my wife, Judy was safe but our house was a disaster. I didn't give a damn about the house but I was so relieved to know that Judy and my daughter, Jennie, and her husband Scott, were all right. Perry insisted that the rest of the day be spent just relaxing—no work. My sons, Danny and Terry were on the earliest plane back to Los Angeles. They had made phone contact with Shelia Lewis, Danny's girlfriend (now his wife), and she and her family were OK. I still had another week to be in Ireland before I could return home. What an emotional time this was for both Bob Wynn and myself.

When I walked into the rehearsal room the evening after the Los Angeles earthquake, the entire choir stood up and started shouting, "Is your family OK? Is everything all right back home?" They didn't want to know about rehearsing until I assured them that I was fine and my family was safe and sound. It was another "teary" experience for me.

After the final taping of the television show, I went backstage to say goodbye to all the musicians and singers who were just mingling around. One older gentleman approached me and asked, "Kin ah 'ave a picture with ya', mate?" After that, he asked, "Mind if ah give ya' a hug?" Well, after an hour of hugging and taking photos with practically everyone on the stage, I sadly said goodbye. What a wonderful human experience that was for me—such dear people!

Thanks to the efforts of a lovely Irish lady performer named Twink, the cooperation of a great orchestra, Dick Willians and the Glasnevin choir, and various other Irish performers—Bob was again able to make magic and we walked away with another television winner. Unfortunately, I am sad to say, it was not one of Como's better performances and when the television special aired, ten months later, it was the most widely viewed show of his entire career. Bob Wynn deserves a special medal for having to solve so many unexpected problems that arose at the very last moment.

Being in Ireland and dealing with all the local folks was indeed a heart-warming experience. They all possessed a great sense of humor and yet, they were very proper and serious when the situation called for it.

I am forever hopeful that one day, before *I take the midnight train*, I will have an opportunity to go back to Dublin, Ireland and again make music with my dear Irish friends.

I left Ireland on Saturday, January 22, the day after our videotaping and flew home to Los Angeles. I was scheduled to conduct the Cerebral Palsy telethon, as I had done many years before. Even though I missed the opening Saturday night portion of the show, Marty Pasetta, the producer insisted I conduct the long portion on Sunday. Mrs. Pat Mitchell, our dear family friend, picked me up at the airport late Saturday night (everyone was trying to keep me away from seeing my devastated home) and gave me shelter for that evening. The next morning, she drove me to the studio for the Sunday portion of the telethon. In spite of the fact that I was in somewhat of a daze, everything went well. After the show, Joe Soldo drove me home. It was the longest ride of my life. He assured me that my family was all right, but he warned me to be prepared for the horror of seeing what the earthquake had done to my house. I was in shock for several days afterward, but thanks to the help and kindness of many of my dear neighbors and friends, we all survived. After one year and over four hundred thousand dollars in damages, we were back to normal.

HARRY CRANE

This man was one of the funniest and most prolific comedy writers in television. He told me that on one occasion, he got very upset at a production meeting because a producer cut out several portions of the script that Harry felt were very funny. Nobody seemed to care about his new suggestions. He then knew he had to go home and do a lot of rewriting. Just before the meeting came to an end, he received his weekly paycheck, which amounted to a tidy sum. He stormed out of the room and while walking out to the parking lot, he kept grumbling to himself about how nobody appreciated his talent and life was a big drag. When he climbed into his beautiful big Mercedes Benz, he threw his briefcase down on the passenger's seat beside him and his check accidentally fell out. He angrily drove away and while waiting for the red light to change at a big intersection, he couldn't help but notice the car next to him. It was an old beat-up jalopy with many different coats of paint and it had big dents all over it. There were rosary beads and a little Jesus figure hanging down from the rearview mirror above the dashboard. An old Mexican laborer was in the driver's seat. They exchanged glances and just as the light turned green, the poor guy waved to Harry and gave him a big smile. At that moment, Harry accidentally glanced down on the seat next to him and he couldn't help but notice the dollar amount of his check. It gave him cause to reconsider his frustration and anger. As his car slowly started up across the intersection, he suddenly found himself singing—"Zip-a-dee-do-da, zip-a-dee-ay—my oh my, what a wonderful day"—and he happily sang that song all the way home.

Harry enjoyed telling a story about Forrest Tucker, a handsome old movie star. One afternoon after a round of golf, he was showering and many of his show business friends were in the locker room with him. Forrest was gifted in the "male appendage department," and Bob Hope was supposed to have asked him, "Aren't you afraid that *thing* might turn on you one day?"

RICHARD MATHESON and DICK WILLIAMS

Matheson is a famous author of more than forty books. He is a giant in the sci-fi field and along with Rod Serling, he was one of the writers of the old television thriller series *Twilight Zone*. Two of his most popular movie stories are *Somewhere In Time* and *Duel*, which was one of Steven Spielberg's first film projects. Since we are also neighbors, we have spent many joyous social hours together with his wife, Ruth and our dear friends, Bunny and Dr. Brian Herdeg and Dody and Walt Steiner. I am thankful to this group for their encouragement and making it possible for me to accomplish one of my greatest secret desires. And that was, to be a director of a theatrical production. My dream came true when I was able to stage and direct two plays with our local theatre group. *Same Time Next Year* was followed by Neil Simon's *California Suite*. I have always loved the challenge of taking audiences to different emotional places by means of the dramatic power of the spoken word. If their imaginations can be provoked, they can be whoever they want to be and travel to places that are truly magical—the wonderful world of "Make Believe." It was and will always be a very exciting aspect of being in show business. "I Wish It Could Be Christmas Forever" and "Do You Remember Me" are two of the many songs Rich and I have written together. I look forward to writing many more songs with this literary master.

Dick Williams and I first worked together in the commercial jingle business in New York City, but it wasn't until we both moved to California in the early seventies, that I realized he was not just a great singer and musician, but also a very talented composer and lyricist. He has been a big help to his famous brother Andy in preparing his theatre and television projects. We have written several songs together and I love the fact that he is brutally candid about our collective efforts. One day I played a simple melody that I had hurriedly sketched out for a song we were working on. When I asked him how he liked it, he paused for a moment and then said, "It stinks." After we both stopped laughing, I realized he was right—it definitely was not one of my better efforts. Dick was the choral director on the last three Como Christmas television specials and in the process, his great sense of humor helped us all get through some difficult situations. Three of the many songs we have written together are "Sing Along With Me," "I'm Dreaming of Hawaii," and "Let's Have a Party."

My family in the early 1980's—daughter Jennie, son Danny, wife Judy, son Terry and me

THE COMO CREW

RAY CHARLES

He was the most important person in the success of Perry's early recording hits. It was Ray who laid out the routines to all of the songs, wrote the choir parts and made sure everything was in order, musically and lyrically. He played the same role on Perry's early television shows along with Mitch Ayres, Joe Lipman, and Jack Andrews. My favorite special material song that Ray wrote the music and lyrics to is "If I Could Read Your Minds." Perry sang that song at every concert we did starting in 1970. It is a remarkable composition, and the audiences loved it.

I've already mentioned, in previous chapters, my love and respect for this talented man. Now I must repeat that he, more than anyone else in my professional life, was responsible for getting me started as a conductor. In our early days together in New York City, he was always very encouraging and supportive, whether it be for my playing, arranging, or conducting. We have written several songs together, and his enormous talent as a singer, musician and lyricist has always been an inspiration to me.

MICKEY GLASS

Mickey deserves special acknowledgment when it comes to anything involving Perry Como. He was originally a song plugger on Tin Pan Alley. Shortly after he and Perry met, a friendship developed that lasted forever. Their personalities were so alike that Mickey soon became Perry's manager and an all-around right-hand man. This was in addition to his running Roncom Music, the Como music publishing firm. The expression "to know him is to love him" is certainly true of Mickey. He was very responsible for helping to create the image of "Mr. Nice Guy" for Perry. It wasn't a difficult job for him, because he just did what came naturally. Promoters, agents, fellow performers, fans—everybody loves Mickey. A real pal and friend to all who have had the good fortune to know him.

SCOTT RECORD

In 1984, this fabulous young entertainer (singer, dancer, comedian, and impressionist) took Jay Leno's place as the opening act for Perry's summer tours. He is one of the biggest talents I have ever known because his performances appeal to audiences of all ages. Perry loved him, as did all of the people connected with our summer concerts. To me, one of the mysteries of show business is why this man, with such great natural ability as an entertainer, has not become a television star in households all over the world.

This is what Scott wrote as a tribute to Perry for the Como statue unveiling in Cannonsburg, Pennsylvania, on May 15, 1999:

"It was my first year of opening the show for Perry Como, a gentle man, a loving man, a benevolent man, a man adored by the entire world. I was fortunate to receive a standing ovation after each of my performances, and he would then take those audiences from that level and bring them to the upper stratosphere." Scott went on to mention that he was unaware that a particular afternoon concert was going to start one hour earlier than usual. After a shopping tour with his wife, Lucy and their young daughter, Elizabeth, they returned to the hotel and were surprised to see Perry and Mickey standing by the front door. Perry and Mickey were also surprised to see Scott, who they thought was already on stage at the theatre. Realizing there had been a terrible mix-up regarding the starting show time, Scott, along with Mickey and Perry, jumped into his non air-conditioned little car and sped off to the theatre. Scott continued:

"Perry asked me to slow down because the audience wasn't going anyplace. As soon as we arrived at the theatre, I jumped out of our car and raced to my dressing room. Perry, dressed in his chino pants and sneakers, yellow windbreaker and fishing hat, walked into the theatre where two thousand people were patiently waiting for the show that was supposed to have started thirty minutes before. When the audience recognized him, the place went crazy. They gave him a standing ovation. When the roar died down, he apologized for the late start, blaming some ambiguous technical problem, and then proceeded to sing several songs with just Nick Perito accompanying him on the piano. When he saw me standing at the back of the theatre all dressed and ready to go, he said, 'My opening act is a young man who sings, tells jokes, and does impressions. You are gonna love him. In fact, I've known that one day I would be opening for him, but I didn't realize it would be this soon.' He called me down to the stage, gave me a big hug and I began to perform. I have never ever met such a gracious person, in or out of show business!"

Pat Boone and Richard Carpenter, both devoted Como fans, also wrote very touching and witty tributes to Perry that I had the pleasure to deliver, on their behalf, at the statue unveiling.

RUSSELL ETLING and CARL MARLOWE

Another person who contributed greatly to the success of the Como summer tours in the late eighties was Russell Etling, a talented young stage manager, lighting engineer, singer, and all-around great guy. Perry never liked to rehearse, so Russell happily took over for him. Like Ray Charles before him, he sang several of Como's songs during our sound-check rehearsals. Perry would finally come up on stage and sing just a few bars of a song—most of the time with just me at the piano. Then he would walk out into the theatre, listen to the orchestra and choir rehearse for a very short while, give us the thumbs up signal and leave. Perry and Mickey would then go out and try to find a place to hit some golf balls. Russell always managed to get everything organized so that when show time came, all was in order.

Carl Marlowe was the cue card man on Perry's early live television shows. He also loved to sing. On one particular program, Carl accidentally mixed up the cue cards and Perry sang the wrong lyrics to "Night and Day." But as always, he just kept on going, making up his own version of what Cole Porter had written. When the show ended, Carl apologized profusely and nothing more was said. On the next week's program, Perry surprised everyone by admitting to the audience that due to a cue-card mix-up, he had made several lyrical mistakes while singing a song the previous week—and now, he was asking Carl to come up in front of the camera and sing the next song for him. Perry then took the cue cards and while Carl nervously started singing the song, Perry intentionally mixed up all of the cards and dropped several of them on the floor. The television and live audiences loved the entire caper—as did Carl.

In later years, he became Como's valet on all of our concert tours. He provided us with lots of laughs because of the fact that he could double-talk in any language.

CHAPTER 25

THE "REAL" PERRY COMO

Rehearsing with Perry for his RCA Today *album, 1988*

The question I've been asked most often is, "What was Perry really like when he was offstage?" Flip Wilson provided me with the perfect answer and that was, "What you see is what you get." Basically, Perry was the same person both on and offstage. He never vocalized and rehearsing was not one of his favorite pastimes. He sang only when he had to. I remember a few occasions when he was with good friends and maybe after a glass or two of wine, he would consent to sing a couple of songs. Those were really very special moments and I am sorry those vocal renditions were never recorded. Otherwise, he much preferred to sit back, listen to some good jokes, have some laughs and let everyone else do the talking. He had great respect for anyone who could tell a good story.

His favorite hobbies were golf and fishing, and he was very good at both. We played a lot of golf together. His easy natural swing made it all look so simple. When it came to fishing, he had great patience, and that is what it takes to be a good fisherman. His definition of a true friend was a person you could go fishing with, sit next to for hours, and not feel it necessary to say one word. That too, we did on occasion when I went to visit him in Florida in later years.

While growing up in Cannonsburg, Pennsylvania in a strict Italian family, he was led to believe that men were supposed to be the workers in the family. They had to have regular physical jobs like laborers, craftsmen, or businessmen who went to work every day in order to earn enough money to support their families. Singing, on the other hand, was *fun*. That was something you did when you *weren't working*. Work was work and fun was fun. That was it.

As he became more successful as a singer, he had difficulty in reconciling that old preconceived idea. Strange as it may seem. I think he sometimes felt embarrassed for getting so much attention and making lots of money doing something he originally thought was just *fun*. It was certainly not a "man's job."

BIG DADDY

Perry had been known by many different nicknames. Perhaps the most popular was "Mr. Nice Guy." Jackie Gleason called him "Silver Throat," and many of his Jewish lady fans fondly referred to him as "Perilla." I remember telling him about a great movie I had seen that starred Burl Ives, who was affectionately referred to in the film as "Big Daddy." For some unknown reason, Perry found that expression to be very touching so I began calling him by the same name. Thereafter, he started calling me "Lil' Daddy." We had accidentally renamed each other.

Perry loved surprises and here was another one he pulled on me. In the early eighties, after an ambitious summer tour, we met in New York City to discuss the music for a new album we were about to record. At our first rehearsal, I couldn't help but notice an elaborately wrapped package on top of the piano. He pretended not to know what it was or who it was for. Mickey insisted that I open it up. You can imagine my surprise when I discovered it was a beautiful gold Rolex wristwatch. Still, they both seemed to be very surprised, as I was. But after I read aloud the inscription on the back of the watch, they both smiled and gave me a big hug! It read:

LIL' DADDY
LOVE,
BIG DADDY

*   *   *

COMO'S PERSONALITY

Perry was always polite, especially when ladies were present—and even humble at times. He definitely was not a show-off. Receiving excessive compliments often made him uncomfortable. During the many years we did summer concert tours, various organizations honored him with plaques and trophies which he reluctantly accepted—then left under the bed of whatever hotel we were staying at the time, hoping they would get lost in the shuffle. But somehow, at the end of every concert tour, they found their way to his home in Florida. He ended up with a garage full of all that kind of stuff. He was modest to a fault.

EGO

Yes, he had an ego, *but* he never flaunted it. He was very proud of his Italian heritage and he also had great respect for other ethnic groups and their respective customs—especially at Christmas time. He made a point of singing songs of all religions. One Christmas, in addition to the usual carols we all know, he donned a yarmulke and sang "Kol Nedra," a serious song of the Hebrew faith. Well, you can't imagine the *hate* mail he received. Sad, but true. Sometimes you are damned if you do and damned if you don't.

Religion was a very personal thing for him. Although he and his family were Catholic, he had great respect for everyone else's religion. Privacy was something else he strongly felt every family should have.

HIS "ACTING" CAREER

In spite of his good looks and great voice, his Hollywood career never really took off. Personally, I thought his performances in "Words and Music" and the other films he appeared in were very good. However, he was convinced that the acting profession was not for him. Deep down in his heart, he couldn't pretend to be someone he wasn't. A movie director once told him that he had to move his arms a lot more while he was singing and "ham it up a little bit." Perry tried his best, but after one take the director came back to him and said, "Never mind, do it your way." He had to *believe* the lyrics before he would sing a song—whether it was humorous or serious. Singing silly songs gave him almost as much pleasure as the very emotional love ballads or religious songs.

DANCING

This was definitely not one of his strong points. He was uncomfortable doing it because he felt it was like "showing off," and that he could not do. However, I know he still had fun trying to do all the correct dance steps. During the opening numbers of many television specials and concerts, we all saw Perry moving about and very often, he was out of sync with the rest of the dancers and singers. The audience loved that because they felt that he was really just like "the guy next door"—and he never tried to dispel that belief.

AUDIENCE'S AFFECTION

Women all over the world loved this man. He was gentle, kind, mild-mannered, good-looking, and he made a woman feel like he was singing only to her. He was also a man's man—guys loved him too, because as I said before, he wasn't a show-off. When Perry was honored on the *Kennedy Center Honors* television show in 1987, Don Ameche said something to the effect that "Como is the only man in the world whose picture can appear on a woman's night table, and her husband will understand." That kinda' said it all.

CHAPTER 26

MORE COMO STORIES

THE BARITONE HORN

When he was in his early teens, he enjoyed strumming on a guitar, but his main instrument was the baritone horn (double barreled), which he played in a local band in Cannonsburg, Pennsylvania. He also owned his own barbershop and was making over sixty dollars a week cutting hair. The band was booked for a weekend job out of town and he was forced to close the shop for a few days. His father took a dim view of that, but Perry went anyway. When he came home, he said his lips were all puffed up from blowing on the horn all weekend and that made his father all the more unhappy. When Perry told him that he only made fifteen dollars for the entire weekend, Papa Como took Perry's horn out to the shed in the backyard and sawed off both bells of the instrument. He made a wine flask out of one and a spittoon out of the other. That ended Perry's career as a horn player.

LONDON, ENGLAND (LATE-NIGHT WALK)

No matter where we were or what time it was, Perry, Mickey Glass, Ray Charles and I always took a long walk before we went to bed. We entertained ourselves with funny stories and old memories. One night in Knightsbridge (London), we walked for over an hour and because the streets were very twisty-turny, Mickey and I both agreed that we were lost. We had no idea how to get back to our hotel, but Perry insisted that he knew exactly where we were and not to worry. Another thirty minutes went by before he finally gave up and we hailed a cab. When the cabbie was told where we wanted to go, he gave us a strange look, shrugged his shoulders and then said, "Hop in, mates." He drove us around the corner— and there was our hotel. We were embarrassed, and the driver was giggling under his breath all the while. He didn't want any money but I know Perry gave him a handsome tip. We all had a good laugh.

RAINSTORM

Another heartwarming event took place after we finished a concert at the Palladium Theatre in London. Many fans were outside the stage door in a pouring rainstorm, waiting to get Perry's autograph. When the manager of the theatre informed us of that fact, Perry suggested that someone tell them to go to the front of the theatre and stand under the marquee. There, they would be sheltered from the storm and he would happily give each of them his autograph. I was chosen to deliver that message. When I went outside and made that announcement to the crowd, they didn't believe me. Someone yelled from the back, "If we all do that, he'll come out this door and get away before we can see him!" I reiterated what I originally said and then went back into the theatre. Shortly thereafter, we left through the front entrance and the few fans that were there got Perry's autograph.

Traffic was intense as we slowly made our way back to the hotel in the limo. Looking out of a side window, we were surprised to see a large gathering of people standing in an alleyway. The driver informed us that it was the crowd still waiting at the stage door, hoping to see Perry. Obviously, the majority of them did not believe what I had told them. Perry immediately asked the driver to turn around. When our car slowly pulled up to the backstage area, the crowd recognized Como and they went crazy! Mickey escorted Perry out into the pouring rain and the fans kindly tried to protect them with their umbrellas. Perry gave his autograph to everyone and they were thrilled to be able to shake his hand. I stayed inside the warm limo, along with Ray Charles, and poured myself a double scotch on the rocks. I sipped it slowly and enjoyed watching all their smiling, happy faces.

MY CAR KEYS

Late in October of 1972, we were filming another Como Christmas show at the CBS studios in West Los Angeles. A large parking lot surrounded the studio and one evening, after a long rehearsal, I got to my car and discovered that I didn't have my keys. It was very dark and I guessed that I had accidentally locked them inside my car. I returned to the guard's counter at the studio and I met Perry and Mickey Glass coming down the hall. When they heard about my predicament, Perry said, "Don't worry, I know exactly what to do about that." He asked the guard to find him a bendable coat hanger. Luckily, the young man was able to produce one. Then he followed us out to my car, talking nonstop to Perry about how much his mom and granny loved him. He didn't seem to be concerned about the fact that we were going to break into an automobile. All he wanted was two tickets to the taping of the TV show for his family. Mickey would take care of that later. Perry, in the meantime, had inserted the coat hanger through a tiny opening over the window and, miraculously, opened the door of a 1966 Caddy. I happily sat down in the driver's seat, but I slowly realized that something was wrong. Mickey, seeing the strange look on my face yelled out, "Don't tell me that this is not"—I nodded. We had broken into the wrong car! The guard couldn't have cared less. He was thrilled just being able to talk and stand next to Perry Como.

We hurriedly locked up the *wrong car* and went looking for the right one. Sure enough, six cars further down the line was my Caddy, the exact same year, color and model of the one we had just broken into. Perry again performed his magic opening-car-door trick. Thank goodness there were no photographers or reporters around. Later on, I enjoyed reminding Perry of the possible headlines in some trash newspapers that would have read, "Mister

Nice Guy Is a Car Thief. He Was Found Breaking into Automobiles in a CBS Parking Lot."

TWO ELDERLY LADIES

Perry sang "It's Impossible" at some point during almost every concert. If I felt he might accidentally skip singing it, I would quietly remind him of the song by noodling the melody on the piano, while he was bantering with the audience. Still, he often ignored my suggestion and omitted the song entirely.

After one such afternoon concert in Chicago, I walked out of the stage door and was immediately accosted by two elderly ladies who began hitting me with their purses and yelling, "He didn't sing 'It's Impossible.'" All of the other Como fans, who were waiting for Perry's autograph, were amused by the whole incident. The ladies kept yelling, "We drove one hundred miles to see his show, and he didn't sing our favorite song!" I did my best to console them, but I think I lost.

Later that evening, Perry enjoyed hearing about my encounter with his two old fans. He really broke up when I told him I needed "hazard pay" to cover any future stage-door attacks. I went on to tease him about the fact that I was also being blinded, night after night, by all the white-and-blue tinted hair of his lady admirers in the audience.

His fans at the Westbury Theatre in Long Island, New York were the most devoted of all. It was necessary for him to walk down a long aisle, in the middle of the theatre-in-the-round, in order to gain access to the revolving stage. The ladies always mobbed him, trying to get a kiss or a hug. I suggested that if he walked more slowly, maybe some of them would pin dollar bills on him like they do on the robed statues at Italian-Catholic feast celebrations. Since it was my idea, I demanded I get 50 percent of the take.

WRONG CHORDS

Both Perry and I grew up knowing that in the southern Italian culture, the purest form of flattery is a put-down. I know that it may sound a bit strange to a lot of people, but it worked fine for both of us. We hardly ever discussed a concert once it was over. Of course, we rehearsed a lot before our tour began, but once a routine was set, *it was set.* Unless we were forced to make a last-minute change, we never discussed the show we were about to do. He loved spontaneity and he knew I did too. That made our concerts fun because he would sing some songs a little differently every night—and I loved the challenge.

As an example, many times after a very successful concert, Perry's dressing room was filled with lots of admiring friends and family, all sipping coffee or wine. Perry would eventually make his entrance from a small side room and many times, he would yell over to me, "Nick, do you have to keep playing all those damn wrong chords?" Not knowing he was kidding, the guests would get embarrassed. Particularly when I would respond with something like, "I'm sorry, but do you have to keep singing so loudly over all the arrangements I've written? Why don't you try to hum more—and use less words." Those few who knew that we were joking, enjoyed our kibitzing. But many times, people would come over to me and quietly offer some comforting words like, "I thought you played rather well tonight." When I tried to explain that it was an old Italian custom and he really meant that he loved what I played, the confused look on many of their faces told me to quickly change the subject and pour them more wine.

JAPANESE MISPRONUNCIATIONS

It is a known fact that many Japanese have difficulty pronouncing the American letters "R" and "L." They often get them mixed up and funny things can happen. For example, on our first trip to Japan, Perry was concerned because audiences were not responding like they did in other parts of the world. We knew that they loved him dearly, but they were more subdued in their outward reactions. He explained his concern to a very attractive Japanese lady theatre owner. She told him that he should not worry because all of Japan "roved him." She went on to say, "In America, audience stand up and make noise, but in Japan, they just stay seated and 'crap a rot.'" I wish I could have taken a photo of Perry's face when she said that. Mickey and I quickly turned and walked away, trying to suppress our laughter. Perry was stuck there with a silly look on his face and he just kept talking, as though nothing had happened. Later on, he jokingly chastised Mickey and me for abandoning him. He proved again, that he was Mr. Nice Guy—even in Japan. We all enjoyed the sign on Mickey Glass's dressing room door which read: "Mr. Mickey *Grass*." We referred to him by his new name for many years after that.

BLIND BLAKE

While filming a springtime television special in the Bahamas, a funny thing happened that involved guest star Loretta Swit (one of the stars of *M*A*S*H*), Perry and an interesting Bahamian singer and guitarist named Blind Blake. He was famous because he wrote a song that was a favorite of both Prince Edward and Wally Simpson when they lived there many years ago.

Perry, Loretta, and Blind Blake, who was truly blind, were seated by the side of a large swimming pool. The cameras were rolling and Perry asked Blake what inspired him to compose the song that Prince Edward was so fond of. After a few sentences, he said something like, "One day I picked up my guitar and I just started fucking around with this tune and I kinda' liked it so I . . . ," etc. Everyone pretended they didn't hear what he actually said until Loretta couldn't hold back any longer. She burst out laughing, as did the entire technical crew. At one point, I thought Perry was going to fall off his chair from laughing so hard. After a short break, the taping of the show continued. Yes, Blake's little comment definitely hit the cutting room floor. However, judging from the dialogue I hear on television now, I think the producers should have left that line in the show.

UNEXPECTED GIFTS

In the early nineties, Como did several live concert tours just before Christmas. I will never forget one particular performance at the Syrian Mosque, an old ornate theatre in Pittsburgh. What we didn't know was that a large flock of pigeons had somehow gained entrance to the building and were nesting in the upper regions of the structure—directly above the stage.

The performance was sold out and the audience was definitely in a happy Christmas mood—a real Como crowd. I conducted the overture, which featured the great Al Cobine orchestra and all of our talented backup singers. Perry made his entrance to thunderous applause and he proceeded to enchant the entire audience. The show was going beautifully until I noticed that the percussionist was waving his arms and trying to tell me something. It seemed that the pigeons were—uh—well—maybe they didn't like the music we were playing, but whatever it was, they all started to "relieve themselves." The percussionist and the top row of brass players were directly in their *line of fire*. Many people in the audience also became aware of the dilemma on stage, but nobody could do a damn thing about it. In the middle of a lovely Christmas carol, Perry became the recipient of an unexpected pigeon's *present*. After he cleaned off his *direct hit*, he shyly admitted that that wasn't exactly what he was expecting as a gift from heaven. The audience roared with laughter. He then advised them all to put their paper programs over their heads and join him in a rousing sing-a-long finale that featured songs like "Jingle Bells," "Santa Claus Is Coming to Town" and "Angels We Have Heard on High."

This turned out to be a very special concert and I think even Santa himself would admit that it wasn't the kind of Christmas surprise he had in mind for all of Perry's fans.

LATE-NIGHT DINNERS

In every city, after an evening performance, there seemed to be a committee or a special host who would invite Perry and a few of us to dinner at a fancy local restaurant—very often it was an Italian restaurant. The menus were always lavish because the chefs all wanted to impress Mr. Como with their best dishes. Perry found this difficult to handle because all he really wanted was a simple plate of pasta with no garlic in the sauce—can you imagine that— an Italian not liking garlic? The chefs never believed that, and as a result, they served us all kinds of food, excellently prepared and highly spiced.

This kind of cuisine was difficult for Perry to handle late at night, because it always upset his stomach, and having to perform the next day, he was apprehensive about getting sick. In order not to hurt the feelings of his benefactors, he often made up excuses. The first time he did this, Mickey, Ray, Carl, and I were totally taken by surprise. One night after the show, a local sponsor extended us a very tempting dinner invitation and Perry answered, "Thank you very much, but Nick and I still have a lot of rehearsing to do tonight." I tried not to look surprised, but I *got the message* and answered, "Oh yeah, I forgot about that."

After everyone left the dressing room, Perry asked the limo driver to take us to the nearest Denny's restaurant. He knew the food there would be simply prepared—not spicy—and he could enjoy his usual late-night snack of scrambled eggs and toast, coffee ice cream for dessert, and a cup of decaf coffee. When we got back to the hotel, we took our usual forty-five-minute walk and then we all went to bed. That was our routine after each night's performance. Pretty wild and crazy, eh?

P.S. I later learned that Perry really enjoyed eating food cooked with garlic, but while he was on the road meeting many different people, he didn't want his breath to be offensive.

CRAZY COMMENTS

While on the road during our summer concert tours, he loved to go down to a local mall in the afternoon and casually shop around. He used the excuse that he needed toothpaste or some underarm deodorant. Mickey and I happily tagged along and we had some funny encounters with a couple of his older fans. *Very casual* was his mode of dress and as a result, he was not immediately recognized.

However, after staring at us for quite a while, one old lady came up to Perry and yelled, "Do you know who you are?" Before he could answer, she went on to tell him where he lived, the color of his home, his mother's maiden name, etc., and if Mickey hadn't intervened, she would still be there pointing her finger and talking to him. Perry politely gave her his autograph and we moved on.

On another occasion, we were standing in a long line waiting to pay our bill. A lady standing behind Perry suddenly recognized him, and screamed out, "My God, I thought you were dead!" After the surrounding customers stopped laughing, Perry quietly answered, "I'm sorry to disappoint you madam, but I am feeling just fine, thank you." Mickey and I waited patiently beside him, as Perry graciously signed autographs for practically every woman in the mall.

CHAPTER 27

MY CLOSING THOUGHTS OF PERRY

Perry giving me a bow at one of our concerts

After the Christmas television special in Ireland in 1994, Perry made it clear to all of us that he was giving up his singing career. He was tired and had lost all interest in performing. When his beloved wife, Roselle suddenly passed away in 1999, it seemed he gave up his desire to live.

After that, I flew to Florida several times to see Perry and do my best to cheer him up. His health was failing badly. In the spring of 2001, he was confined to his bed and under twenty-four-hour medical surveillance. Even though he was practically comatose at that time, his medical attendants were surprised at how he'd perk up whenever I came to see him. Acting as if nothing was wrong, I said things like, "Hey, Big Daddy, we have a big summer tour all booked, and I brought down some new songs that I know you're anxious to learn." Upon hearing my voice, he would open his eyes, give me a big smile and pretend to listen to my silly comments reminding him of all the laughs and fun times we shared in the previous thirty-six-plus years. I spent the better part of three days with him. The last morning I was there, we exchanged hugs and I tearfully said goodbye. I knew the end was near.

One month later, while on tour in Japan conducting the Percy Faith orchestra, I received the sad news of Perry's death on May 14, 2001. Thanks to the support and consolation I received from my musician friends, I was able to get through a very difficult emotional time in my life.

Perry was more than just an employer to me. He was my cousin, my uncle, my friend. The fact that we were both raised in a strict Italian family only solidified our relationship because of all the similar situations we had to deal with while we were growing up.

Whether it was a ballad or a rhythm tune, Perry had his own special way of interpreting the lyrics that gave each song a very *personal* meaning. His personality, along with the warm, friendly quality of his voice made everyone feel like he was a member of their family. He brought so much joy and happiness to fans all over the world. His closing theme song was "You Are Never Far Away From Me," and that's how I will always feel about him.

EPILOGUE

One night in the early fifties, I saw a television show hosted by Walter Cronkite. His guest was a famous Italian author named Luigi Barzini, who had just written a book called *The Italians*. In the course of their conversation, Barzini said something to the effect that all the people in Italy are great actors, each and every one of them. He humorously added that perhaps "only one hundred of their least talented have become famous in films."

I totally agree with that statement. My father would easily have been my exhibit A. Like so many of his contemporaries and other poor immigrants, namely the African Americans, Irish and Jews, they often chose to *make believe* in their respective lives and use humor and drama as distractions from the hard realities of everyday life. Whenever possible, *make light of stressful situations* was the order of the day for most of them. Fate has been kind to me because I've had the opportunity to associate with many people like that in every phase of my life. They have taught me so much about humor and being able to communicate, even under stressful conditions.

Another interesting television show in the late fifties was hosted by David Susskind. One night his guests were several English playwrights, each of whom had written a play that was running on Broadway at the time. Susskind found it to be rather strange because no American writers were represented that season. When he asked his guests to account for that fact, one of them answered, "Because *we* dared to be wrong." They obviously went beyond the ordinary and found new and exciting ways and things to write about.

I have encouraged many young people to do exactly that. Don't sit back and wait for something to happen—ask questions, probe new areas, go out and make it happen. Whatever it is, get off the fence and charge straight ahead—try it, you might like it—*dare to be wrong*! But above all, practice, study, and continue to develop your talents to the fullest so that you will be prepared for that moment in life when opportunity knocks and the red light goes on. After that, remember to say thank you.

Many music lovers have often told me that they used to play the piano and wish they had continued to practice, "but now, it's too late." It is *never* too late. The old clichés are true: where there's a will, there's a way—nothing ventured, nothing gained. My advice is to just sit down at your piano and play. Don't be too judgmental of your performance. Learn from your mistakes and try to relax and enjoy yourself. In the process, you will realize that the more you practice, the better you will play. Regardless of your vocation or your purpose in life, and no matter what instrument you play, have *fun* with music. When you let your imagination run wild, it can stimulate all kinds of wonderful emotions in you *and* your audience. Music has allowed me to express my innermost feelings in a way I could never describe in words.

It's always fun playing jazz with some of my musician friends. We just sit and jam (musically improvise) with very little verbal communication. One of us will start a song, and then we let our imaginations take us to whatever key or mood we want to pursue. When I am in New York City, I enjoy doing exactly that with my bass player pal, Jerry Bruno. Because of his incredible ears and natural harmonic sense, he joins right in and always knows exactly what I am playing. Occasionally, we meet with another old friend, Bucky Pizzarelli, the great guitarist and the three of us have a ball improvising together.

Several musicians, writers and performer friends of mine have suffered greatly from what I felt was the unjust criticism they received from various critics in the media. In the early years of the *Johnny Carson Show*, I had the pleasure of hearing a very talented girl singer question a New York City critic (both of whom shall remain nameless) on what qualified him (the critic) to pass judgment on *any* theatrical artist or performance. Her very logical questions were interrupted by a television commercial break but minutes later, when the show came back on the air, she was still blistering him with queries like, "What have *you* ever written? What have *you* ever produced? Where have *you* ever performed?" Carson did his best to change the subject, but to no avail. I loved it all because it made me see the true wisdom in the immortal words of George Bernard Shaw who said, "A critic is a legless man who teaches *running.*"

Two of the many technological changes that have occurred in the entertainment world are *synthesis* and *amplification.* Both have been terribly abused. The basic theories and principles of music are still the same, but many of today's pop musicians and producers refuse to deal with those facts. Experience has taught me that the old adage—*truth will win out*—depends a great deal on where you are, who you are with, and what demands are being made upon you at the time. On several occasions, I have suffered, both professionally and socially for opening my big mouth and saying what I felt and *knew* to be the truth.

Years ago, an astrologist told me that I would spend a great deal of my musical life in foreign countries, namely Japan. That prophecy soon became a reality for me. My work in Japan began with the Como concert tours in the seventies, followed by the record albums with Matsuo Kazuko and Kayama Yuzo, then three lengthy tours with the Percy Faith Orchestra. In addition to the concerts with Domingo, Carreras and Ross, I also had the pleasure to conduct the orchestra for Richard Carpenter of the famous "Carpenters" on an extended tour of Japan in 1997. Audiences all over the world adored Richard and the music he and his sister Karen brought to them through the years.

Thanks to another Japanese promoter friend named Yutaka Kawana and his lovely wife, Ayako, I was chosen to take a large Hollywood orchestra to Himeji, Japan in the fall of 2001 and do five concerts as part of a week long celebration acknowledging the 400th anniversary of the magnificent Himeji Castle. I orchestrated and conducted a lengthy composition written by Asei Kobayashi featuring our orchestra, a vocal soloist, and a choir from Tokyo. After that, we played several arrangements of mine featuring the

"Music of Hollywood." A personal thank you from me to all of the Japanese audiences who have such great appreciation and love for American music.

I want to acknowledge some of the truly unsung heroes in the music world. First, the copyists who have strained their eyes extracting from my scores all of the individual notes and parts for each member of the orchestra. Their accomplishments, often under very stressful time limitations, constantly amaze me. I am also eternally grateful to the many brilliant musicians that I have had the honor to conduct in recording studios, concert halls, night clubs, and theatres all over the world. Every composer, orchestrator, and arranger I've ever known will agree that all music copyists and orchestral musicians deserve our deepest thanks.

My life in music was, and still is very exciting—starting with my early years back in Denver, Colorado, playing the accordion for free firecrackers and watermelons, all the way up to conducting, composing, and arranging music for large symphonic orchestras while accompanying famous musical artists all over the world. At times, it was almost like being on a magic carpet ride.

Writing this book has been a very emotional experience for me. Some old memories have brought me great sadness, while others have been very amusing and uplifting. I hope you've enjoyed reading the story of my journey, and I also like to think that it has brought an occasional smile to your face.

Good fortune has allowed me to be an observer and a participant in many of the incredible social, political, artistic, and technological changes that have occurred during my lifetime, simply because *I just happened to be there.* Again, thanks to all my dear friends and family members for their love and support, but most important— thank you, Mama, and thank you, Papa.